READERS GUIDES TO ESSENTIAL CRITICISM

CONSULTANT EDITOR: NICOLAS TREDELL

Published

Philippa Lyon	Twentieth-Century War Poetry
Merja Makinen	The Novels of Jeanette Winterson
Matt McGuire	Contemporary Scottish Literature
Timothy Milnes	Wordsworth: *The Prelude*
Jago Morrison	The Fiction of Chinua Achebe
Carl Plasa	Tony Morrison: *Beloved*
Carl Plasa	Jean Rhys: *Wide Sargasso Sea*
Nicholas Potter	Shakespeare: *Antony and Cleopatra*
Nicholas Potter	Shakespeare: *Othello*
Steven Price	The Plays, Screenplays and Films of David Mamet
Andrew Radford	Victorian Sensation Fiction
Berthold Schoene–Harwood	Mary Shelley: *Frankenstein*
Nick Selby	T. S. Eliot: *The Waste Land*
Nick Selby	Herman Melville: *Moby Dick*
Nick Selby	The Poetry of Walt Whitman
David Smale	Salman Rushdie: *Midnight's Chidren –The Satanic Verses*
Patsy Stoneman	Emily Brontë: *Wuthering Heights*
Susie Thomas	Hanif Kureishi
Nicolas Tredell	F. Scott Fitzgerald: *The Great Gatsby*
Nicolas Tredell	Joseph Conrad: *Heart of Darkness*
Nicolas Tredell	Charles Dickens: *Great Expectations*
Nicolas Tredell	William Faulkner: *The Sound and the Fury–As I Lay Dying*
Nicolas Tredell	Shakespeare: *Macbeth*
Nicolas Tredell	The Fiction of Martin Amis
Matthew Woodcock	Shakespeare: *Henry V*
Angela Wright	Gothic Fiction

Forthcoming

Pascale Aebischer	Jacobean Drama
Annika Bautz	Jane Austen: *Sense and Sensibility – Pride and Prejudice – Emma*
Matthew Beedham	The Novels of Kazuo Ishiguro
Jodi–Anne George	*Beowulf*
Sarah Haggarty & Jon Mee	Willam Blake: *Songs of Innocence and Experience*
Matthew Jordan	Milton: *Paradise Lost*
Stephen Regan	The Poetry of Philip Larkin
Mardi Stewart	Victorian Women's Poetry
Michael Whitworth	Virginia Woolf: *Mrs Dalloway*
Gina Wisker	The Fiction of Margaret Atwood

Readers' Guides to Essential Criticism
Series Standing Order
ISBN 1–4039–0108–2
(outside North America only)

You can receive future titles in this series as they are published by placing a standing order. Please contact your bookseller or, in the case of difficulty, write to us at the address below with your name and address, the title of the series and the ISBN quoted above.

Customer Services Department, Macmillan Distribution Ltd
Houndmills, Basingstoke, Hampshire RG21 6XS, England

F. Scott Fitzgerald

The Great Gatsby

EDITED BY NICOLAS TREDELL

Series editor: Richard Beynon

Published by
PALGRAVE MACMILLAN
Houndmills, Basingstoke, Hampshire RG21 6XS and
175 Fifth Avenue, New York, N.Y. 10010
Companies and representatives throughout the world

PALGRAVE MACMILLAN is the global academic imprint of the Palgrave Macmillan division of St. Martin's Press, LLC and of Palgrave Macmillan Ltd. Macmillan® is a registered trademark in the United States, United Kingdom and other countries. Palgrave is a registered trademark in the European Union and other countries.

First published 1997 by Icon Books Ltd

ISBN-10: 1-874166-67-6
ISBN-13: 978-1-874166-67-2

This book is printed on paper suitable for recycling and made from fully managed and sustained forest sources. Logging, pulping and manufacturing processes are expected to conform to the environmental regulations of the country of origin.

A catalogue record for this book is available from the British Library.

Printed by the MPG Books Group in the UK

Short Loan Collection

Contents

A NOTE ON REFERENCES

Cross-references to the extracts printed in this Guide, and page references to the Cambridge University Press 1991 edition of *The Great Gatsby*, are given in brackets in the text of the Guide. Other page references are given in the endnotes. All quotations from the novel have been amended to accord with the CUP edition, apart from the use of English rather than American spellings.

INTRODUCTION

THE GREAT *Gatsby* has generated enormous critical debate since its first
publication in 1925. Like its near-contemporary *The Waste Land*
(1922), which it echoes in notable ways, it is a relatively short work that
has proved remarkably fertile, offering seemingly endless grain for critics
to garner. This Guide aims to trace the history of that critical harvest and
to offer a selection of the best that has been thought and said about
Gatsby from the 1920s to the 1990s. The intention has been to choose
criticism from past decades that was significant in its own day and which
remains alive in our own, and to locate in the present decade the growth
points of *Gatsby* studies. This Introduction offers an account of
Fitzgerald's career and reputation as a novelist up to the publication of
Gatsby, and then outlines the critical material in the rest of the Guide.

Scott Fitzgerald was already famous when *The Great Gatsby* came out.
Five years before, in the summer of 1919, he had thrown up his job with
the Barron Collier advertising agency in New York and returned home to
his parents' house in St Paul, Minnesota, to work on the novel that
became *This Side of Paradise*. He had previously published a number of
short stories in magazines, but he wanted a larger literary success. *This
Side of Paradise*, an engaging, straggling tale of the life and loves of Amory
Blaine from childhood to early manhood, drew on two earlier versions
of a novel called *The Romantic Egotist*, both of which had been rejected by
the publishing house of Scribner's. When Fitzgerald had finished the
new novel, he sent it once more to Scribner's. They remained reluctant
to publish him. But Maxwell Perkins, the Scribner's editor who was to
become famous for his support of Fitzgerald, applied pressure, and they
agreed. Fitzgerald recalls how, when the postman brought him the news
of the novel's acceptance, he 'ran along the street, stopping automobiles
to tell friends and acquaintances about it'.[1] He predicted that the novel
would sell well and make him famous.

He was right. When *This Side of Paradise* appeared on 26 March 1920,
the first printing of 3,000 copies sold out within three days.[2] Further
printings rapidly followed. In its relaxed portrayal of privileged young
people in pursuit of pleasure, and sometimes of art, the novel caught,
and helped to create, a mood of hedonism and rebellion that suited the

times. The immediate success of the novel enabled Fitzgerald quickly to achieve another ambition. In the previous month, he had written to Maxwell Perkins 'I'm almost sure I'll get married as soon as my book is out',[3] and on 3 April, a week after the novel's publication, he duly did so. His bride was Zelda Sayre, a southern belle from Montgomery, Alabama, whom he had met in 1918 when he had been a second lieutenant in the US Army. Together they plunged into the glamorous life that 1920s New York offered to its well-off celebrities, going to parties, featuring in newspapers and magazines, riding on the roofs of taxis, leaping into fountains. No wonder that Fitzgerald said, looking back: 'It seemed a romantic business to be a successful literary man'.[4] Talented, young and handsome, he had got the book, the fame, the girl and the money all at once. Events appeared to bear out the view which he recollected having held at that time: 'Life was something you dominated if you were any good'.[5]

But the 'media success' that Fitzgerald enjoyed after the publication of his first novel did not fully satisfy him. As a student at Princeton, he had told his friend Edmund Wilson 'I want to be one of the greatest writers who have ever lived, don't you?',[6] and he was serious. A claim to greatness, however, could not rest on *This Side of Paradise*. The novel had received a largely enthusiastic review response, but it had been seen, inevitably, as a young man's novel – 'a convincing chronicle of youth by youth', as Margaret Emerson Bailey put it[7] – and it had sometimes been criticised as callow and imitative. On the strength of *This Side of Paradise*, Fitzgerald had become a novelist to watch; but the future direction of his talent remained uncertain. His very success seemed to pose a danger. Edmund Wilson had already sounded the alarm after a pre-publication reading of *This Side of Paradise* in typescript in November 1920; in a patronising letter to Fitzgerald, he had said: 'I believe you might become a very popular trashy novelist without much difficulty'.[8]

In the midst of his hectic life, and the production of numerous short stories, Fitzgerald hastily wrote a long second novel, *The Beautiful and Damned*, which came out in March 1922. Rich in style and incident, but still episodic and structurally and stylistically unstable, *The Beautiful and Damned* was darker in tone than *This Side of Paradise*. It traced the story of its protagonist, Anthony Patch, from decadent bachelorhood into glamorous but destructive marriage and drunken disintegration. Reviewers were fairly favourable, and some recognised that Fitzgerald had, as H. L. Mencken put it in his review, 'tried something much more difficult' than *This Side of Paradise* and deserved credit even if the result was not wholly successful.[9] But Gilbert Seldes's review charged that Fitzgerald still lacked 'a full respect for the medium he works in' and accused him of an 'irrelevance [that] destroys his design' and 'a carelessness about structure and effect'.[10] *The Beautiful and Damned* showed that Fitzgerald wanted to resist becoming a popular, trashy novelist; but his desire to be a great writer still seemed some way from fulfilment.

In July 1922, thinking about his third novel, Fitzgerald wrote to Maxwell Perkins: 'I want to write something *new* – something extraordinary and beautiful and simple + intricately patterned'.[11] Critics have often used this as a direct statement of intent about *The Great Gatsby*, but Matthew J. Bruccoli suggests that it refers to another, lost project whose relationship to *Gatsby* is impossible to determine.[12] It does, nonetheless, indicate the way Fitzgerald was thinking about his own future fiction after the publication of *The Beautiful and Damned*. It seems that he began writing the draft of what was to become *The Great Gatsby* in the summer of 1923, while living at Great Neck, Long Island. In September 1923, he diverted his attention to work on the production of his unsuccessful play, *The Vegetable* (1923), and then, needing money to clear his debts, he wrote eleven short stories in the winter of 1923–4, one of which, 'Absolution', bears a close relation to *Gatsby*. He then returned to the novel, which at this time was provisionally called *Among Ash-Heaps and Millionaires*. In a letter to Maxwell he declared: 'I feel I have an enormous power in me now' and he affirmed that his book would be 'a consciously artistic achievement'.[13]

On 27 October, Fitzgerald, now living in France, wrote to Perkins to tell him he was sending him, under separate cover, 'my third novel: *The Great Gatsby*', and immediately added, in brackets: 'I think that at last I've done something really my own'.[14] Perkins replied in detail in a famous letter of 20 November, calling the book 'brilliant' but offering some criticisms of the structure and saying that 'Gatsby is somewhat vague'.[15] Fitzgerald tried to respond to these criticisms in revising the galley proofs, which he returned to Perkins in mid-February.[16] *The Great Gatsby* appeared on 10 April 1925.

This Guide traces the critical reception of *Gatsby* from its first appearance into the 1990s. It is a complex and fascinating story. As the first chapter of this Guide shows, the early reviews were mixed, and the novel did not sell well. Although reviews of Fitzgerald's subsequent books sometimes mentioned *Gatsby* in positive terms, the novel did not, in the later 1920s and the 1930s, receive sustained critical attention. Copies from the second 1925 printing remained available, but most of them stayed in the publisher's warehouse. The Modern Library edition in 1934, with an introduction by Fitzgerald that is reprinted later in this Guide, failed to sell and was dropped from the series. When Fitzgerald died in 1940, the chances of *Gatsby's* survival might well have seemed slim.

But death brought Fitzgerald to life again as an author, and in the 1940s essays and articles started to appear that argued for a higher estimate of his work than he had enjoyed in the last decade of his lifetime.

A consensus began to emerge that *Gatsby* was his best novel, and the reasons for that judgement began to be explored. The extracts in this Guide from essays of the mid-1940s by Arthur Mizener and William Troy offer analyses of *Gatsby* that remain perceptive and provocative and which helped, in their time, to stimulate critical debate, providing formulations that others could build on or dissent from. They helped to prepare the ground for the growth in *Gatsby* studies in the 1950s.

The 1950s was the golden age of academic literary criticism in America and, on an inevitably lesser scale, in England. The profession was expanding, a powerful technique of evaluation and interpretation emerged in the shape of the New Criticism, the teaching and criticism of literature could be felt to be socially and politically important, and there was a desire, in the USA, to construct a canon of great American writers and great American novels. In this context, Fitzgerald studies, and interpretations of *Gatsby* in particular, mushroomed. In Fitzgerald, biographers and critics had a writer who had enjoyed a spectacular success and a subsequent failure that was very American but which could also strike a universal chord. In *Gatsby* they had a novel that was eminently readable, widely accessible, easily teachable, intricately patterned, and about the American Dream. This Guide traces the evolution of the 'American Dream' interpretation from its formulation by Lionel Trilling, through its development by Edwin S. Fussell, to its apotheosis in Marius Bewley. But dominant interpretations provoke dissent, and this Guide looks at two notable examples from the 1950s: John W. Bicknell's redefinition of *Gatsby* as a pessimistic elegy rather than an American tragedy, and R. W. Stallman's immensely lively essay that seeks to show that there is much, much more in *Gatsby* than Bewley had cared to notice. The story of Fitzgerald studies in the Fifties culminates in the first full-length critical study of Fitzgerald by James E. Miller, Jr, and this Guide contains an excerpt from his thorough and illuminating analysis of *Gatsby*'s narrative technique.

In the 1960s and 1970s, biographical and critical books and essays on Fitzgerald continued to proliferate. Many reworked old ground, often usefully, but unspectacularly. Others achieved new insights by looking more closely at specific aspects of Fitzgerald's work. The essays by J. S. Westbrook and Victor A. Doyno in this Guide are examples of the latter approach; Westbrook's investigation of nature and optics in *The Great Gatsby*, and Doyno's exploration of patterns in the novel, remain fascinating, and are still open to development by critics today. These essays, however, take the stature of *Gatsby* for granted: not so Gary J. Scrimgeour, who in 1966 launched a scathing attack on Nick Carraway's character and, more radically, on Fitzgerald's craftsmanship. Scrimgeour had been anticipated, in his assault on Nick, by R. W. Stallman, and his attack on Fitzgerald's craftsmanship was to be taken up again in the

1970s by Ron Neuhaus.[17] But Scrimgeour's essay remains the most powerful and provocative statement of the case against the classic status of *Gatsby*. The extract included in this Guide conveys the force and pertinence of Scrimgeour's attack. No critic who wants to give a positive account of *Gatsby* can afford to ignore it.

From the mid-1960s other, uncomfortable questions began to be raised about Fitzgerald's fiction, relating especially to his representations of ethnic minorities, of sexuality, and of women. In 1967, Robert Forrey addressed the issue of Fitzgerald's portrayal of African-Americans, an issue that is more than ever active today, when American literature has been reshaped by African-American writers and critics. His essay is discussed and quoted in this Guide. The same year saw the publication of Leslie A. Fiedler's critical blockbuster *Love and Death in the American Novel* which vividly opened up the question of sexuality in Fitzgerald's fiction, particularly in relation to the significance of Daisy in *The Great Gatsby*. This Guide includes his discussion of the matter. At the start of the 1970s, Milton R. Stern and John F. Callahan, in their respective ways, looked again at the question of Fitzgerald's relationship to American history, and excerpts from both their books are provided. These are followed by a discussion of Peter Gregg Slater's essay 'Ethnicity in *The Great Gatsby*', which quotes his concise and penetrating analysis of the exclusions of Nick Carraway's 'American Dream'. Two essays, by Joan S. Korenman and Leland S. Person, Jr, focus, like Leslie A. Fiedler but with rather different emphases, on Fitzgerald's representation of Daisy in *The Great Gatsby*, and raise challenging questions. Their essays are followed by a powerful psychoanalytic account of the novel by A. B. Paulson, which reads it in terms of the psychological mechanisms of splitting. The examples of important 1970s' criticism conclude with an excerpt from Keath Fraser's provocative essay, which offers us a gay Gatsby.

In the 1980s, *Gatsby* studies marked time to some extent. A number of biographical and critical books on Fitzgerald appeared, including Matthew J. Bruccoli's magisterial biography, and there was a continuing stream of essays on *Gatsby*, but among much competent work, little new ground was broken, despite the large changes that were then coming over literary studies. An exception is Richard Godden's essay in which Bertolt Brecht comes to West Egg, and finds that Jay Gatsby is an actor in the alienation style. This Guide provides an extract from Godden's stylish interpretation. In the late 1980s, Michael Holquist invited Mikhail Bakhtin to meet Gatsby, and the results of the encounter are also recorded in these pages. That brings us to present times: and it is good to be able to report that, in the 1990s, we seem to have entered a new era of *Gatsby* studies. The final chapter of this Guide gives excerpts from three important pieces of criticism: Patti White's brilliant post-modernist/(post)-structuralist reading, which sees *Gatsby*'s guest list as a model of narrative; Ronald Berman's vivid, perceptive mapping of the intricate network of connections between the novel and the high and popular culture of its time; and Frances Kerr's richly suggestive interpretation of *Gatsby* as a challenge to modernist gender constructions.

This Guide offers itself as a history, an anthology and a contribution to a dialogue. It is a history in that it provides a selection of primary sources, in the form of extracts from the original critical documents, with a linking commentary between them; it is an anthology in that it gathers together and arranges choice examples of living criticism, from the past and from the present; and it is a contribution to that ongoing, many-voiced dialogue between *The Great Gatsby*, its readers, and its critics, which is surely the most exciting, and the most enduring, of all *Gatsby*'s parties.

CHAPTER ONE

The Road from West Egg: Early Reviews to Posthumous Revival, 1925–49

T HE GREAT *Gatsby* was not hailed as a masterpiece on its first appearance in April 1925. The responses of reviewers ranged from dismissal to qualified praise. *The New York World* headed its anonymous brief review: 'F. Scott Fitzgerald's Latest a Dud',[1] while Ruth Snyder in the *New York Evening World* concluded: 'We are quite convinced after reading *The Great Gatsby* that Mr Fitzgerald is not one of the great American writers of today'.[2] In the *Brooklyn Daily Eagle*, Ruth Hale, responding to the Scribner's book-jacket blurb that called *Gatsby* 'a magical, living book, blended of irony, romance and mysticism', challenged: 'Find me one chemical trace of magic, life, irony, romance or mysticism in all of *The Great Gatsby* and I will bind myself to read one Scott Fitzgerald book a week for the rest of my life'.[3] Harvey Eagleton, in a longer and more considered review in the *Dallas Morning News* did acknowledge that *Gatsby* was Fitzgerald's attempt to move into a different fictional field, but he judged it a failure; like all his books, in Eagleton's view, it has nothing constructive to offer and for that reason cannot hope to rise above being '"popular fiction" of the most ephemeral variety'.[4] Eagleton finds the 'creative faculty' lacking in Fitzgerald, seeing him as 'continuously auto-biographic',[5] and identifying *Gatsby*'s narrator, Nick Carraway, with Fitzgerald himself. His review concludes: 'The Roman candle which sent out a few gloriously coloured balls at the first lighting seems to be ending in a fizzle of smoke and sparks'.[6]

Other reviewers shared Eagleton's recognition that Fitzgerald had tried to write a different kind of novel from his earlier work, but gave a more positive verdict. Fanny Butcher's review in the *Chicago Daily Tribune* was headed: 'New Fitzgerald Book Proves He's Really a Writer'. Like Eagleton, Butcher related *Gatsby* to Fitzgerald's previous novels, but found *The Great Gatsby* 'as different from [those] as experience is from innocence'.[7] The idea that *The Great Gatsby* was a novel of 'experience' rather than of 'innocence' was echoed by a number of reviewers who found that it showed, to a greater or lesser extent, a more mature Fitzgerald. An anonymous review in the editorial section of the *Raleigh News and Observer* discerned 'a new note in Fitzgerald's latest book – just a hint of maturity that is not to be found in his other books'.[8] Laurence Stallings in the *New York World* felt that Fitzgerald's novel fell short of 'full maturation' because of the 'lack of breadth in the portrait' of Gatsby, but nonetheless found in the work an unquestionable 'maturity of viewpoint'.[9] In a review in the *Baltimore Evening Sun,* headed 'Scott Fitzgerald's Latest Novel Is Heralded as His Best', Hunter Stagg declared that *Gatsby* showed Fitzgerald to be 'a man really progressing toward artistic maturity'.[10] Two clippings in Fitzgerald's scrapbooks, the sources of which have not been identified, felt that, with *Gatsby*, maturity had been achieved. In one clipping, Edward Shenton called *Gatsby* 'a mature conception',[11] and in a second, an anonymous reviewer saw Fitzgerald assuming, with *Gatsby*, the 'role of mature artist'.[12] Other reviewers made a similar point in different words. William Curtis, in *Town and Country*, felt that, after Fitzgerald's previous novels, meeting Fitzgerald in *The Great Gatsby* was 'somewhat like realizing that a hopeful child has become adult',[13] while Gretchen Mount, in the *Detroit Free Press* affirmed: 'Scott Fitzgerald has grown up'.[14]

The Great Gatsby also won praise from reviewers for its style and structure. While Ruth Snyder of the *New York Evening World* found the style 'painfully forced',[15] Phil. A. Kinsley in the *Philadelphia Record* called it 'superb',[16] and Laurence Stallings in the *New York World* claimed that Gatsby showed 'an interest in the colour and sweep of prose, in the design and integrity of the novel . . . like nothing else he has attempted'.[17] 'H. B.' of the *New York Post* felt the novel 'demonstrat[ed] an admirable mastery of his medium both in style and construction', though he found the construction wanting in that '[t]he plot and its developments work out too geometrically and too perfectly for *The Great Gatsby* to be a great novel'; the book was 'as perfectly constructed as a good short story, and even the best short stories have something of the managed and diagrammed about them'.[18] In one unidentified clipping in Fitzgerald's scrapbook, Walter K. Schwinn applauded 'the masterly organization of the narrative',[19] and Edward Shenton, in the same review in which he called *Gatsby* 'a mature conception', said that the novel showed that Fitzgerald had 'discovered how to mould a story and then conceal the structure'.[20] Shenton's view that the structure of *Gatsby* was well-crafted but unobtrusive was echoed by a third unidentified, and this time anonymous, review in Fitzgerald's scrapbook. This review is interesting both in itself and because, in the brief passage quoted opposite, it offered the beginnings of an analysis of Fitzgerald's technique that would be developed in James E. Miller, Jr's 1957 study of Fitzgerald, part of which is reprinted later in this book (see pp. 65–72):

■ The building up of our knowledge of Gatsby through the eyes of the young man whose house is next door is a remarkable exhibition of technique, but unlike most performances of this kind it does not obtrude itself as a device more important than the story itself. It is like the knowledge we build up through current gossip and confirm through sudden and dramatic incident.[21] □

This reviewer also homed in on one of the motifs that would provoke much later critical discussion – the eyes of Dr T. J. Eckleburg that 'seem at first an unjustifiable animism, but in the end their very grotesqueness in the presence of the final tragedy becomes something like a mockery, a grim and inevitable death mask'.[22] S/he was, in fact, among the few reviewers who picked out one or more of those passages in *Gatsby* that would become prominent in future critical debate. Harvey Eagleton does cite the 'list of . . . visitors' at Gatsby's parties, but he dismisses it as 'characteristically unnecessary'.[23] An unnamed reviewer in *The Outlook*, however, sees 'the catalogue of guests' as evidence of 'a vein of satiric invention'.[24] It is notable that, in the forty-nine reviews reprinted in Jackson R. Bryer's collection,[25] the remarks by Gatsby that would later become famous – that Daisy's '"voice is full of money"' (p. 94) and that, even if she did love Tom, '"it was just personal"' (p. 119) – are not discussed, and that only one review – that of Gilbert Seldes, printed on pages 29–31 – refers to the concluding passage of the novel that would later become so celebrated and so crucial to the claim that the primary theme of *The Great Gatsby* was 'the American dream': a claim whose most influential exponent was Marius Bewley in his essay 'Scott Fitzgerald's Criticism of America', an extract from which appears later in this book (see pp. 57–61).

A number of reviews made comparisons between *The Great Gatsby* and the work of other writers. References to Henry James occur more than once. Edwin Clark, for instance, in the *New York Times Book Review*, compares *Gatsby* to Henry James's *The Turn of the Screw* (1898), both because it is 'more a long short story than a novel', and because of its 'method of telling': in James's tale, 'the evil . . . which so endangered the two children was never exactly stated beyond a suggested generalization', and, similarly, 'Gatsby's fortune, business, even his connection with underworld figures, remain vague generalizations'.[26] A comparison between James and Fitzgerald is also made in Carl Van Vechten's review, printed on pages 27 and 28, but Vechten sees the work as resembling, not *The Turn of the Screw*, but *Daisy Miller* (1879). A brief anonymous item in the *St. Paul Pioneer Press* compares the 'ironic compassion' with which Fitzgerald handles his characters to that of the English novelist May Sinclair,[27] while Laurence Stallings finds that Willa Cather's novel *A Lost Lady* (1923) shares two of the elements that, as we noted earlier, Stallings identifies in *Gatsby* – a 'maturity of viewpoint' combined with a 'lack of breadth' in the portrait of its central protagonist.[28] William Curtis sees Fitzgerald in *Gatsby* as having 'definitely abandoned the school' of Sinclair Lewis's *Main Street* (1920) and 'turned to the studiedly brilliant style' of the French novelist Paul Morand and the English novelist Ronald Firbank.[29] John McClure, judging *Gatsby* to have 'merit' but finding it 'half-baked', sees Fitzgerald as 'still where he was five years ago' and 'still fac[ing] the necessity of a decision between writing in the fashion like Mr Rupert Hughes, or according to his inner lights like James Branch Cabell and Sherwood Anderson'.[30] Gilbert Seldes, in the review printed below, found *Gatsby* 'passionate as [Ford Madox Ford's] *Some Do Not* (1924) is passionate'; much later, in an essay published in 1970, Richard Foster was to develop a comparison between Fitzgerald and Ford, though he would compare *Gatsby* with *The Good Soldier* (1915) rather than with *Some Do Not*.[31]

The first review reprinted here is by Isabel Paterson, from the *New York Herald Tribune*. It is one of two reviews of *Gatsby* that she wrote in 1925 – the other review, later and briefer, was for *McNaught's Monthly*.[32] Twenty-six years later, in his introduction to his famous collection, *F. Scott Fitzgerald: The Man and His Work* (first published 1951), Alfred Kazin cited Paterson's final verdict, in the *New York Herald Tribune Review*, that *Gatsby* was 'a book of the season only',[33] and called it, with irony, an 'historic pronouncement'[34] – implying that Paterson had been obtusely in error. But, in fact, the review, taken as a whole, is judicious, maintaining what Paterson herself recognises as an uneasy ambivalence between dismissing the novel completely and praising it unequivocally. She does commend its balance and shapeliness, and she does usefully set it in the broader cultural context of the time, in which there was a strong sense of a division between life, which is formless, and fiction, which is, or ought to be, patterned: a sense that we might now see as distinctively modernist, and which can be found in, for example, T. S. Eliot's praise of James Joyce's use of myth in *Ulysses* (1922) as 'a way of controlling, of ordering, of giving a shape and a significance to the immense panorama of futility and anarchy which is contemporary history'.[35] But Paterson's admiration for some aspects of *Gatsby* does not overcome her doubts as to the overall value of the novel, and these doubts do not make her review a superseded curiosity, as Kazin implies: they are doubts that have been felt, both in 1925 and subsequently, by a number of readers and critics, and her attempts to explain and justify them are still worth considering.

She offers four main reasons for her negative responses to *Gatsby*. First, there is her feeling that the characters about whom Fitzgerald writes are lightweight, and that Gatsby is their archetype – 'a man from nowhere, without roots or background', as she calls him, a dismissal of Gatsby that seems, significantly, to echo Tom Buchanan's. Then there is the charge that Fitzgerald is a virtuoso at reproducing surfaces but that 'he has not, yet, gone below that glittering surface' – a charge that, as we shall see, is echoed by H. L. Mencken's review, but which might be rethought today, when post-modernism has challenged the distinction between 'surface' and 'depth' in which 'depth' is a privileged term. Thirdly, Paterson dismisses the implication that Gatsby's passion for Daisy might be related to her 'superior social status' and 'wealth'; this is a valuable corrective to any attempt to explain Gatsby's passion wholly in such terms, but a questionable one insofar as it seeks to exclude consideration of the complex relations between social and financial inequality and desire that the novel dramatises. Paterson's aversion to sociological explanations – she uses the adjective 'sociological' in her review to suggest the limitations of *This Side of Paradise* – is also evident in her fourth objection, when she challenges the contrast Nick implies between the wild East and the sober West, and affirms that profligate pleasure-seekers are to be found everywhere. While this unduly plays down the sociological aspect of *Gatsby*, it also displays a salutary scepticism about taking the East/West contrast too simply: twenty years later, in 1955, R. W. Stallman was to argue vigorously, and in detail, that such a contrast could not be sustained (see pp. 62–5). In her own challenge to the contrast, Paterson also, taking a hint from the novel itself (p. 88), makes a comparison that will be developed in later criticism between Gatsby and Trimalchio, the extravagant and fabulously wealthy party host in Petronius's first-century AD Latin novel *Satyricon* (about AD 54–68).[36]

■ For a reviewer with a conscience, here is a nice problem – to give Scott Fitzgerald's new novel its just due without seeming to overpraise it, or, contrariwise, to say plainly that it is neither profound nor durable, without producing the impression that it is insignificant (which it is not).

This is like announcing a decision on points, when the public has been expecting a knock-out. The former method of winning is quite as honourable, but not so showy. *This Side of Paradise* was put over with a punch of a very special kind. But *The Great Gatsby* is the first convincing testimony that Mr. Fitzgerald is also an artist.

The reason why *This Side of Paradise* created such a furore was not its intrinsic literary worth, but its rare combination of precocity and true originality. The universal difficulty for beginning novelists is to use what they know. Fiction must be shaped to a pattern. Life appears to be formless, incoherent, fantastically irrelevant. In the individual experience episodes don't seem to hang together; cause and effect are not even on speaking terms; apparently things just happen. The technical tricks of foreshortening for perspective, of working to scale, of selecting and composing, and, above all, of using documentary facts simply as a painter employs a model for his imaginative figure paintings, these things are usually learned by a long process of trial and error. For this reason youth has seldom been articulate of its own emotions and ideas. The young are busy drawing from casts, from 'the antique', learning the craft. By the time they have skill enough to work from the life – the first fine, careless rapture has faded. It has to be done from memory.

Mr. Fitzgerald managed somehow to pour his glowing youth on the page before it could escape forever. His natural facility was so extraordinary that he could get along with a minimum of conscious technique. Even the inevitable crudities and banalities of his first novel were a part of its authenticity. They were genuine echoes of the gaucheries of his age and environment. The smart, swaggering, callow cubs of 1915 (was it?) were like that; such were their amusements, catchwords, standards and point of view.

It was really a sociological document. Not even a personal confession, in the main, but a snapshot of one aspect of the crowd mind.

So is *The Great Gatsby* in a sense. But it is first and foremost a novel, which its predecessor wasn't. It is beautifully and delicately balanced; its shapeliness is the more praiseworthy for the extreme fragility of the material. It is an almost perfectly fulfilled intention. There is not one accidental phrase in it, nor yet one obvious or blatant line.

And to work at all with such people, such types and backgrounds, is something of a feat. They are the froth of society, drifting sand, along the shore. Can one twist ropes of sand? Decidedly not; but one may take the sand and fuse it in the warmth of fancy, and with skill enough one may blow it into enchanting bubbles of iridescent glass.

The Great Gatsby is just such an imponderable and fascinating trifle. Gatsby himself is the archetype of the species of ephemerides who occupy the whole tale. He was a man from nowhere, without roots or background, absolutely self-made in the image of an obscure and undefined ideal. You could not exactly call him an impostor; he was himself an artist of sorts, trying to remould himself. His stage was a Long Island summer colony, where he came in contact with the realities of his dream and was broken by them. That he was a bootlegger, a crook, maybe a killer (all on the grand scale) is part of the irony of things; for it wasn't his sins he paid for, but his aspirations. He was an incurable romanticist (I would draw a distinction between that and a romantic, as between sentimentality and sentiment), and his mistake was to accept life at its face value.

There, too, is the chief weakness of Mr. Fitzgerald as a novelist. In reproducing surfaces his virtuosity is amazing. He gets the exact tone, the note, the shade of the season and place he is working on; he is more contemporary than any newspaper, and yet he is (by the present token) an artist. But he has not, yet, gone below that glittering surface except by a kind of happy accident, and then he is rather bewildered by the results of his own intuition. Observe how he explains the duration and intensity of Gatsby's passion for Daisy Buchanan. He says it was because of Daisy's superior social status, because she was a daughter of wealth – Gatsby hadn't realized 'how extraordinary a "nice" girl could be' (p. 117); and the revelation dazzled him, made him Daisy's slave forever. Pooh, there is no explanation of love. Daisy might have been a cash girl or a mill hand, and made as deep a mark – it is Carmen and Don José over again. There isn't any why about that sort of thing.

Again, Mr. Fitzgerald identifies the strange rout who came of [sic] Gatsby's incredible parties as 'the East', in contrast to a more solid, integrated society of the Middle West. But these drunken spenders and migratory merrymakers exist proportionately everywhere; there are more of them in and around New York because there is more of New York, and they congregate chiefly where there is easy money – like midges dancing over a pool. And they come from all quarters. They are not even peculiar to this age; they made up the guests at Trimalchio's supper, and Lucian satirized them.

But Gatsby hasn't the robust vitality of the vulgar Trimalchio. He and his group remain types. What has never been alive cannot very well go on living; so this is a book of the season only, but so peculiarly of the season, that it is in its small way unique.[37] □

The kind of ambivalence exemplified by Paterson's review is absent from the short but perceptive review by 'E. K.' that follows. The anonymous reviewer does not call *Gatsby* a masterpiece; but s/he commends it highly, finding, like a number of other reviewers, a more mature Fitzgerald in the novel, a Fitzgerald who combines detachment with a new sense of values and a new emotion, that of pity. 'E. K.' touches on an important issue when s/he alludes to the mixture of genres in *Gatsby* – s/he identifies melodrama, detective fiction, satire and what s/he calls 'jazz-age extravaganza', but other genres, for example the 'novel of manners', could be proposed: there is still room today for an extensive study of *Gatsby* in terms of genre. 'E. K.'s praise of the efficiency of the novel was, however, to be echoed sixty years later in 1985, when Kenneth E. Eble, in a discussion of how far *Gatsby* could be considered an example of 'the great American novel', said that 'one can, only half facetiously, propose that [it] is an *efficient* novel, and thereby identifiably and pleasingly American'.[38]

■ Reading F. Scott Fitzgerald's new novel, *The Great Gatsby*, one has an impression that the author entertained in his urbane and ever more polished imagination ideas for a melodrama, a detective story, and a fantastic satire, with his usual jazz-age extravaganza adding its voice to the mental conversation. And the result is not confusion, but a graceful, finished tale, as if each of the four had contributed a keen, well-timed remark to a good-mannered and highly efficient committee meeting.

Jay Gatsby is a mysterious and slightly sinister figure, who emerges from nowhere to buy a twentieth-century palace at West Egg, Long Island, from which he dispenses hospitality with lavish and dazzling extravagance – a modern Solomon erecting a bizarre temple to the wayward god Popularity. Fitzgerald has painted with swift, sure strokes the pictures of his bewildering parties, where crowds of people, many of them unknown to the host, come and go, drinking his champagne, flitting through his gorgeous rooms, velvet lawns, and bright gardens like greedy moths around a cool flame, warranted not to singe their wings. And with a noticeable difference from his attitude toward similar frolics in other books, it is as an observer rather than as a participant that Fitzgerald describes these parties. There is a new awareness of values in his attitude toward the dubious Croesus of West Egg and the careless men and women who cast aspersions on Gatsby's career with a mordant wit stimulated by Gatsby's liquor. Very deftly he suggests that Gatsby, for all his uncertain background and the haziness in which his vague business connections and pre-sumably ill-gotten wealth envelop him, is far more real than the men and women who stoop from the security of their own well-ordered business and social worlds to play with him and to spend his money. His is a vitality which they lack – the inner fire which comes from living with an incorruptible dream, even if extraordinary material corruption has been practised in its realization.

Gatsby's dream centres on Daisy, an alluring creature who deserted him for wealth and safety in the person of Tom Buchanan in the days before Gatsby had begun the shady business operations which have earned him his vast fortune. And Daisy, with the casual cruelty of her class, lets him hope for an instant, and then when events have rushed her toward a crisis, withdraws into her ivory tower, leaving Gatsby to bear the brunt of the havoc she has wrought. She speaks no word of sorrow or regret when the results of his chivalry have swept him to tragedy.

It is a colourful, provocative tale, moving with an excitement that is saved from melodrama by a kind of delicate unreality. The Fitzgerald who tells it is no longer the impudent youngster, glorying in his own sophistication, making rather elaborate and obvious grimaces in the face of whatever Main Street inhibitions he can get to notice him. He is as gay, as extravagant as ever, but not quite as tolerant, and no longer indifferent, for, in the tragic ending of Gatsby's grotesque career, he shows us a new emotion – that of pity.[39] □

The review by H. L. Mencken that follows was inevitably bound to have an impact, because of Mencken's position in American culture. Matthew Bruccoli, in his biography of Fitzgerald, calls the Mencken of 1919 'the most powerful critic in America'.[40] Henry Louis Mencken was an essayist, editor and literary critic, and in 1919, his study of the development of English in the USA, *The American Language*, had made him famous beyond literary circles. From 1908 to 1923, he edited, with the critic George Jean Nathan, *The Smart Set*, a New York magazine with a modest circulation but of great influence; between 1919 and 1922, it had published eleven of Fitzgerald's short stories and plays; the last of these was 'The Diamond as Big as the Ritz', which appeared in June 1922. Mencken and Nathan then went on to found *The American Mercury*, which Mencken edited from 1924 to 1933; two of Fitzgerald's stories appeared in this magazine, including, in June 1924, 'Absolution', a story later collected in *All the Sad Young Men* (1926), and one that Fitzgerald claimed in a letter of 1934 was 'intended to be a picture of [Gatsby's] early life' that he had cut because he 'preferred to preserve the sense of mystery'.[41]

In his review of *Gatsby*, written for a newspaper in his home town of Baltimore, Mencken sometimes indulges in knockabout self-display and caricature, for example in his dismissal of the story of *Gatsby* as a 'glorified anecdote' – a description that might, after all, be derisively applied to many of Henry James's stories and tales. For all his facetiousness, however, Mencken does make some serious points. Like 'E. K.' and several other reviewers, Mencken finds a new Fitzgerald in *Gatsby*. He sets this new Fitzgerald in what he sees as a specifically American context, in which literary success is both very rewarding and very dangerous – indeed, potentially fatal – to a writer's talent. But Mencken feels that Fitzgerald has escaped this, by virtue of facing up to his deficiencies, resisting the temptation to be facile, and working hard at his craft. While he finds that Fitzgerald is still more interested in spectacle – the spectacle of wealthy and idle Americans – than in literary style, he commends the energy and accuracy of Fitzgerald's portrayal. Mencken echoes, however, Isabel Paterson's charge that Fitzgerald remains superficial.

■ Scott Fitzgerald's new novel, *The Great Gatsby*, is in form no more than a glorified anecdote, and not too probable at that. The scene is the Long Island that hangs precariously on the edges of the New York city ash dumps – the Long Island of gaudy villas and bawdy house parties. The theme is the old one of a romantic and preposterous love – the ancient *fidelis ad urrum* [Mencken may mean *fidelis ad unum* – 'faithful to one'] motif reduced to a *macabre* humour. The principal personage is a bounder typical of those parts – a fellow who seems to know everyone and yet remains unknown to all – a young man with a great deal of mysterious money, the tastes of a movie actor and, under it all, the simple sentimentality of a somewhat sclerotic fat woman.

This clown Fitzgerald rushes to his death in nine short chapters. The other performers in the Totentanz [dance of death] are of a like, or even worse quality. One of them is a rich man who carries on a grotesque intrigue with the wife of a garage keeper. Another is a woman golfer who wins championships by cheating. A third, a sort of chorus to the tragic farce, is a bond salesman – symbol of the New America! Fitzgerald clears them all off at last by a triple butchery. The garage keeper's wife, rushing out upon the road to escape her husband's third degree, is run down and killed by the wife of her lover. The garage keeper, misled by the lover, kills the lover of the lover's wife – the Great Gatsby himself. Another bullet, and the garage keeper is also reduced to offal. Choragus fades away [Choragus is the leader of the chorus in ancient Greek drama – 'Choragus' here is Nick Carraway]. The crooked lady golfer departs. The lover of the garage keeper's wife goes back to his own consort. The immense house of the Great Gatsby stands idle, its bedrooms given over to the bat and the owl, its cocktail shakers dry. The curtain lurches down.

II

This story is obviously unimportant, and though, as I shall show, it has its place in the Fitzgerald canon, it is certainly not to be put on the same shelf with, say, *This Side of Paradise*. What ails it, fundamentally, is the plain fact that it is simply a story – that Fitzgerald seems to be far more interested in maintaining its suspense than in getting under the skins of its people. It is not that they are false; it is that they are taken too much for granted. Only Gatsby himself genuinely lives and breathes. The rest are mere marionettes – often astonishingly lifelike, but nevertheless not quite alive.

What gives the story distinction is something quite different from the management of the action or the handling of the characters; it is the charm and beauty of the writing. In Fitzgerald's first days it seemed almost unimaginable that he would ever show such qualities.

His writing, then, was extraordinarily slipshod – at times almost illiterate. He seemed to be devoid of any feeling for the colour and savour of words. He could see people clearly and he could devise capital situations, but as writer *qua* writer [that is, in the capacity of writer] he was apparently little more than a bright college boy. The critics of the Republic were not slow to discern the fact. They praised *This Side of Paradise* as a story, as a social document, but they were almost unanimous in denouncing it as a piece of writing.

It is vastly to Fitzgerald's credit that he appears to have taken their caveats seriously and pondered them to good effect. In *The Great Gatsby* the highly agreeable fruits of that pondering are visible. The story, for all its basic triviality, has a fine texture, a careful and brilliant finish. The obvious phrase is simply not in it. The sentences roll along smoothly, sparklingly, variously. There is evidence in every line of hard and intelligent effort. It is a quite new Fitzgerald who emerges from this little book and the qualities that he shows are dignified and solid. *This Side of Paradise*, after all, might have been merely a lucky accident. But *The Great Gatsby*, a far inferior story at bottom, is plainly the product of a sound and stable talent, conjured into being by hard work.

III

I make much of this improvement because it is of an order not often witnessed in American writers, and seldom indeed in those who start off with a popular success. The usual progression, indeed, is in the opposite direction. Every year first books of great promise are published – and every year a great deal of stale drivel is printed by the promising authors of year before last. The rewards of literary success in this country are so vast that, when they come early, they are not unnaturally somewhat demoralizing. The average author yields to them readily. Having struck the bull's eye once, he is too proud to learn new tricks. Above all, he is too proud to tackle hard work. The result is a gradual degeneration of whatever talent he had at the beginning. He begins to imitate himself. He peters out.

There is certainly no sign of petering out in Fitzgerald. After his first experimenting he plainly sat himself down calmly to consider his deficiencies. They were many and serious. He was, first of all, too facile. He could write entertainingly without giving thought to form and organization. He was, secondly, somewhat amateurish. The materials and methods of his craft, I venture, rather puzzled him. He used them ineptly. His books showed brilliancy in conception, but they were crude and even ignorant in detail. They suggested, only too often, the improvisations of a pianist playing furiously by ear but unable to read notes.

These are the defects that he has now got rid of. *The Great Gatsby*, I seem to recall, was announced a long while ago. It was probably several years on the stocks. It shows on every page the results of that laborious effort. Writing it, I take it, was painful. The author wrote, tore up, rewrote, tore up again. There are pages so artfully contrived that one can no more imagine improvising them than one can imagine improvising a fugue. They are full of little delicacies, charming turns of phrase, penetrating second thoughts. In other words, they are easy and excellent reading – which is what always comes out of hard writing.

IV

Thus Fitzgerald, the stylist, arises to challenge Fitzgerald, the social historian, but I doubt that the latter ever quite succumbs to the former. The thing that chiefly interests the basic Fitzgerald is still the florid show of modern American life – and especially the devil's dance that goes on at the top. He is unconcerned about the sweatings and sufferings of the nether herd; what engrosses him is the high carnival of those who have too much money to spend and too much time for the spending of it. Their idiotic pursuit of sensation, their almost incredible stupidity and triviality, their glittering swinishness – these are the things that go into his notebook.

In *The Great Gatsby*, though he does not go below the surface, he depicts this rattle and hullabaloo with great gusto and, I believe, with sharp accuracy. The Long Island he sets before us is no fanciful Alsatia; it actually exists. More, it is worth any social historian's study, for its influence upon the rest of the country is immense and profound. What is vogue among the profiteers of Manhattan and their harlots today is imitated by the flappers of the Bible Belt country clubs week after next. The whole tone of American society, once so highly formalized and so suspicious of change, is now taken largely from frail ladies who were slinging hash a year ago.

Fitzgerald showed the end products of the new dispensation in *This Side of Paradise*. In *The Beautiful and the* [sic] *Damned*, he cut a bit lower. In *The Great Gatsby* he comes near the bottom. Social leader and jail bird, grand lady and kept woman, are here almost indistinguishable. We are in an atmosphere grown increasingly levantine. The Paris of the Second Empire pales to a sort of snobbish chautauqua [a name, derived from Chautauqua in New York State, for a summer school or other educational course]; the New York of Ward McAllister becomes the scene of a convention of Gold Star Mothers. To find a parallel for the grossness and debauchery that now reign in New York one must go back to the Constantinople of Basil I.[42] □

A less exhibitionist, more thoughtful account of *The Great Gatsby* than Mencken's was provided by William Rose Benét in a review headed 'An Admirable Novel'. Benét, the elder brother of the better-known poet, short story writer and novelist Stephen Vincent Benét, was himself a poet, and won a Pulitzer Prize for his autobiography *The Dust Which Is God* (1941). In 1924, he founded a journal, *The Saturday Review of Literature*, and it was here that his response to *Gatsby* appeared.

Benét sets *Gatsby* in the context of Fitzgerald's previous writing and literary career, and acknowledges, like Mencken, that he has feared for Fitzgerald's artistic well-being. But he is more definite than Mencken as to the nature of the threat – it consists of the commercial pressures of the magazine market for which Fitzgerald had written many short stories. Like Mencken, however, Benét believes that *The Great Gatsby* shows that Fitzgerald has escaped this danger, and displays maturity in its attitude and its craftmanship. Its attitude is one of disillusionment and detachment; Fitzgerald is still able to evoke the glitter of the 1920s but he is no longer dazzled by it; he sees its underlying emptiness and impoverishment. As Benét puts it, '[I]rony has entered his soul'. In terms of craftmanship, Benét recognises – in contrast to, say, Harvey Eagleton – that Nick Carraway is not wholly to be identified with Fitzgerald himself. He also commends Fitzgerald's ability to bring the whole range of his characters to life; and he homes in on two passages of the novel that were later to become famous – the conclusion and the 'catalogue of guests'. He praises the final sentence for its philosophic depth, although he does not explicate this, and he cites the catalogue of guests as a notable example of Fitzgerald's 'astonishing feats' in the novel.

Benét's review is also important for its suggestion that Gatsby is both specifically American, that '[t]he mystery of Gatsby is a mystery saliently characteristic' of this epoch of American life, and that he is also a universal figure, a contemporary incarnation of an archetype, the 'fortunate youth'. The idea that Gatsby is distinctively American, and the idea that he is universal, which Benét juxtaposes in his review, will form two significant threads – sometimes interweaving, sometimes clashing and diverging – in the later critical history of *The Great Gatsby*.

■ The book finished, we find again, at the top of page three [in the first American edition], the introductory remark:

> No – Gatsby turned out all right at the end; it is what preyed on Gatsby, what foul dust floated in the wake of his dreams that temporarily closed out my interest in the abortive sorrows and short-winded elations of men. (p. 6)

Scott Fitzgerald's new novel is a remarkable analysis of this 'foul dust'. And his analysis leads him, at the end of the book, to the conclusion that all of us 'beat on, boats against the current, borne back ceaselessly into the past' (p. 141). There is depth of philosophy in this.

The writer – for the story is told in the first person, but in a first person who is not exactly the author, but rather one of the number of personalities that compose the actual author, – the hypothetical chronicler of Gatsby is one in whose tolerance all sorts and conditions of men confided. So he came to Gatsby, and the history of Gatsby, obscured by the 'foul dust' aforementioned, 'fair sickened' him of human nature.

The Great Gatsby is a disillusioned novel, and a mature novel. It is a novel with pace, from the first word to the last, and also a novel of admirable 'control'. Scott Fitzgerald started his literary career with enormous facility. His high spirits were infectious. The queer charm, colour, wonder, and drama of a young and reckless world beat constantly upon his senses, stimulated a young and intensely romantic mind to a mixture of realism and extravaganza shaken up like a cocktail. Some people are born with a knack, whether for cutting figure eights, curving an in-sheet, picking out tunes on the piano, or revealing some peculiar charm of their intelligence on the typewritten page. Scott Fitzgerald was born with a knack for writing. What they call 'a natural gift'. And another gift of the fairies at his christening was a reckless confidence in himself. And he was quite intoxicated with the joy of life and rather engagingly savage toward an elder world. He was out 'to get the world by the neck' and put words on paper in the patterns his exuberant fancy suggested. He didn't worry much about what had gone before Fitzgerald in literature. He dreamed gorgeously of what there was in Fitzgerald to 'tell the world'.

And all these elements contributed to the amazing performance of *This Side of Paradise*, amazing in its excitement and gusto, amazing in phrase and epithet, amazing no less for all sorts of thoroughly bad writing pitched in with the good, for preposterous carelessness, and amazing as well for the sheer pace of the narrative and the fresh quality of its oddly pervasive poetry. Short stories of flappers and philosophers displayed the same vitality and flourished much the same faults. *Tales of the Jazz Age* inhabited the same glamour. *The Beautiful and Damned*, while still in the mirage, furnished a more valuable document concerning the younger generation of the first quarter of the Twentieth Century. But brilliant, irrefutably brilliant as were certain passages of the novels and tales of which the 'boy wonder' of our time was so lavish, arresting as were certain gleams of insight, intensely promising as were certain observed facilities, there remained in general, glamour, glamour everywhere, and, after the glamour faded, little for the mind to hold except an impression of this kinetic glamour.

There ensued a play [*The Vegetable*], in which the present writer found the first act (as read) excellent and the rest as satire somehow stricken with palsy, granted the cleverness of the original idea. There ensued a magazine phase in which, as was perfectly natural, most of the stories were negligible, though a few showed flashes. But one could discern the demands of the 'market' blunting and dulling the blade of that bright sword wildly whirled. One began to believe that Fitzgerald was coming into line with the purveyors of the staple product. And suddenly one wanted him back in the phase when he was writing so well and, at the same time, writing so very badly. Today he was writing, for the most part, on an even level of magazine acceptability, and on an even level of what seemed perilously like absolute staleness of mind toward anything really creative.

But *The Great Gatsby* comes suddenly to knock all that surmise into a cocked hat. *The Great Gatsby* reveals thoroughly matured craftsmanship. It has structure. It has high occasions of felicitous, almost magic, phrase. And most of all, it is out of the mirage. For the first time Fitzgerald surveys the Babylonian captivity of this era unblinded by the bright lights. He gives you the bright lights in full measure, the affluence, the waste, but also the nakedness of the scaffolding that scrawls skeletons upon the sky when the gold and blue and red and green have faded, the ugly passion, the spiritual meagreness, the empty shell of luxury, the old irony of 'fair-weather friends'.

Gatsby remains. The mystery of Gatsby is a mystery saliently characteristic of this age in America. And Gatsby is only another modern instance of the eternal 'fortunate youth'. His actual age does not matter, in either sense. For all the cleverness of his hinted nefarious proceedings, he is the coney caught. For he is a man with a dream at the mercy of the foul dust that sometimes seems only to exist in order to swarm against the dream, whose midge-dance blots it from the sky. It is a strange dream, Gatsby's, – but he was a man who had hope. He was a child. He believed in a childish thing.

It is because Fitzgerald makes so acid on your tongue the taste of the defeat of Gatsby's childishness that his book, in our opinion, 'acquires merit'. And there are parts of the book, notably the second chapter, that, in our opinion, could not have been better written. There are astonishing feats that no one but Fitzgerald could have brought off, notably the catalogue of guests in Chapter IV. And Tom Buchanan, the '"great big hulking . . . specimen"' (p. 13), is an American university product of almost unbearable reality.

Yet one feels that, though irony has entered into Fitzgerald's soul, the sense of mere wonder is still stronger. And, of course, there is plenty of entertainment in the story. It arises in part from the almost photographic reproduction of the actions, gestures, speech of the types

25

Fitzgerald has chosen in their moments of stress. Picayune souls for the most part, and Gatsby heroic among them only because he is partly a crazy man with a dream. But what does all that matter with the actual narration so vivid and graphic? As for the drama of the accident and Gatsby's end, it is the kind of thing newspapers carry every day, except that here is a novelist who has gone behind the curt paragraphs and made the real people live and breathe in all their sordidness. They are actual, rich and poor, cultivated and uncultivated, seen for a moment or two only or followed throughout the story. They are memorable individuals of today – not types.

Perhaps you have gathered that we like the book! We do. It has some miscues, but they seem to us negligible. It is written with concision and precision and mastery of material.[43] □

Carl Van Vechten, the writer of the next review, shared Benét's liking for *Gatsby*. Van Vechten was himself a novelist closely associated with the representation of American life in New York in the 1920s, in such novels as *Peter Whiffle* (1922) and *The Blind Bow-Boy* (1923). His most praised work, *Nigger Heaven*, set among Harlem soirées and nightclubs, was published the year after *Gatsby*. Like Mencken and Benét, Van Vechten acknowledges the anxiety aroused by Fitzgerald's spectacular literary career, and he concurs with them in seeing *Gatsby* as a hopeful sign. He finds in it a quality of 'mysticism', and though he does not elaborate on what he means by this term, he is perhaps referring to those 'mythical' qualities of the novel that have been explored by some later critics. It is interesting to see that he mentions having read the short story 'Absolution' in the *American Mercury*, a short story that, as we have already noted, has close connections with *Gatsby*, connections that were later to be extensively explored in studies such as Henry Dan Piper's.[44]

Van Vechten also draws some interesting comparisons between Fitzgerald and other writers. One comparison is with the novelist and playwright Booth Tarkington, author of more than forty works of fiction, who between 1915 and 1924 had published three novels dealing with the rise of the *nouveau riche* businessman and its social effects: *The Turmoil* (1915); the Pulitzer Prize-winning *The Magnificent Ambersons* (1918), which was to be filmed in 1942 by Orson Welles; and *The Midlander* (1924); the three were published as a trilogy, *Growth*, in 1927. A second comparison is between Fitzgerald and the American naturalist novelist Frank Norris, best known for his novel *McTeague: A Story of San Francisco* (1899), the story of a physically huge and sluggish man whose inchoate desires drive him finally to murder.[45] The third comparison – and the one that has recurred in some later criticism – is between Fitzgerald and Henry James, in terms of both theme and technique. In particular, Van Vechten suggests, Gatsby is like Daisy Miller – a comparison that is also made, though in a different way, by Leslie A. Fiedler in his study *Love and Death in the American Novel*, from which there is an extract later in this Guide (see pp. 99–103).

■ What will be the future of F. Scott Fitzgerald? This query has been futilely repeated whenever a new book from his pen has appeared, since the initial interrogation which greeted the publication of that sophomoric masterpiece, *This Side of Paradise*. It will be asked more earnestly than before by prescient readers of *The Great Gatsby*, who will recognize therein a quality which has only recently made its debut in the writings of this brilliant young author, the quality vaguely referred to as mysticism. Moreover, this is a fine yarn, exhilaratingly spun.

Mr. Fitzgerald is a born story-teller; his words, phrases, and sentences carry the eye easily through to the end of the book. Further, his work is imbued with that rare and beneficent essence we hail as charm. He is by no means lacking in power, as several passages in the current opus abundantly testify, and he commands a quite uncanny gift for hitting off character or presenting a concept in a striking and memorable manner. The writer he most resembles, curiously enough, despite the dissimilarity in their choice of material and point of attack, is Booth Tarkington, but there exists at present in the work of Mr. Fitzgerald a potential brutality, a stark sense of reality, set off in his case by an ironic polish, that suggests a comparison with the Frank Norris of *Vandover and the Brute* (1914) and *McTeague*.

Up to date, Mr. Fitzgerald has occupied himself almost exclusively with the aspects and operations of the coeval flapper and cake-eater. No one else, perhaps, has delineated these mundane creatures quite as skilfully as he, and his achievement in this direction has been awarded authoritative recognition. He controls, moreover, the necessary magic to make his most vapid and rotterish characters interesting and even, on occasion, charming, in spite of (or possibly because of) the fact that they are almost invariably presented in advanced stages of intoxication. More cocktails and champagne are consumed in the novels of Scott Fitzgerald than a toper like Paul Verlaine could drink in a lifetime. *The Beautiful and Damned*, indeed, is an epic of inebriation beside which [Zola's] *L'Assommoir* (1877) fades into Victorian insipidity.

In *The Great Gatsby* there are several of Mr. Fitzgerald's typical flappers who behave in the manner he has conceived as typical of contemporary flapperdom. There is again a gargantuan drinking-party, conceived in a rowdy, hilarious, and highly titillating spirit. There is also, in this novel, as I have indicated above, something else. There is the character of Jay Gatsby.

This character, and the theme of the book in general, would have appealed to Henry James. In fact, it did appeal to Henry James. In one way or another this motif is woven into the tapestry of a score or more of his stories. In *Daisy Miller* you may find it complete. It is the theme of a soiled or rather cheap personality transfigured and rendered pathetically appealing through the possession of a passionate idealism. Although the comparison may be still further stressed, owing to the fact that Mr. Fitzgerald has chosen, as James so frequently chose, to see his story through the eyes of a spectator, it will be readily apparent that what he has done he has done in his own way, and that seems to me, in this instance, to be a particularly good way. The figure of Jay Gatsby, who invented an entirely fictitious career for himself out of material derived from inferior romances, emerges life-sized and life-like. His doglike fidelity not only to his ideal but to his fictions, his incredibly cheap and curiously imitative imagination, awaken for him not only our interest and suffrage, but also a certain liking, as they awaken it in the narrator, Nick Carraway.

When I read 'Absolution' in the *American Mercury* I realized that there were many potential qualities inherent in Scott Fitzgerald which hitherto had not been too apparent. *The Great Gatsby* confirms this earlier impression. What Mr. Fitzgerald may do in the future, therefore, I am convinced, depends to an embarrassing extent on the nature of his own ambitions.[46] □

The final review is by Gilbert Seldes. Seldes had been American correspondent of the *Écho de Paris* and was now managing editor of the literary magazine *The Dial*, and a regular and long-standing contributor to the New York *Journal* and to the magazine T. S. Eliot edited in London, *The New Criterion*. He had featured with Fitzgerald himself, and other writers such as Edmund Wilson, in a *Vanity Fair* spread in February 1922 announcing 'The New Generation in Literature'.[47] His books included *The Seven Lively Arts* (1924), *The Stammering Century* (1928) and *The Public Arts* (1956). A critic of popular culture as well as a literary critic, he later became director of TV programmes for the Columbia Broadcasting Company and professor and dean of the Annenberg School of Communications at the University of Pennsylvania.[48]

In his review for *The Dial*, Seldes joins Mencken, Benét, and Van Vechten in registering the anxiety that Fitzgerald's career aroused, and his anxiety focuses, like Van Vechten's, on Fitzgerald's short-story writing. He is more emphatic than the three previous reviewers, however, in affirming that *The Great Gatsby* shows that Fitzgerald has transcended his weaknesses. Not only does Seldes note the technical and artistic skill with which the novel is structured; he also specifies, as other reviewers had not done, some of the techniques Fitzgerald employs: the departures from straightforward chronology, the use of flashbacks, or what Seldes calls 'retrospects', and the deployment of selective, significant detail. Seldes makes an interesting attempt to suggest the differences in length and pace between the scenes and the way in which they relate to one another, and in contrast to 'H. B.''s view, cited earlier, that *Gatsby* is too 'diagrammed', he sees it as an organism rather than a puzzle. The technical skill helps to create a tragedy. Seldes finds irony in *Gatsby*, like Benét, pity, like 'E.K.', and one other quality – a consuming passion.

Seldes makes a number of interesting comparisons, as Van Vechten does, between Fitzgerald and other writers: Henry James and Edith Wharton, and, more unusually, the Ford Madox Ford of *Some Do Not* (1924). Conrad, who will become a very important comparison in some later criticism, is mentioned, but only as a source of 'borrowed cadences' rather than a positive and important influence. Seldes also identifies a pathetic 'American' quality in the novel, in the way Gatsby sets out to restore his illusion by becoming vastly and conspicuously rich. In contrast to the charge made by both Isabel Paterson and H. L. Mencken – that Fitzgerald still says on the surface in *Gatsby* – Seldes finds that Fitzgerald has attacked, with irony, the underlying spirit and thus turned his American characters into universal ones. Like Benét, Seldes sees Gatsby as both distinctively American and as universal.

■ There has never been any question of the talents of F. Scott Fitzgerald; there has been, justifiably until the publication of *The Great Gatsby*, a grave question as to what he was going to do with his gifts. The question has been answered in one of the finest of contemporary novels. Fitzgerald has more than matured; he has mastered his talents and gone soaring in a beautiful flight, leaving behind him everything dubious and tricky in his earlier work, and leaving even farther behind all the men of his own generation and most of his elders.

In all justice, let it be said that the talents are still his. The book is even more interesting, superficially, than his others; it has an intense life, it must be read, the first time, breathlessly; it is vivid and glittering and entertaining. Scenes of incredible difficulty are rendered with what seems an effortless precision and crowds and conversation and action and retrospects – everything comes naturally and persuasively. The minor people and events are threads of colour and strength, holding the principal things together. The technical virtuosity is extraordinary.

All this was true of Fitzgerald's first two novels, and even of those deplorable short stories which one feared were going to ruin him. *The Great Gatsby* adds many things, and two above all: the novel is composed as an artistic structure, and it exposes, again for the first time, an interesting temperament. 'The vast juvenile intrigue' of *This Side of Paradise* is just as good subject-matter as the intensely private intrigue of *The Great Gatsby*; but Fitzgerald racing over the country, jotting down whatever was current in college circles, is not nearly as significant as Fitzgerald regarding a tiny section of life and reporting it with irony and pity and a consuming passion. *The Great Gatsby* is passionate as [Ford Madox Ford's] *Some Do Not* is passionate, with such an abundance of feeling for the characters (feeling their integral reality, not hating or loving them objectively) that the most trivial of the actors in the drama are endowed with vitality. The concentration of the book is so intense that the principal characters exist almost as essences, as biting acids that find themselves in the same golden cup and have no other choice but to act upon each other. And the *milieux* which are brought into such violent contact with each other are as full of character, and as immitigably compelled to struggle and to debase one another.

The book is written as a series of scenes, the method which Fitzgerald derived from Henry James through [Edith] Wharton, and these scenes are reported by a narrator who was obviously intended to be much more significant than he is. The author's appetite for life is so violent that he found the personality of the narrator an obstacle, and simply ignored it once his actual people were in motion, but the narrator helps to give the feeling of an intense unit which the various characters around Gatsby form. Gatsby himself remains a mystery; you know him, but not by knowing about him, and even at the end you can guess, if you like, that he was a forger or a dealer in stolen bonds, or a rather mean type of bootlegger. He had dedicated himself to the accomplishment of a supreme object, to restore to himself an illusion he had lost; he set about it, in a pathetic American way, by becoming incredibly rich and spending his wealth in incredible ways, so that he might win back the girl he loved; and a 'foul dust floated in the wake of his dreams' (p. 6). Adultery and drunkenness and thievery and murder make up this dust, but Gatsby's story remains poignant and beautiful.

This means that Fitzgerald has ceased to content himself with a satiric report on the outside of American life and has with considerable irony attacked the spirit underneath, and so has begun to report on life in its most general terms. His tactile apprehension remains so fine that his people and his settings are specifically of Long Island; but now he meditates upon their fate, and they become universal also. He has now something of extreme importance to say; and it is good fortune for us that he knows how to say it.

The scenes are austere in their composition. There is one, the tawdry afternoon of the satyr, Tom Buchanan, and his cheap and 'vital' mistress, which is alive by the strength of the lapses of time; another, the meeting between Gatsby and his love, takes place literally behind closed doors, the narrator telling us only the beginning and the end. The variety of treatment, the intermingling of dialogue and narrative, the use of a snatch of significant detail instead of a big scene, make the whole a superb impressionistic painting, vivid in colour, and sparkling with meaning. And the major composition is as just as the treatment of detail. There is a brief curve before Gatsby himself enters; a longer one in which he begins his movement toward Daisy; then a succession of carefully spaced shorter and longer movements until the climax is reached. The plot works out not like a puzzle with odd bits falling into place, but like a tragedy, with every part functioning in the completed organism.

Even now, with *The Great Gatsby* before me, I cannot find in the earlier Fitzgerald the artistic integrity and the passionate feeling which this book possesses. And perhaps analysing the one and praising the other, both fail to convey the sense of elation which one has in reading his new novel. Would it be better to say that even *The Great Gatsby* is full of faults, and that that doesn't matter in the slightest degree? The cadences borrowed from Conrad, the occasional smartness, the frequently startling, but ineffective adjective – at last they do not signify. Because for the most part you know that Fitzgerald has consciously put these bad and half-bad things behind him, that he trusts them no more to make him the white-headed boy of *The Saturday Evening Post*, and that he has recognized both his capacities and his obligations as a novelist.[49] □

Despite such praise, Fitzgerald was not wholly pleased by the reviews, writing to Edmund Wilson that 'of all the reviews, even the most enthusiastic, not one had the slightest idea what the book was about'[50] – a statement that has challenged literary critics ever since to do better than *Gatsby*'s original reviewers. In fact, as the selection of reviews above suggests, the original reviewers were by no means all clueless, and some were able to offer perceptive comments on the themes, form and style of the novel. The fact that Fitzgerald said, in the same letter to Wilson, that he felt compensated for what he saw as the reviewers' deficiency by letters about the book from Wilson himself and from H. L. Mencken is rather contradictory, since, as we have seen, Mencken was one of the original reviewers and his letter to Fitzgerald seems to have echoed his review in charging that – as Fitzgerald paraphrases it – '[t]he story [of *Gatsby*] is fundamentally trivial'.[51]

Other letters about *Gatsby* that seemed to please Fitzgerald came from James Branch Cabell, Edith Wharton, Gertrude Stein, and, most famously, T. S. Eliot, who set literary critics another challenge – and provided excellent promotional copy – when he said that *Gatsby* 'seems to me to be the first step that American fiction has taken since Henry James' but, pleading lack of time, did not expound on the reasons for this judgement.[52]

If *The Great Gatsby* was a qualified success with reviewers and with Fitzgerald's fellow writers, its sales were disappointing. The novel came out in April with a first printing of 20,870 copies; but on 20 April 1925, Maxwell Perkins, Fitzgerald's editor at Scribner's, sent him a cable about Gatsby that began: 'Sales situation doubtful'. The first printing made $6,261, enough to cancel Fitzgerald's $6,000 debt to Scribner's, but although there was a second printing in August of 3,000 copies, it soon became clear that the prediction of high sales would not be fulfilled.[53] By 1926, *Gatsby* was dead commercially;[54] when Fitzgerald died in 1940, copies of the second printing were still unsold. His final royalty statement of 1 August 1940 recorded sales of seven copies.[55]

In 1925, Fitzgerald had turned down an offer of $10,000 for pre-publication rights from the magazine *College Humor*, hoping for a higher price, but *Cosmopolitan* and *Liberty*, which might have paid more, turned it down, the fiction editor of *Liberty* feeling that it was '[t]oo ripe' with its proliferation of mistresses and adultery.[56] *Gatsby* was, however, serialised in *Famous Story Magazine* in 1926,[57] though only for $1,000.[58] In 1926, Owen Davis dramatised the novel and, as was probably inevitable, altered its time-scheme, for example by providing a prologue about the meeting of Daisy and Gatsby in Louisville.[59] Produced by William Brady, the play opened on Broadway, at New York's Ambassador Theatre, on 2 February 1926,[60] and ran for 112 performances.[61] The first of three film versions to date of *The Great Gatsby* appeared in 1926 – a silent movie, starring Warner Baxter as Gatsby, Lois Wilson as Daisy, Hale Hamilton as Tom Buchanan, Neil Hamilton as Nick Carraway, Carmelita Geraghty as Jordan Baker, and a then-new actor, William Powell, as Wilson.[62] But the stage and screen versions of *Gatsby* did nothing to help the sales of the book.

In February 1926, in accordance with Scribner's custom of following a novel with a volume of short stories, Fitzgerald's collection *All the Sad Young Men* appeared. This included two stories closely connected with *Gatsby*: 'Absolution' and 'Winter Dreams'. Some of the reviews of *All the Sad Young Men* also passed judgement on *Gatsby*, although, as in the original reviews of the novel, opinions were mixed. Baird Leonard said that he had found *Gatsby* 'a bewildering and tawdry performance',[63] and a number of other references damned with faint praise. Harry Hansen – who had given *This Side of Paradise* a rave review – felt that *Gatsby* had proved Fitzgerald 'a competent painter of the American scene',[64] and an unnamed writer in the *Philadelphia Record*, although s/he did not find *Gatsby* 'epoch-making' and felt that it offered 'freakish specimens of humanity', nonetheless judged it 'alluring as an effective picture of certain phases of life – the merry life – in the suburbs of a great American city'.[65] More positively, but ambiguously, an anonymous reviewer in the *Cleveland Plain Dealer* said that *The Great Gatsby* 'was so good that it should have been better'.[66] Other endorsements were less equivocal. The *New York Times Book Review* spoke of 'the perfection and success of *The Great Gatsby* of last Spring' and of its 'high excellence'.[67] The *Milwaukee Journal* characterised Fitzgerald as the 'man who in *The Great Gatsby* brilliantly, pitilessly, scathed a phase of modern life that had not been treated before'.[68] E. C. Beckwith observed that *The Great Gatsby* 'added to our conviction that Fitzgerald's future place as a literary artist would be among Willa Cather, Dreiser and Sherwood Anderson' and referred to 'the brilliant level' of *Gatsby*.[69] Leon Whipple felt that *Gatsby* 'clearly said something about one part of our time, and said it with glamorous art',[70] and Brooks Cottle called *Gatsby* 'a novel of keen satire written with a fine economy'.[71] William Rose Benét, who had, as we have seen, reviewed *Gatsby* so favourably, began his piece in the *Saturday Review of Literature* with a paragraph on *Gatsby*, praising its maturity, formal control, reticence and sharpness, and later calling it 'an undeniable achievement' which perhaps made us, in judging *All the Sad Young Men*, 'exorbitant in our demands'.[72] But these favourable comments on *Gatsby*, in the course of reviews of *All the Sad Young Men*, were no more successful than the stage and screen dramatisations in encouraging sales of the novel.

The year 1926 also saw the publication of the British edition of *Gatsby*. William Collins and Sons, the London publishers of Fitzgerald's two previous novels, had rejected it, saying that the British public would not understand, believe or buy it – 'the atmosphere of the book is extraordinarily foreign to the English reader'[73]. Chatto and Windus brought it out in 1926, and, as in America, it received mixed reviews. Some of the favourable responses came from those who had already reviewed it positively in the USA – for example, Edward Shanks in the *London Mercury*, who, as if anticipating the British reaction William Collins had feared, acknowledged that '[t]he story leaves one with a queer nightmarish idea of the possibilities of life in America' but affirmed that Fitzgerald 'handles his grotesque material with an artist's discretion'.[74] *Gatsby* was twice reviewed in Eliot's *New Criterion*, once by Gilbert Seldes in January and again by the American poet, novelist and short-story writer Conrad Aiken in October. Aiken praised the novel's 'excellence of form' and, in identifying some of its narrative techniques, he made an interesting comparison that brought together a new medium and a distinguished author of an earlier generation, whose name had already been associated with Fitzgerald in some American reviews of *Gatsby*: '[t]echnically, [the novel] appears to owe much to the influence of the cinema; and perhaps also something to Henry James – a peculiar conjunction, but not so peculiar if one reflects on the flash-backs and close-ups and parallel themes of that "little experiment in the style of Gyp", *The Awkward Age* (1889)'.[75] The anonymous reviewer in the *Times Literary Supplement* called *Gatsby* 'undoubtedly a work of art and of great promise' and praised Fitzgerald's 'economical construction', his 'power of telling conciseness' and his capacity to 'use words like living things, instead of like dead counters'. It also called Gatsby himself 'a Conradian hero . . . like Almayer or the hero [presumably Kurtz] of "Heart of Darkness"'.[76] A much less enthusiastic review came from a writer who was later to become a well-known English novelist. L. P. Hartley, who had published his first volume of short stories, *Night Fears*, in 1924, and his first novel, *Simonetta Perkins*, in 1925, wrote in *The Saturday Review*:

■ Mr. Scott Fitzgerald deserves a good shaking. Here is an unmistakable talent unashamed of making itself a motley to the view. *The Great Gatsby* is an absurd story, whether considered as romance, melodrama, or plain record of New York high life . . . [At the end,] [a]ll the characters behave as if they were entitled to grieve over a great sorrow, and the book closes with the airs of a tragedy. Mr. Fitzgerald seems to have lost sight of O. Henry [an American short-story writer famous for his 'twist-in-the-tail' stories] and hitched his wagon to Mr. Arlen's star [Michael Arlen was a popular fiction writer whose novel *The Green Hat* had been a bestseller in 1924]. It is a great pity, for even in this book, in the dialogue, in many descriptive passages, there are flashes of wit and insight, felicities of phrase and a sense of beauty. His imagination is febrile and his emotion over-strained; but how good, of its kind, is his description of Gatsby's smile . . . (p. 40) *The Great Gatsby* is evidently not a satire; but one would like to think that Mr. Fitzgerald's heart is not in it, that it is a piece of mere naughtiness.[77] □

Such reviews were unlikely to encourage sales. Of the 1,616 copies printed by Chatto and Windus, 1,100 were sold in 1926, and 350, at a reduced price, in 1927. The total royalties were £32.15s.2d.[78] A complete version of the novel was published in the British fiction magazine *Argosy* in 1937,[79] but it was 1948 before another edition in book form, this time from Grey Walls Press, appeared in the UK.[80]

After *Gatsby*, Fitzgerald did not publish another novel for nine years. He was later to regret this, as a famous comment in a letter of 12 June 1940 to his daughter, Scottie, shows: 'I wish now I'd *never* relaxed or looked back – but said at the end of *The Great Gatsby*: "I've found my line – from now on this comes first. This is my immediate duty – without this I am nothing"'.[81] Had a novel appeared more quickly after *Gatsby*, it might have enhanced Fitzgerald's general literary reputation, and the standing of *Gatsby* itself. But it was not to be. His personal and professional life became increasingly troubled as he moved between Europe, Hollywood and Baltimore, writing film scripts and short stories, and trying without success to complete another novel; his wife Zelda experienced her first nervous breakdown in 1930 and her second in 1932, writing, in between time, her own novel, *Save Me the Waltz*, which came out in 1932. Zelda had her third breakdown in 1934, the year in which Fitzgerald's fourth novel, *Tender is the Night*, did eventually emerge.

The publication of *Tender is the Night* offered an occasion for further critical comment on *Gatsby*, and a number of reviews of the new work – though by no means all – took up the opportunity. Some of them referred to *Gatsby* in order to highlight the length of time that had elapsed since Fitzgerald's last novel; *Time*, for example, began its anonymous review: 'For many a US reader a nine-year period of suspense ended last week when F. Scott Fitzgerald, bad boy of US letters, published his first novel since *The Great Gatsby* (1925)'.[82] Others used *Gatsby* as a novel with which to compare and contrast *Tender is the Night*. For example, Edward Weeks felt that *Gatsby*, in particular, had been 'overpraised' but welcomed *Tender is the Night*;[83] James Gray, in contrast, saw *Tender is the Night* as a relapse into the immaturity of Fitzgerald's pre-*Gatsby* fiction from which *Gatsby* itself had 'so triumphantly escaped'. This contrast prompted Gray to an interesting brief analysis of *Gatsby*. He acknowledged that *Gatsby*, like *Tender is the Night*, 'had its tempestuous melodrama, its undisciplined characters', but argued that, in the earlier novel, 'Fitzgerald, standing aside, understood the pathos of the impulse that carried his central character stubbornly toward a quite unobtainable goal. The quality of compassion which he got into that admirable record was completely touching and persuasive.' *Tender is the Night* is vitiated, Gray charges, because Fitzgerald 'was not willing to submit himself to the stern self-discipline which made him rewrite and rewrite *The Great Gatsby* many times until he had eliminated all its irrelevances'[84] – a point that relates to Fitzgerald's own emphasis, in the Modern Library introduction reprinted on pages 37–9, on what he had cut out of the earlier novel.

John Chamberlain was less disappointed in *Tender is the Night*. Announcing himself '[a]s one who would rather have written *The Great Gatsby* than any other American novel published in the Twenties' and praising it as 'so perfect in its feeling and its symbolism' and as 'such a magnificent evocation of the spirit of a whole decade', Chamberlain confessed that he had approached *Tender is the Night* 'with anticipation and trepidation' – but had felt enthusiastic about it, though judging it to be less technically perfect than *Gatsby*.[85] Other reviewers, however, praised *The Great Gatsby* but found *Tender is the Night* surpassed it and fully realised the potential that Fitzgerald had shown in his previous novel.

Gordon Lewis judged that, with *Gatsby*, 'Fitzgerald had arrived at a point of remove and perspective that would some time bring into being a first-rate literary production', and affirmed that, although it had been 'a long wait', *Tender is the Night* 'fulfils the bright promise'.[86] And Gilbert Seldes, who, as we saw earlier, had praised *Gatsby* in both England and America, took a similar line, affirming that *Gatsby* was 'the turning point in [Fitzgerald's] career, the first novel which indicated that he could control all his powers and would eventually write a great novel. Now he has written the great novel: *Tender is the Night*'.[87]

Whatever judgements were made of the relative merits of the two novels, the very fact that *Gatsby* was mentioned at all was bound to help to bring it back to public notice, if only in a small way. A potentially more significant form of exposure was the republication in 1934 of *Gatsby* itself, in a 95-cent Modern Library edition, with an introduction by Fitzgerald. If this introduction was an opportunity for Fitzgerald to explain and to promote the importance of *Gatsby*, it was not one that he seized in any obvious way: instead, to use the metaphor he himself employed in the introduction, he circled round the book itself, approaching it but never quite alighting on it. He uses much of his limited space to complain about the critical reception of his books, and although he initially claims that he has 'no cause to grumble' about this, he does spend a disproportionate amount of time grumbling, and sounding rather peevish, about reviewers. His tribute to H. L. Mencken, whom he uses as a measure of the defects of more recent reviewers, has a certain irony, in view of Mencken's reservations about *Gatsby* in his original review (see pp. 19–22).

Fitzgerald attributes what he now seems to see as the poor response to *Gatsby* to the novel's avoidance of 'big' social and political issues and its focus on millionaires rather than peasants and workers ('farmers'). Here he seems, to some extent, to be transferring back to the mid-1920s the literary context of the decade in which the introduction was written – the decade of literary commitment, of novels that dealt with social and political issues and focused on the poor and dispossesed, the decade of Steinbeck and Dos Passos. This offers an interesting insight into the kind of pressure Fitzgerald felt himself to be under in the 1930s from what he calls 'political diehards', and the politicised cultural context he invokes may partly account for the neglect of *Gatsby* in the decade leading up to the Second World War. It does less, however, to explain its critical reception in the 1920s.

When Fitzgerald, in this introduction, does get to *Gatsby* itself, he offers some fascinating glimpses of his own memories of its genesis and growth: his assertion that he tried to keep his 'artistic conscience' 'pure' when he was writing the novel; his re-reading of Conrad's Preface to *The Nigger of the 'Narcissus'* (1897); his irritation at the accusations of immaturity that had been levelled at his pre-*Gatsby* fiction and his defiant feeling that, even if the material with which he dealt seemed to preclude maturity, it was *his* material, 'and it was all [he] had to deal with'; his sense of how much he had cut out of the novel, not only in terms of words but also in terms of feelings; and his affirmation of the book's imaginative honesty. These are important hints, which critics would later take up and develop in a range of ways. Fitzgerald, however, does not talk directly about the novel's structure, style or themes. If, as he complained, not one of the original reviewers had had the slightest idea what the book was about, he was clearly not now going to enlighten them. This may have been due to a kind of modernist pride, a sense that *Gatsby* could not be paraphrased and that it should speak for itself, through its art; or it may be – and this seems a more likely explanation – that Fitzgerald was unable to articulate his sense of the book's themes. Possibly both of these reasons played their part. What we have is an oblique, enigmatic preface that tantalises but does not deliver, so that, if we want to penetrate *Gatsby*'s secrets, we must go back to the novel itself, equipped with the few but invaluable hints that Fitzgerald gives us. With a certain kind of writer – though probably not with Fitzgerald – this might have been a complex strategy to achieve just such an end.

■ To one who has spent his professional life in the world of fiction the request to 'write an introduction' offers many facets of temptation. The present writer succumbs to one of them; with as much equanimity as he can muster, he will discuss the critics among us, trying to revolve as centripetally as possible about the novel which comes hereafter in this volume.

To begin with, I must say that I have no cause to grumble about the 'press' of any book of mine. If Jack (who liked my last book) didn't like this one – well then John (who despised my last book) *did* like it; so it all mounts up to the same total. But I think the writers of my time were spoiled in that regard, living in generous days when there was plenty of space on the page for endless ratiocination about fiction – a space largely created by Mencken because of his disgust for what passed as criticism before he arrived and made his public. They were encouraged by his bravery and his tremendous and profound love of letters. In his case, the jackals are already tearing at what they imprudently regard as a moribund lion, but I don't think many men of my age can regard him without reverence, nor fail to regret that he got off the train. To any new effort by a new man he brought an attitude; he made many mistakes – such as his early undervaluation of Hemingway – but he came equipped; he never had to go back for his tools.

And now that he has abandoned American fiction to its own

devices, there is no one to take his place. If the present writer had seriously to attend some of the efforts of political diehards to tell him the values of a métier he has practised since boyhood – well, then, babies, you can take this number out and shoot him at dawn.

But all that is less discouraging, in the past few years, than the growing cowardice of the reviewers. Underpaid and overworked, they seem not to care for books, and it has been saddening recently to see young talents in fiction expire from sheer lack of a stage to act on: [Nathanael] West, [Vincent] McHugh and many others.

I'm circling closer to my theme song, which is: that I'd like to communicate to such of them who read this novel a healthy cynicism toward contemporary reviews. Without undue vanity one can permit oneself a suit of chain mail in any profession. Your pride is all you have, and if you let it be tampered with by a man who has a dozen prides to tamper with before lunch, you are promising yourself a lot of disappointments that a hard-boiled professional has learned to spare himself.

This novel is a case in point. Because the pages weren't loaded with big names of big things and the subject not concerned with farmers (who were the heroes of the moment), there was easy judgement exercised that had nothing to do with criticism but was simply an attempt on the part of men who had few chances of self-expression to express themselves. How anyone could take up the responsibility of being a novelist without a sharp and concise attitude about life is a puzzle to me. How a critic could assume a point of view which included twelve variant aspects of the social scene in a few hours seems something too dinosaurean to loom over the awful loneliness of a young author.

To circle nearer to this book, one woman, who could hardly have written a coherent letter in English, described it as a book that one read only as one goes to the movies around the corner.[88] That type of criticism is what a lot of young writers are being greeted with, instead of any appreciation of the world of imagination in which they (the writers) have been trying, with greater or lesser success, to live – the world that Mencken made stable in the days when he was watching over us.

Now that this book is being reissued, the author would like to say that never before did one try to keep his artistic conscience as pure as during the ten months put into doing it. Reading it over one can see how it could have been improved – yet without feeling guilty of any discrepancy from the truth, as far as I saw it; truth or rather the *equivalent* of the truth, the attempt at honesty of imagination. I had just re-read Conrad's preface to *The Nigger*, and I had recently been kidded half haywire by critics who felt that my material was such as to preclude all dealing with mature persons in a mature world. But, my

God! it was my material, and it was all I had to deal with.

What I cut out of it both physically and emotionally would make another novel!

I think it is an honest book, that is to say, that one used none of one's virtuosity to get an effect, and, to boast again, one soft-pedalled the emotional side to avoid the tears leaking from the socket of the left eye, or the large false face peering around the corner of a character's head.

If there is a clear conscience, a book can survive – at least in one's feelings about it. On the contrary, if one has a guilty conscience, one reads what one wants to hear out of reviews. In addition, if one is young and willing to learn, almost all reviews have a value, even the ones that seem unfair.

The present writer has always been a 'natural' for his profession, in so much that he can think of nothing he would have done as efficiently as to have lived deeply in the world of imagination. There are plenty other people constituted as he is, for giving expression to intimate explorations, the:

— Look – this is here!

— I saw this under my eyes.

— This is the way it was!

— No, it was like this.

— "Look! Here is that drop of blood I told you about."

— "Stop everything! Here is the flash of that girl's eyes, here is the reflection that will always come back to me from the memory of her eyes."

— "If one chooses to find that face again in the non-refracting surface of a washbowl, if one chooses to make the image more obscure with a little sweat, it should be the business of the critic to recognize the intention."

— "No one felt like this before – says the young writer – but *I* felt like this; I have a pride akin to a soldier going into battle; without knowing whether there will be anybody there, to distribute medals or even to record it."

But remember, also, young man: you are not the first person who has ever been alone and alone.

F. SCOTT FITZGERALD

Baltimore, Md.
August, 1934.[89] □

Fitzgerald himself was dissatisfied with the introduction, and asked if he could rewrite it for a second printing. This was too optimistic; no second printing took place. The Modern Library dropped *Gatsby* from its list due to lack of sales.[90]

Fitzgerald published only one further book in his lifetime, the short-story collection *Taps at Reveille*, which appeared in 1935. Of the review responses to this volume collected by Jackson R. Bryer, most do not mention *Gatsby* at all. Of those that do, William Troy – who would write a landmark essay on Fitzgerald in 1945 (see pp. 43–5) – spoke of a 'tempt-ation that has caused certain critics, grateful that anything possessing so many of the features of a great work of fiction could be written in America, to speak of *The Great Gatsby* as if it were *Madame Bovary* or *War and Peace*'.[91] Such a temptation, Troy seems to imply, should be resisted. James Gray and Arthur Coleman used *Gatsby* in the same way as some reviewers of *Tender is the Night*, as a book with which to compare and contrast Fitzgerald's latest production. Gray, for whom *Tender is the Night* was an 'intense disappointment', found, in the story 'Crazy Sunday' in *Taps at Reveille*, 'an echo of [Fitzgerald's] achievement in *The Great Gatsby*'.[92] Coleman regretted the publication of *Taps at Reveille*, seeing it as a record of 'the petrifaction of a talent that in 1925 looked like one of the best bets in American literature'; he felt that he 'would rather remember Fitzgerald by *Gatsby* and *Tender is the Night*' and by a few 'really glittering short stories'. While admiring four of the stories in the collection – 'Crazy Sunday', 'Two Wrongs', 'The Last of the Belles' and 'Babylon Revisited' – he saw 'only rarely' in the others 'a flash of that spontaneity and objectivity which materialized in *The Great Gatsby*'.[93]

In 1936, Fitzgerald published in the magazine *Esquire* the auto-biographical essays that were later collected under the title of the first of them, *The Crack-Up*. These chastened reflections on his life and career, his early success and later breakdown, were measured, moving, and mem-orably phrased – 'in a real dark night of the soul it is always three o'clock in the morning, day after day'.[94] But they helped to reinforce the impres-sion that his literary career had been a failure. As Henry Dan Piper points out, Fitzgerald received little attention from critics and scholars in the 1930s, and when he was mentioned, it tended to be in limiting terms. For example, Vernon Louis Parrington's *Main Currents in American Thought* (1930), a history of American letters much used in US universities in the 1930s and 1940s, summed up Fitzgerald as 'a short candle already burnt out',[95] while Harlan Hatcher's *Creating the Modern American Novel* (1935) claimed Fitzgerald's fiction was ephemeral, lacking 'the permanent searching of the soul that makes one generation read another's novels'.[96] Fitzgerald's declining reputation in the 1930s might well have seemed to uphold Isabel Paterson's verdict that *Gatsby* was 'a book of the season only' (see p. 17). As the decade drew to a close, it would have been rash to predict that Scott Fitzgerald's name, or Jay Gatsby's, would endure.

On 21 December 1940, Fitzgerald died in Hollywood of a heart attack. He was 44. Obituary assessments varied in their opinion of *Gatsby*. A *New York Times* editorial said: '[i]t was not a book for the ages, but it caught superbly the spirit of a decade'.[97] In the *St. Paul Dispatch*, James Gray, while praising *Gatsby*, indicated how it had fallen into relative obscurity when he ventured that '[p]erhaps some day it will be rediscovered'.[98] *The New Yorker*, in its survey of the obituaries, called it 'one of the most scrupulously observed and beautifully written of American novels'.[99] In the two 1941 issues of the magazine *The New Republic* which were devoted to recollections and re-evaluations of Fitzgerald, the novelist John Dos Passos affirmed that *Gatsby* was 'one of the few classic American novels'.[100] But in the aftermath of Fitzgerald's death, his own posthumous fate, and that of *Gatsby*, remained uncertain.

An important impetus to the rediscovery of *Gatsby* was its republication by Scribner's in 1941 in a volume that also contained some short stories and the novel Fitzgerald had been working on at the time of his death, *The Last Tycoon*. This was likely to encourage reviewers and readers of *The Last Tycoon* to give fresh attention to *Gatsby* and to compare and contrast the two novels. Most of the reviews collected by Bryer referred to *Gatsby*. Two mentioned that it was generally regarded as Fitzgerald's 'masterpiece' without committing themselves to such a judgement – indeed, one anonymous review summarised it dismissively as 'a tale of the Long Island gin and jitters set'.[101] John T. Appleby delivered a hostile verdict on Fitzgerald's overall achievement: 'he had very little [to] say . . . he said that very little, perhaps most effectively in *The Great Gatsby*'; and to compare *The Last Tycoon* with *Gatsby* 'demonstrates conclusively the shallowness and the limitations of Fitzgerald's abilities'.[102] Clifton Fadiman, on the other hand, felt that *The Last Tycoon*, even in its unfinished state, was an advance on *Gatsby* but he nonetheless observed, almost in an aside, that *Gatsby* 'by the way, is unexpectedly re-readable'.[103] Other reviewers suggested grounds for a more positive evaluation of *Gatsby*, although they vary with regard to the question of whether it is better than *The Last Tycoon*. Milton Rugoff, for example, accepted that Fitzgerald 'concerned himself with the outward behaviour of his contemporaries' but pre-empted the charge of superficiality to which such a concern might give rise by claiming: 'the truer a transcription of outward behaviour is the closer it is likely to come to those inner mysteries; and at his best Fitzgerald crossed the line. He did it in *The Great Gatsby*; he does it again in this last work'.[104] James Gray called *Gatsby* 'a beautifully articulated piece of craftsmanship' against which *The Last Tycoon* is found wanting: '[i]t would not have been another *Great Gatsby*'; the love affair it describes 'seems like a worried imitation of effects that Fitzgerald achieved with warmth and spontaneity' in *Gatsby*.[105] Margaret Marshall, however, felt that with *The Last Tycoon* 'he had not only returned to the level of *The Great Gatsby*' but that the finished chapters and working notes (included in Scribner's volume) showed 'that he would have gone beyond it'. In *Gatsby*, Marshall claimed, 'Fitzgerald reached that plateau of objectivity and control in fiction which few American novelists attain', rising above the plane of the autobiographical and creating, in Jay Gatsby, an independent character. She found, however, that, in *The Last Tycoon* 'Fitzgerald shows an even greater freedom and power in the creation of a character. Gatsby walks by himself – he still does – but we see him, so to speak, in silhouette. Monroe Stahr of the present book is much more thoroughly realized.'[106] Arnold Gingrich, however, still upheld the supremacy of *Gatsby*, devoting most of the first half of his review to praising it and affirming that, while *The Last Tycoon* 'is a very fine, if unfinished novel', *The Great Gatsby* 'is a masterpiece'. He seized on the republishing of *Gatsby* in the same volume as *The Last Tycoon* as a way of promoting *Gatsby*: 'Your reason for buying this book should be to read *The Last Tycoon*. But your reason for keeping it should be to read again, and again, and again, *The Great Gatsby*'.[107]

Gingrich's desire that *The Great Gatsby* should be read again and again and again was to be amply fulfilled in the years to come. Further American editions of the novel appeared in the 1940s: a small reprint by Scribner's in 1942 and, in 1945, five new editions or editions. These comprised a reprint of the edition containing both *Gatsby* and *The Last Tycoon*; two impressions of a Viking Portable Fitzgerald that included *Gatsby*; a twenty-five cent Bantam paperback; and an Armed Services edition of 155,000 copies that were given away free to military personnel. In 1946, New Directions published *Gatsby* in the New Classics series, with an introduction by Lionel Trilling on which he was later to draw for his essay on Fitzgerald in *The Liberal Imagination* (1951) (see pp. 51–6), and in the same year, *Gatsby* was included in *Great American Short Novels*, and the Bantam paperback was twice reprinted.[108] Grey Walls Press brought out a new English edition of *Gatsby* in 1948, as we have already noted, and the first Penguin paperback version came out in 1950.[109] In the USA in 1949, the Portable Fitzgerald went into a third and fourth impression, and Grosset and Dunlap bought out another edition of the novel to tie in with the movie adaptation, starring Alan Ladd, which was released in that year.[110]

It seemed that more and more people were reading *Gatsby*, or at least possessed copies of the book. But critical and scholarly opinion still tended to be dismissive, as Henry Dan Piper points out. Carl Van Doren, in his popular history *The American Novel: 1789–1930*, published in 1940, the year of Fitzgerald's death, felt that *Gatsby* was his best work but categorised it, reductively, as 'a short realistic novel about a romantic bootlegger'.[111] Joseph Warren Beach's *American Fiction* (1941) did not mention Fitzgerald's fiction at all.[112] George Snell mentioned *Gatsby* in *Shapers of American Fiction* (1947) but felt that after 1925 Fitzgerald's 'genius burned out like a meteor'.[113] Alexander Cowie's large history, *The Rise of the American Novel* (1948), mentioned only one of Fitzgerald's books, *This Side of Paradise*.[114] On the other hand, Maxwell Geismar's *The Last of the Provincials: The American Novel, 1915-1925*, which came out in 1943, devoted a substantial chapter to Fitzgerald, 'Orestes at the Ritz'. Geismar discussed *Gatsby* seriously, although he had reservations about the novel, as his final judgement suggests: '*The Great Gatsby* fades a little with its last "dying fall" – but it is still the warm and touching chronicle of our deceptive native romance'.[115]

It was through essays more than through books, however, that Fitzgerald's critical reputation would begin to be revived in the 1940s. Extracts from two of the most important are printed below. The first is from William Troy's 'Scott Fitzgerald – The Authority of Failure', which appeared in *Accent* magazine in Autumn 1945, as people were starting to turn their thoughts from war to peace and to rebuilding a devastated world.

Troy begins by pointing out that Fitzgerald, given what he produced, was not a failure at all. He goes on to argue, however, that Fitzgerald contributed to his own image as a failure by a kind of heroism – 'by daring to make failure the consistent theme of his work from first to last'.[116] That daring gave him authority and strength. Already, Troy was preparing the ground for a refurbished image of Fitzgerald that could appeal to a chastened postwar mood and chime in with those popularised versions of existentialist philosophies that proposed that the path of apparent 'failure' might lead to human and artistic success.

In the extract below, Troy focuses on *The Great Gatsby*, and he makes a case for it as a work that successfully achieves the kind of 'objective correlative' that Eliot had sought to define in his 1919 essay 'Hamlet'. Eliot had written:

■ The only way of expressing emotion in the form of art is by finding an 'objective correlative'; in other words, a set of objects, a situation, a chain of events which shall be the formula of that particular emotion; such that when the external facts, which must terminate in sensory experience, are given, the emotion is immediately evoked.[117] □

Eliot's poetry and aesthetic notions were to be profoundly influential in postwar literary criticism; by applying one of the best-known of those notions to *Gatsby*, Troy was offering a way in which the novel could become academically respectable – and the comparison was further legitimated by Eliot's own praise of *Gatsby*, which was cited earlier, as 'the first step that American fiction has taken since Henry James' (see pp. 31-2 above). Troy goes on to explain *Gatsby*'s achievement of an 'objective correlative' in terms of Fitzgerald's adoption of a technique – that of 'the intelligent but sympathetic observer' – derived from Conrad and James; he thus links Fitzgerald not only with Eliot but also with the two early modern novelists who were to be most highly rated by postwar literary critics. Having made these exalted comparisons, Troy further enhances his claims for *Gatsby* by suggesting that it can be read in relation to both an American, and a more universal, mythology; Gatsby himself comes to stand for the American dream and the novel, like Eliot's *The Waste Land*, becomes a kind of Grail-romance.

In his concise comments on *The Great Gatsby*, Troy thus succeeds in sowing the seeds of at least four approaches to *Gatsby* that will bear fruit in subsequent and more elaborated criticism: *Gatsby* as an example of an achieved 'objective correlative'; *Gatsby* as an instance of the effective deployment of a powerful narrative technique; *Gatsby* as creating a symbol of the American dream; and *Gatsby* as a modern version of ancient and universal myth.

■ Not until *The Great Gatsby* did Fitzgerald hit upon something like Mr. Eliot's 'objective correlative' for the intermingled feeling of personal insufficiency and disillusionment with the world out of which he had unsuccessfully tried to write a novel.

Here is a remarkable instance of the manner in which adoption of a special form or technique can profoundly modify and define a writer's whole attitude toward his world. In the earlier books author and hero tended to melt into one because there was no internal principle of differentiation by which they might be separated; they respired in the same climate, emotional and moral; they were tarred with the same brush. But in *Gatsby* is achieved a dissociation, by which Fitzgerald was able to isolate one part of himself, the spectatorial or aesthetic, and also the more intelligent and responsible, in the person of the ordinary but quite sensible narrator, from another part of himself, the dream-ridden romantic adolescent from St. Paul and Princeton, in the person of the legendary Jay Gatsby. It is this which makes the latter one of the few truly mythological creations in our recent literature – for what is mythology but this same process of projected wish-fulfilment carried out on a larger scale and by the whole consciousness of a race? Indeed, before we are quite through with him, Gatsby becomes much more than a mere exorcizing of whatever false elements of the American dream Fitzgerald felt within himself: he becomes a symbol of America itself, dedicated to 'the service of a vast, vulgar and meretricious beauty' (p. 77).

Not mythology, however, but a technical device which had been brought to high development by James and Conrad before him, made this dissociation possible for Fitzgerald. The device of the intelligent but sympathetic observer situated at the centre of the tale, as James never ceases to demonstrate in the Prefaces, makes for some of the most priceless values in fiction – economy, suspense, intensity. And these values *The Great Gatsby* possesses to a rare degree. But the same device imposes on the novelist the necessity of tracing through in the observer or narrator himself some sort of growth in general moral perception, which will constitute in effect *his* story. Here, for example, insofar as the book is Gatsby's story it is a story of failure – the prolongation of the adolescent incapacity to distinguish between dream and reality, between the terms demanded of life and the terms offered. But insofar as it is the narrator's story it is a successful transcendence of a particularly bitter and harrowing set of experiences, localized in the sinister, distorted, El Greco-like Long Island atmosphere of the later twenties, into a world of restored sanity and calm, symbolized by the bracing winter nights of the Middle Western prairies. 'Conduct may be founded on the hard rock or the wet marshes', he writes, 'but after a certain point I don't care what it's founded on. When I came back from the East last autumn I felt that I wanted the world to be in uniform and at a sort of moral attention forever; I wanted no more riotous excursions with privileged glimpses into the human heart ever recurring' (p. 5). [The last two words that Troy includes in his quotation are not, in fact, in the text of *Gatsby*, either in this passage or elsewhere.] By reason of its enforced perspective the book takes on the pattern and the meaning of a Grail-romance – or of the initiation ritual on which it is based. Perhaps this will seem a far-fetched suggestion to make about a work so obviously modern in every respect; and it is unlikely that Fitzgerald had any such model in mind. But like [Herman Melville's] *Billy Budd* (1924, published posthumously), [Stephen Crane's] *The Red Badge of Courage* (1895), or [Willa Cather's] *A Lost Lady* – to mention only a few American stories of similar length with which it may be compared – it is a record of the strenuous passage from deluded youth to maturity.[118] ☐

A second very important essay of the 1940s was Arthur Mizener's essay 'F. Scott Fitzgerald 1896–1940: The Poet of Borrowed Time'. This essay was one of a number that Mizener wrote about Fitzgerald in the 1940s and early 1950s. It was first published in 1946 in the book *Lives of Eighteen from Princeton*, and subsequently reprinted as the opening essay in Alfred Kazin's influential collection *F. Scott Fitzgerald: The Man and His Work*. Mizener was to go on to become Fitzgerald's first biographer with *The Far Side of Paradise* which, like Kazin's collection, appeared in 1951, and was a further important step in establishing Fitzgerald's posthumous reputation.

In 'The Poet of Borrowed Time', Mizener combines biographical and critical approaches; but, despite the biographical element of his essay, Mizener is concerned to suggest that Fitzgerald's fiction can be judged independently of his life, and he also wants him to be seen as more than a sensitive recorder of his era. His central claim is that 'Fitzgerald's great accomplishment is to have realized in completely American terms the developed romantic attitude, in the end at least in that most responsible form in which all the romantic's sensuous and emotional responses are disciplined by his awareness of the goodness and evilness of human experience'.[119] Mizener thus presents Fitzgerald both as a quintessentially American writer, and, in a more general sense, as a romantic writer whose romanticism is chastened by his grasp of human reality.

The section of the essay in which Mizener homes in on *Gatsby* is printed opposite. It suggests a number of topics that future critics would take up. One major topic is the link between *Gatsby* and Conrad. We saw earlier that Fitzgerald had himself implied a connection with Conrad when, in his introduction to the Modern Library edition of *Gatsby*, he had spoken of re-reading Conrad's preface to *The Nigger of the 'Narcissus'* around the time he was writing the novel (see p. 38). Mizener alludes to Fizgerald's remark and expands on it by locating the influence of Conrad in Fitzgerald's use, in *Gatsby*, of 'the modified first-person form' for which Conrad would have provided a model. The exploration of the relationship of *Gatsby* to Conrad's fiction will be pushed much further in future criticism – a notable example is Robert E. Long's 1966 essay '*The Great Gatsby* and the Tradition of Joseph Conrad'.[120] Fitzgerald's use of the 'modified first-person form' is carefully analysed by James E. Miller, Jr in 1957, in the first full-length study of Fitzgerald's fiction. An extract from Miller's book, incorporating that analysis, appears later in this Guide.

Mizener also coins a phrase that will offer scope for development, and dissent, by future critics: that *Gatsby* is 'a kind of tragic pastoral' that sets up a contrast between the sophistication and corruption of the urban East, and the simplicity and virtue of the rural West. Gatsby, Mizener argues, is 'great' insofar as he represents the latter; insofar as he represents the former, he is absurd. These oppositions, in Mizener's view, structure the whole novel and provide its formal order. Here, too, Mizener offers suggestions that will prove fertile in future criticism. Like William Troy, he has both offered a high estimate of the novel and suggested ways in which its themes and techniques may be more deeply explored and analysed. Even the one reservation he makes about *Gatsby* offers scope for further critical debate: he contends that Fitzgerald identifies too completely with Gatsby's romanticism and fails to ask whether there may not be a 'fundamental moral inadequacy in Gatsby's attitude'. *The Great Gatsby*, Mizener concludes, does not provide a vision of order of the kind Ulysses offers in his famous speech on 'degree' in Shakespeare's *Troilus and Cressida*.

We join Mizener's essay at the start of section three, as he turns his attention to Gatsby, having argued in section two that *The Beautiful and*

Damned was 'an enormous improvement on *This Side of Paradise*'.[121]

■ *The Great Gatsby* was another leap forward for Fitzgerald. He had found a situation which would allow him to exploit without loss of probability much more of his feeling about his material, and he had arrived at the point where he understood the advantage of realizing his subject dramatically. He had been reading Conrad and as a result adopted the modified first-person form which suited his purpose so well. For Fitzgerald needed a form which would at once allow him to colour the scene with the feelings of an observer and yet hold the feelings within some determined limits. In earlier stories he had splashed whatever colours he wished over the scene without much regard for the structure as a whole or for the disruptive effect on the dramatic representation of the constant interference of the author's own person. But here, as later in *The Last Tycoon*, he selected a narrator sufficiently near the centre of things to know all he needed to know, tied into the action by the affair with Jordan Baker which is, though muted, carefully made parallel to the affair between Gatsby and Daisy. By means of this narrator he was able to focus his story, the story of a poor boy from the Middle West who, in the social confusion of the first World War, met and fell in love with a rich girl. Daisy marries while he is in France, but he never ceases to dream of making enough money to be 'worthy' of her, taking her from her husband, Tom Buchanan, and starting their life again exactly where it had stopped when he had gone to France. He therefore devotes himself to making money in whatever way he can, not because he wants money, but because he wants his dream of a life with Daisy.

Nick Carraway, the narrator, is equally carefully placed so far as his attitude is concerned. He has come East to be an Easterner and rich, but his moral roots remain in the West. In the most delicate way Fitzgerald builds up these grounds for his final judgement of the story and its people. In the book's first scene, Nick's humorous awareness of the greater sophistication of these people is marked: '"You make me feel uncivilized, Daisy," I confessed . . . "Can't you talk about crops or something?"' (pp. 13–14). But only a moment later, when Daisy has confessed her unhappiness with Tom, he has an uneasy sense of what is really involved: 'The instant her voice broke off, ceasing to compel my attention, my belief, I felt the basic insincerity of what she had said . . . I waited, and sure enough, in a moment she looked at me with an absolute smirk on her lovely face as if she had asserted her membership in a rather distinguished secret society to which she and Tom belonged' (p. 17).

Nick's father has told him that '"Whenever you feel like criticizing anyone . . . just remember that all the people in this world haven't had the advantages that you've had"' (p. 5). Nick does not forget; when, at the end of the book, he meets Tom, 'I couldn't forgive him or like him but I saw that what he had done was, to him, entirely justified . . . I shook hands with him; it seemed silly not to, for I felt suddenly as though I were talking to a child. Then he went into the jewellery store to buy a pearl necklace – or perhaps only a pair of cuff buttons – rid of my provincial squeamishness forever' (pp. 139–140).

Nick goes back to the West, to the country he remembered from the Christmas vacations of his childhood, to 'the thrilling, returning trains of my youth and the street lamps and sleigh bells in the frosty dark and the shadows of holly wreaths thrown by lighted windows on the snow. I am part of that, a little solemn with the feel of those long winters, a little complacent from growing up in the Carraway house in a city where dwellings are still called through decades by a family's name'. The East remains for him 'a night scene by El Greco' in which '[i]n the foreground four solemn men in dress suits are walking along the sidewalk with a stretcher on which lies a drunken woman in a white evening dress. Her hand, which dangles over the side, sparkles cold with jewels. Gravely the men turn in at a house – the wrong house. But no one knows the woman's name, and no one cares' (p. 137).

Thus, though Fitzgerald would be the last to have reasoned it out in such terms, *The Great Gatsby* becomes a kind of tragic pastoral, with the East the exemplar of urban sophistication and culture and corruption, and the West, 'the bored, sprawling, swollen towns beyond the Ohio' (p. 137), the exemplar of simple virtue. This contrast is summed up in the book's title. In so far as Gatsby represents the simple virtue which Fitzgerald associates with the West, he is really a great man; in so far as he achieves the kind of notoriety which the East accords success of his kind, he is great about as Barnum was. Out of Gatsby's ignorance of his real greatness and his misunderstanding of his notoriety, Fitzgerald gets much of the book's irony. These terms, then, provided the occasions for all Fitzgerald's feelings, so that he was able to say everything he had to say within the terms of a single figure and to give his book the kind of focus and freedom which comes only from successful formal order.

His hero, Gatsby, is frankly romantic, a romantic, like Fitzgerald, from the West, who has missed the girl on whom he has focused all his 'heightened sensitivity to the promises of life' (p. 6) because he had no money. He gets it, by all sorts of corrupt means, and comes back five years later to find Daisy and to fulfil 'his incorruptible dream' (p. 120). '"I wouldn't ask too much of her,"' Nick says to him once, '"[y]ou can't repeat the past"'. '"Can't repeat the past?" he cried incredulously. "Why of course you can!"' (p. 86). But he could not repeat the past with Daisy, changed by her momentary passion for Tom at the time of their marriage and corrupted all her life by her dependence on the protection of wealth and the conventions of the wealthy life which have preserved and heightened her beauty, until in the end she lets Gatsby die for the murder she has committed. He dies waiting for a telephone message from Daisy, and Nick observes: 'I have an idea that Gatsby himself didn't believe it would come and perhaps he no longer cared. If that was true he must have felt that he had lost the old warm world, paid a high price for living too long with a single dream. He must have looked up at . . . [a] new world, material without being real, where poor ghosts, breathing dreams like air, drifted fortuitously about' (p. 126).

Against Nick's gradual understanding of the incorruptibility at the heart of Gatsby's corruption, Fitzgerald sets his gradual penetration of the charm and grace of Tom and Daisy's world. What he penetrates to is corruption, grossness, and cowardice. In contrast to the charm and grace of this world, Gatsby's fantastic mansion, his absurd pink suits, '[his] elaborate formality of speech [which] just missed being absurd' (p. 40) appear ludicrous; against the corruption which underlies this grace, Gatsby's essential moral incorruptibility is heroic. To the representation of this double contrast Fitzgerald brings all his now mature powers of observation, of invention, of creating for the scenes and persons the quality and tone the story requires. Because of the formal perfection of *The Great Gatsby*, this eloquence is given a concentration and intensity Fitzgerald never achieved again. The art of the book, in the narrow sense, is nearly perfect. Its limitation is the limitation of Fitzgerald's nearly complete commitment to Gatsby's romanticism. This commitment is partly concealed by Gatsby's superficial social insufficiency, and our awareness of this insufficiency is strengthened as much as Fitzgerald dares strengthen it by Nick's constant, ironic observation of it: Gatsby is, as a cultured '"Oggsford man"' (p. 57), after all a fake. But this is a romantic irony which touches only the surface; it does not cut to the heart of the matter, to the possibility that there may be some fundamental moral inadequacy in Gatsby's attitude. The world of Daisy and Tom which is set over against Gatsby's dream of a world is beautiful and appealing but in no sense justified: Tom's muddled attempts to offer a reasoned defence for it are only a proof that it is indefensible. Fitzgerald's book is a *Troilus and Cressida* with an Ajax but no Ulysses.[122] □

Both Mizener and Troy, in their accounts of *Gatsby*, provided important preliminary outlines for more extended critical explorations of the novel. With these outlines, with a growing body of other critical and biographical writing about Fitzgerald,[123] and with several editions of

Gatsby now in print, it began to seem by the later 1940s that Gatsby might prove to be more than 'a book of the season only'. The 1950s would put the matter to the proof.

CHAPTER TWO

Dream, Time and Craft: Interpreting *Gatsby* in the 1950s

IT SOON became clear in the Fifties that *Gatsby* would not go away. The tentative Fitzgerald revival of the previous decade started to turn into an industry. This was undoubtedly helped by the expansion of literary studies in American higher education, especially in the shape of the New Criticism, which focused closely upon the structure and style of literary works and upon their moral significance. This focus on structure and style could link up with the interest, generated by the Modernist work of Eliot and Joyce, in the mythical and archetypal patterns that might be discerned in literature. The intricate patterning of *Gatsby* offered many opportunities for the analysis of style and structure and for the detection of broader mythic patterns, while its mixture of explicit moral concern and profound moral ambiguity offered rich opportunities to debate its ethical significance and the ways in which this related to its aesthetic structure.

The literary form that the New Criticism favoured above all was the short lyric poem, which could be conveniently analysed as a whole in a seminar or essay. A compressed, poetic novel such as *Gatsby*, however, was probably the next best thing. The elevation of the novels of Conrad and James to high status also benefited *Gatsby*, in view of the connections that could be established between their fictional techniques and thematic concerns, and those of Fitzgerald. And, in a USA that was booming, immensely powerful, but still uncertain of its underlying values, the idea, already embryonically formulated by writers such as Mizener, that *Gatsby* was in a crucial sense about America, could provide an oblique way of exploring contemporary aspirations and anxieties.

The first major contribution to Fitzgerald studies in the 1950s was an essay by Lionel Trilling. This essay combined two pieces previously published in 1945: a review article on the Edmund Wilson edition of *The Crack-Up* and the introduction to the New Directions edition of *Gatsby*.[1]

By fusing them into one essay, however, and by publishing the essay in his book *The Liberal Imagination* (1951), Trilling gave his appraisal of Fitzgerald greater force and wider currency.

Born in 1905, Lionel Trilling taught for most of his life at Columbia University. In the 1930s and 1940s, however, he had many literary and political connections outside the university, and was never a narrowly academic critic; he always sought to relate literature to wider social and cultural concerns. He had published a study of Matthew Arnold, developed from his PhD thesis, in 1939, a book about E. M. Forster in 1943, and a novel of his own, *The Middle of the Journey*, in 1947; but he made his reputation during the 1940s by the essays he contributed to literary and cultural magazines such as *Partisan Review, Kenyon Review*, and, in England, Cyril Connolly's *Horizon*. It is these essays, for the most part, that are collected in *The Liberal Imagination*.

The Liberal Imagination contributed to – indeed, probably helped to create – the liberal humanist ideology that would come to dominate literary criticism in both the USA and England during the 1950s. Trilling's liberal humanism at that time was not, however, of a kind that denied any link between literature and politics; indeed, he claimed that the essays collected in *The Liberal Imagination* 'assume[d] the inevitable intimate, if not always obvious, connection between literature and politics'.[2] He suggested that the essays – on topics ranging from Kipling to the Kinsey Report, Tacitus to Freud – were unified by an interest in the ideas of liberalism, especially in relation to literature. Writing at a time when he could confidently claim that 'there are no conservative or reactionary ideas in general circulation',[3] Trilling felt that the interests of liberalism would be best served by questioning some of its current ideas and assumptions – for example, its tendency towards 'a denial of the emotions and the imagination'[4] – and that '[t]he job of criticism would seem to be . . . to recall liberalism to its first essential imagination of variousness and possibility, which implies the awareness of complexity and difficulty'.[5]

Possibility, complexity and difficulty were all terms that could be applied to Scott Fitzgerald, in both his life and his work, especially *The Great Gatsby*. But, in his essay on Fitzgerald in *The Liberal Imagination*, Trilling goes further, presenting him as an heroic figure, a sort of tragic hero, like Milton's Samson. He groups together *The Great Gatsby* and *Tender is the Night* as Fitzgerald's two 'mature' novels,[6] and, in his discussion of *Gatsby*, which is printed on page 54, he develops his positive estimate of this novel. First of all, he seeks to establish that, while *Gatsby* can be read as a novel of manners about the 1920s, it is more than that; Trilling compares Fitzgerald to French nineteenth-century novelists – presumably writers such as Balzac and Stendhal – because Fitzgerald is concerned, like them, with the moral realities and implications of the society he evokes and explores. Trilling then goes on to make the crucial claim that *Gatsby* represents America, and he offers an interesting definition of the two polarities that define and divide both *Gatsby* and the USA: power and dream. The implication that *Gatsby* was a characteristically American novel had been made by others, for example William Troy (see pp. 43–5). Trilling crystallises and develops this implication by suggesting that Fitzgerald, in *Gatsby*, may be both the equal of Balzac or Stendhal, *and* quintessentially American.

A large claim; but one that would carry weight, for two reasons: because of the critical authority that Trilling already possessed, and which *The Liberal Imagination* had augmented; and because such a claim offered American culture something that, in the 1950s, it probably desired: a novel that could show that the USA had a cultural achievement that was distinctively its own but which was also the equal of the Europeans; a cultural achievement that would complement and enhance America's political dominance in the postwar world. To say that Trilling's large claim for *Gatsby* could function in this way is not to suggest that Trilling consciously intended that it should do so; it is, however, significant that he writes as if he were primarily addressing American readers, as the phrases 'ours is the only nation' and 'our national life' in the excerpt below demonstrate.

Trilling's discussion of *Gatsby* also mentions form and style; the use of 'foreshortening' and what he calls 'ideographs'. In the *Concise Oxford Dictionary* definition, an ideograph is a 'character symbolising [the] idea of a thing without expressing the sequence of sounds in its name' – for example, a Chinese character. Trilling appears to use the term to mean those symbols, setting and scenes in *Gatsby* – for example, the valley of ashes, Eckleburg's eyes, the parties – that seem to concentrate, often in a strongly visual form, many ideas and feelings without explicating them, rather in the manner of the definition of the 'Image' attributed to the poet Ezra Pound, in the aesthetic manifesto 'A Few Don'ts by An Imagiste' first published in 1913: 'An "Image" is that which presents an intellectual and emotional complex in an instant of time'.[7] It was Pound who was to edit and compress T. S. Eliot's *The Waste Land*, and it is significant that, in his account of *Gatsby*, Trilling slips in a comparison between *The Waste Land* and Fitzgerald's novel in terms of their ideographic technique, and also alludes to the reciprocal admiration of Eliot and Fitzgerald. In invoking *The Waste Land* and Eliot in this way, Trilling further enhances the status of both Fitzgerald and *Gatsby*.

Trilling goes on to praise Fitzgerald for 'the voice of his prose', a voice that is defined in terms of an attitude rather than a rhythm – an attitude in which firm moral judgement is qualified by a tenderness towards human desires. This 'voice', Trilling then declares, is both the 'normal' and the 'ideal' voice of the novelist. It is also, as it happens, not unlike Trilling's own voice in his critical prose – and in this respect, Trilling not only enters a covert, and probably unconscious, claim for himself, but also assimilates Fitzgerald to the 'liberal imagination'.

At the end of his account, Trilling returns to the exemplary character of Scott Fitzgerald himself, a character that, as Trilling presents it, turns out to be remarkably like *Gatsby's*, in its gift for hope and its heroic lack of prudence. This is also the end of an essay in which Trilling has, masterfully, raised Fitzgerald's ranking in several ways: by suggesting a partial identity between Fitzgerald, *Gatsby*, and the USA itself; by linking Fitzgerald, in his life, with a tragic hero such as Samson; by comparing him, as a novelist of society, with nineteenth-century European giants such as Stendhal and Balzac; by likening his technique to that of the then-heroic icon of Modernist poetry, T. S. Eliot; and by implying that Fitzgerald's prose is the epitome of the novelist's voice and that, in this dimension at least, Fitzgerald achieved that combination of the ideal and the everyday that eluded Gatsby.

Two further aspects of Trilling's account should be noted; one is a hint, the other a silence. The hint is of a gay subtext in *Gatsby*, when Trilling calls Jordan Baker 'vaguely homosexual', a subtext that will be explored much more fully in Keath Fraser's 'Another Reading of *The Great Gatsby*' in 1979, from which an extract is printed later in this book. The silence is in regard to Fitzgerald's portrayal of the Jew, in the figure of what Trilling himself calls 'the dim Wolfsheim' – an omission which may relate to Trilling's own complex relationship to his own Jewish ancestry and to his desire for assimilation into the American mainstream.[8]

■ *The Great Gatsby* . . . after a quarter-century is still as fresh as when it first appeared; it has even gained in weight and relevance, which can be said of very few American books of its time. This, I think, is to be attributed to the specifically intellectual courage with which it was conceived and executed, a courage which implies Fitzgerald's grasp – both in the sense of awareness and of appropriation – of the traditional resources available to him. Thus, *The Great Gatsby* has its interest as a record of contemporary manners, but this might only have served to date it, did not Fitzgerald take the given moment of history as something more than a mere circumstance, did he not, in the manner of the great French novelists of the nineteenth century, seize the given moment as a moral fact. The same boldness of intellectual grasp accounts for the success of the conception of its hero – Gatsby is said by some to be not quite credible, but the question of any literal credibility he may or may not have becomes trivial before the large significance he implies. For Gatsby, divided between power and dream, comes inevitably to stand for America itself. Ours is the only nation that prides itself upon a dream and gives its name to one, 'the American dream'. We are told that '[t]he truth was that Jay Gatsby, of West Egg, Long Island, sprang from his Platonic conception of himself. He was a son of God – a phrase which, if it means anything, means just that – and he must be about His Father's Business, the service of a vast, vulgar and meretricious beauty' (pp. 76–7). Clearly it is Fitzgerald's intention that our mind should turn to the thought of the nation that has sprung from its 'Platonic conception' of itself. To the world it is anomalous in America, just as in the novel it is anomalous in Gatsby, that so much raw power should be haunted by envisioned romance. Yet in that anomaly lies, for good or bad, much of the truth of our national life, as, at the present moment, we think about it.

Then, if the book grows in weight of significance with the years, we can be sure that this could not have happened had its form and style not been as right as they are. Its form is ingenious – with the ingenuity, however, not of craft but of intellectual intensity. The form, that is, is not the result of careful 'plotting' – the form of a good novel never is – but is rather the result of the necessities of the story's informing idea, which require the sharpness of radical foreshortening. Thus, it will be observed, the characters are not 'developed': the wealthy and brutal Tom Buchanan, haunted by his 'scientific' vision of the doom of civilisation, the vaguely guilty, vaguely homosexual Jordan Baker, the dim Wolfsheim, who fixed the World Series of 1919, are treated, we might say, as if they were ideographs, a method of economy that is reinforced by the ideographic use that is made of the Washington Heights flat, the terrible 'valley of ashes' seen from the Long Island Railroad, Gatsby's incoherent parties, and the huge sordid eyes of the oculist's advertising sign. (It is a technique which gives the novel an affinity with *The Waste Land*, between whose author and Fitzgerald there existed a reciprocal admiration.) Gatsby himself, once stated, grows only in the understanding of the narrator. He is allowed to say very little in his own person. Indeed, apart from the famous '"Her voice is full of money"' (p. 94), he says only one memorable thing, but that remark is overwhelming in its intellectual audacity: when he is forced to admit that his lost Daisy did perhaps love her husband, he says, '"In any case . . . it was just personal"' (p. 119). With that sentence he achieves an insane greatness, convincing us that he really is a Platonic conception of himself, really some sort of Son of God.

What underlies all success in poetry, what is even more important than the shape of the poem or its wit of metaphor, is the poet's voice. It either gives us confidence in what is being said or it tells us that we do not need to listen; and it carries both the modulation and the living form of what is being said. In the novel no less than in the poem, the voice of the author is the decisive factor. We are less consciously aware of it in the novel, and, in speaking of the elements of a novel's art, it cannot properly be exemplified by quotation because it is continuous and cumulative. In Fitzgerald's work the voice of his prose is of the essence of his success. We hear in it at once the tenderness toward human desires that modifies a true firmness of moral judgement. It is, I would venture to say, the normal or ideal voice of the novelist. It is characteristically modest, yet it has in it, without apology or self-consciousness, a largeness, even a stateliness, which derives from Fitzgerald's connection with tradition and with mind, from his sense of what has been done before and the demands which this past accomplishment makes. ' . . . I became aware of the old island here that flowered once for Dutch sailors' eyes – a fresh, green breast of the new world. Its vanished trees, the trees that had made way for Gatsby's house, had once pandered in whispers to the last and greatest of all human dreams; for a transitory enchanted moment man must have held his breath in the presence of this continent, compelled into an aesthetic contemplation he neither understood nor desired, face to face for the last time in history with something commensurate to his capacity for wonder' (p. 140). Here, in the well-known passage, the voice is a little dramatic, a little *intentional*, which is not improper to a passage in climax and conclusion, but it will the better suggest in brief compass the habitual music of Fitzgerald's seriousness.

Fitzgerald lacked prudence, as his heroes did, lacked that blind instinct of self-protection which the writer needs and the American writer needs in double measure. But that is all he lacked – and it is the generous fault, even the heroic fault. He said of his Gatsby, 'If personality is an unbroken series of successful gestures, then there was something gorgeous about him, some heightened sensitivity to the promises of life, as if he were related to one of those intricate machines that register earthquakes ten thousand miles away. This responsiveness had nothing to do with that flabby impressionability which is dignified under the name of the "creative temperament" – it was an extraordinary gift for hope, a romantic readiness such as I have never found in any other person and which it is not likely I shall ever find again' (p. 6). And it is so that we are drawn to see Fitzgerald himself as he stands in his exemplary role.[9] □

The idea that *The Great Gatsby* was an evocation and evaluation of the American Dream received considerable elaboration during the 1950s. An early and important stage in this process was Edwin S. Fussell's essay 'Fitzgerald's Brave New World', which appeared in the journal *English Literary History* in December 1952. Fussell argued that Fitzgerald's literary status depended above all on his critique of the American Dream; a critique that appears in what Fussell regards as his best work in an 'almost archetypal' story that has two dominant patterns: the quest for romantic wonder, in the terms that contemporary America offers; and the seduction by those terms.[10] Fussell's account of *Gatsby* anticipates, in some respects, an essay published two years later that was to become the best-known interpretation of the novel in terms of the American Dream. This was Marius Bewley's 'Scott Fitzgerald's Criticism of America', which appeared in the *Sewanee Review* in Spring 1954 and was incorporated, in expanded form, in Bewley's *The Eccentric Design: Form in the Classical American Novel*, which came out in 1959.[11] Bewley's essay, in its original version, has enjoyed a long afterlife, having been reprinted, in full, in four later anthologies of criticism.[12]

It is, in fact, open to question whether Bewley's essay quite merits the classic status it seems to have attained. Though it remains valuable in some respects – that is why it is discussed and quoted in this Guide – its overall approach is not original, and its elaborations are sometimes ponderous. In the 1950s, however, Bewley was a significant figure in developing a vision of American literature for consumption in the USA and beyond. He had lived in England and had studied at Cambridge University with the figure who was then the most dominant British literary critic, F. R. Leavis; he had become Leavis's friend – not an easy thing to do, since Leavis was notoriously prickly; and he had contributed to Leavis's major critical journal *Scrutiny*. Bewley shared Leavis's view that a great work of fiction was both morally significant and artistically accomplished – indeed, that the artistic accomplishment and moral significance were inseparable – and, as Leavis had sought to establish a 'great tradition' of English novels, so Bewley was trying, in the 1950s, to establish a 'great tradition' of American novels. He had already made a reputation with his book *The Complex Fate* (1952), to which Leavis had contributed an introduction. *The Complex Fate* focused mainly on James and Hawthorne and took its title from James's remark '[i]t's a complex fate, being an American'. Scott Fitzgerald could be seen as one of the twentieth-century explorers, in fiction, of that 'complex fate'.

Bewley could hardly have failed to be aware, however, that Leavis took a dim view of Fitzgerald, since in his introduction to *The Complex Fate*, he had pronounced this damning diagnosis:

■ Scott Fitzgerald . . . shows that a writer, while using English as unquestionably a native inheritance, may yet have inherited little else with it. As the one positive alternative to the actual and very unideal kinds of relation between the sexes ordinary in the milieu he depicts, he never gets beyond the teen-age Romeo-and-Juliet notion of romantic love. Such love is what the hero is baulked of by social snobbery in

The Great Gatsby. And it is not merely that, in Fitzgerald's world, no vestige, and no suspicion, of any standard of maturity exists. The extremity of the destitution that disqualifies him as a novelist and a creative writer (in spite of the almost classical status that has been conferred on him) is what can be seen in the accounts of his life; those accounts which, offered us so often in apparent unawareness of their implication, have the closest critical bearings on what he wrote. The state of dispossession they illustrate – dispossession of the interests, the awarenesses, the impulsions and the moral perceptions out of which a creative rendering of human life might come – is such that he seems to have had hardly any sense of even the elementary decencies that one had thought of as making civilized intercourse possible (if he was aware of them, it was to show – the relevant episodes are very striking – resentful hostility to any regard for them in others). There is nothing in his writings to contradict what we know of the life.[13] □

It may be that Bewley's essay on *The Great Gatsby* was, to some degree, a kind of 'hidden polemic' against Leavis's view of Fitzgerald, in which Bewley tried to prove that Gatsby possessed those very qualities that Leavis said Fitzgerald lacked. This may partly account for the lengthy elaborations of the essay, as Bewley sought to make his case as strong as possible.

While Bewley feels, like Mizener and Trilling, that *The Great Gatsby* is distinctively American, he rejects, at the outset of his essay, the suggestion, whose unacknowledged source is presumably Mizener, that the novel is in some sense 'pastoral'. He makes a claim for *Gatsby* as belonging to a great tradition of American novels and as providing, in a way that is inseparable from its artistic form, a radical criticism of a fundamental American attitude with a long historical pedigree. But as well as emphasising the distinctively American quality of Gatsby's romanticism, Bewley also argues that Gatsby is a 'mythic' character – Bewley himself encloses the adjective in inverted commas – in a specific sense that he derives and develops from the cultural critic Jacques Barzun. In Barzun's 'materialist' (though not 'historical materialist') definition, as paraphrased by Bewley, figures, whether real or fictional, who 'express destinies, aspirations, attitudes typical of man or particular groups' take on a mythical character.[14] Gatsby becomes mythical in this sense both because he embodies the core conflict in the American Dream between illusion and reality and because he heroically personifies the American romantic hero. Bewley also finds in Gatsby a Renaissance quality, as if he were a Shakespearean 'Duke in disguise'.[15]

The elevation of Gatsby to mythical status is coupled, in Bewley's essay, with a denigration of Daisy as representative of the decadence of the American world within which Gatsby tries to satisfy his aspirations.

Bewley seems remarkably hostile to Daisy, charging her with 'vicious emptiness'[16] and 'monstrous moral indifference';[17] and his claim that her failure is not to be seen in 'human or personal' terms,[18] which might seem to suggest that she is not, in herself, the target of Bewley's attack, could also appear to negate her. Bewley further implies that Daisy, or what she represents, is an aesthetic as well as a moral failure; like William Troy in the extract quoted earlier (see pp. 43–5), Bewley employs T. S. Eliot's notion of the 'objective correlative', but rather than applying it to the novel itself, as Troy did, he applies it to a character in the novel, to Daisy, who fails 'to represent the objective correlative of Gatsby's vision'.[19] It is interesting to compare Bewley's version of Daisy with those offered later in this Guide by Leslie A. Fiedler, by Joan S. Korenman and Leland S. Person, Jr (see pp. 99–103, 112–15 and 115–22).

Despite its length, there is a notable omission in Bewley's essay; he rarely discusses Nick Carraway, or analyses his role in the narrative. Nick becomes the almost transparent medium through which we see, on the one hand, Gatsby, and, on the other, Fitzgerald. For example, Bewley (like Edwin S. Fussell),[20] interprets the passage in which Nick speculates on Gatsby's state of mind after Daisy's desertion as if it were a report by an omniscient narrator, privy to his character's secret thoughts – whereas it is Nick's thoughts on what Gatsby 'must have' thought that we are offered, and they may be telling us something about Nick as well as Gatsby. So Bewley valuably elaborates one influential interpretation of the novel that nonetheless leaves important aspects undiscussed – for example, the function and character of Nick, which will be explored later in the 1950s, and the representation of women, which will be taken up in the 1970s.

The excerpt from Bewley's essay that follows begins with a discussion of the novel's famous guest list and goes on to develop the idea of Gatsby as a 'mythic' figure:

■ The names of [Gatsby's] guests could have been recorded nowhere else as appropriately as in the margins of a faded timetable. The embodiment of illusions, they are as ephemeral as time itself; but because their illusions represent the distortions and shards of some shattered American dream, the timetable they adorn is 'in effect July 5th' (p. 49) – the day following the great national festival when the exhausted holiday crowds, as spent as exploded firecrackers, return to their homes. The list of names which Fitzgerald proceeds to enumerate conjures up with remarkable precision an atmosphere of vulgar American fortunes and vulgar American destinies . . . After two pages and more, the list ends with the dreamily elegiac close: 'All these people came to Gatsby's house in the summer' (p. 51).

Why did they come? There is the answer of the plotted story – the free party, the motor-boats, the private beach, the endless flow of cock-tails. But in the completed pattern of the novel one knows that they came for another reason – came blindly and instinctively – illusions in pursuit of a reality from which they have become historically sepa-rated, but by which they might alone be completed or fulfilled. And why did Gatsby invite them? As contrasted with them, he alone has a sense of the reality that hovers somewhere out of sight in this nearly ruined American dream; but the reality is unintelligible until he can invest it again with the tangible forms of his world, and relate it to the logic of history. Gatsby and his guests feel a mutual need of each other, but the division in American experience has widened too far, and no party, however lavish, can heal the breach. The illusions and the real-ity go their separate ways. Gatsby stands at the door of his mansion, in one of the most deeply moving and significant paragraphs of the novel, to wish his guests good-bye:

> The caterwauling horns had reached a crescendo and I turned away and cut across the lawn toward home. I glanced back once. A wafer of a moon was shining over Gatsby's house, making the night fine as before and surviving the laughter and the sound of his still glowing garden. A sudden emptiness seemed to flow now from the windows and the great doors, endowing with complete isolation the figure of the host who stood on the porch, his hand up in a formal gesture of farewell. (p. 46)

[F]rom th[is] . . . scene there opens a perspective of profound meaning. Suddenly Gatsby is not merely a likable, romantic hero; he is a creature of myth in whom is incarnated the aspiration and the ordeal of his race.

'Mythic' characters are impersonal. There is no distinction between their public and their private lives. Because they share their meaning with everyone, they have no secrets and no hidden corners into which they can retire for a moment, unobserved. An intimacy so universal stands revealed in a ritual pattern for the inspection and instruction of the race. The 'mythic' character can never withdraw from that air which is his existence – that is to say, from that area of consciousness (and hence of publicity) which every individual shares with the members, both living and dead, of his group or race. Gatsby is a 'mythic' character in this sense – he has no private life, no meaning or significance that depends on the fulfilment of his merely private destiny, his happiness as an individual in a society of individuals. In a transcendent sense he touches our imaginations, but in this smaller sense – which is the world of the realistic novel – he even fails to arouse our curiosity. At this level, his love affair with Daisy is too easily 'placed', a tawdry epic 'crush' of no depth or interest in itself. But Gatsby not only remains undiminished by what is essentially the meanness of the affair: his stature grows, as we watch, to the proportions of a hero.[21] □

Later in the same year in which Bewley's essay appeared, John W. Bicknell published an essay that staked out a different position. In 'The Waste Land of F. Scott Fitzgerald', published in *The Virginia Quarterly Review* of Autumn 1954, Bicknell agrees that *Gatsby* is an evocation and an indictment of the American Dream – indeed he suggests that it is easier to recognise this in the 1950s than in the 1920s – but he takes issue with the kind of interpretation represented by Bewley. He sees the novel as a profoundly pessimistic elegy, and Gatsby himself as a pathetic victim, not a doomed mythic hero embodying the American Dream. Bicknell develops Trilling's brief reference to the similarities between *Gatsby* and Eliot's *The Waste Land,* and also suggests a link between Eliot, Fitzgerald and Conrad, especially through 'Heart of Darkness'. But he argues that while Conrad could summon up stoicism against the heart of darkness, and Eliot in the waste land could shore up fragments against his ruins, Fitzgerald's valley of ashes is void of the means of either transcendence or endurance.[22]

Bicknell's analysis of *Gatsby* offers a more restricted Fitzgerald than Bewley's; but both critics share a sobriety of tone and approach that, while it is appropriate to some aspects of *Gatsby*, hardly does justice to the exuberance of the novel. In November 1955, however, an essay appeared in the fourth issue of the journal *Modern Fiction Studies* that did echo that exuberance and which conveyed the richness of the novel more effectively than any previous account: R. W. Stallman's 'Gatsby and the Hole in Time'.

While Bewley is highly selective in the aspects of *Gatsby* he discusses, and firmly subordinates his chosen aspects to his overall interpretation, Stallman is like a voracious magpie, seizing on all kinds of bright curiosities and heaping them up for our inspection. His essay resembles an overstuffed Aladdin's cave which constantly bids to exceed the order he tries to impose on it. This in itself is valuable, in that it does help to bring across the multiplicity and variousness of *Gatsby* and offers much material for future critical investigation. It is, however, not only the details Stallman accumulates, but also his more general arguments, that are worth our attention.

Stallman starts by agreeing with Bewley that *Gatsby* is a criticism of the American Dream rather than, as Mizener put it, a tragic pastoral of the Jazz Age. But he then proceeds to charge Bewley himself with oversimplifying the matter. The novel, Stallman proposes, is not only about the American Dream; Gatsby is 'a myth-hero', 'a modern Icarus' who 'transcends reality and time' and 'belongs . . . to all history inasmuch as all history repeats in cycle form what Gatsby represents – America itself'.[23] In other words, the dreams, aspirations and disappointments that 'America' has, in our time, come to represent recur, in different forms, throughout history. This large claim might seem to risk dissolving the specific details of the novel into some vague general archetype. Stallman goes on, however, to argue that Gatsby, although a transcendent figure, has one notable quality that makes him very specific to his epoch: his confused sense of time. Thus the very way in which Gatsby tries to be transcendent, by attempting to deny the logic of time, locates him in a particular historical moment, brands him as being of his epoch. Stallman contends that in *Gatsby*, Fitzgerald renders a hole, or breach, in time, the 'void of the corrupted present cancelled out by the corrupted past',[24] and his essay explores the way in which time is referred to and symbolised in the novel.

The time theme is not Stallman's only topic, however. He challenges two assumptions that, by 1955, had become fairly dominant in *Gatsby* criticism. One assumption is that Nick Carraway is to be respected, even admired, for his moral concern and perception. But Stallman provocatively characterises Nick as 'a defunct archpriest in the confessional-box, a prig with holier-than-thou airs'.[25] His attack stirred up a debate about Nick that continues, in various forms, to this day. The other assumption Stallman challenges is that *Gatsby* opposes a corrupt East to a virtuous West (see Mizener, pp. 46–9). With close attention to detail, Stallman argues that this opposition cannot hold: that East and West echo and mirror each other in all kinds of ways.

Stallman identifies a wide range of other oppositions in *Gatsby* but suggests how these oppositions, like the opposition between East and West, cannot stay rigid: '[b]lurred or confused identity patterns everything in the book'. He also points out the doubling that occurs in the novel, the proliferation of twos or pairs (two eggs, two eyes) that subverts the notion of a unique identity: '[n]othing is complete and whole as a thing in itself'. Although Stallman claims that his interpretation of *Gatsby* results from 'explor[ing] it as an integrated whole',[26] his analysis seems, in this respect, to anticipate a deconstructionist approach in which oppositions and doublings are identified but are then shown to infiltrate and contaminate each other in such a way that their rigid boundaries cannot be maintained. It is this part of his analysis that we can now read:

■ East is West, night is day, reality is unreality. Reality, substance without substance, is overwhelmed by dream and confounded by illusion. Nothing in the novel is not confused. Even geography is scrambled. The cagey Nick probes Gatsby as to what part of the West he comes from: '"What part of the middle-west?" I inquired casually'. And Gatsby just as casually replies: '"San Francisco"' (p. 52). The confused identity of West and East is epitomized in the figure of Dan Cody as 'the pioneer debauchee who . . . brought back to the eastern seaboard the savage violence of the frontier brothel and saloon' (p. 78). Blurred or confused identity patterns everything in the book. McKee's over-enlarged portrait of Mrs. Wilson's dead mother hovers like an ectoplasm on the wall, looking like 'a hen sitting on a blurred rock. Looked at from a distance however the hen resolved itself into a bonnet and the countenance of a stout old lady beamed down into the room' (p. 25).

Confused and divided selfhood, exemplified notably in Gatsby and Nick, has its counterpart motif in mistaken and crossed identity. Everyone's identity overlaps another's . . . Jordan is misidentified as Daisy by Myrtle; Wilson substitutes for Tom Buchanan as the murderer of Gatsby; and in the enigmatic book entitled *Simon Called Peter* self-identity is similarly repudiated. The unknown Gatsby, known only by his false name, confounds identity and, being mistaken for the 'murderer' of Myrtle, he is murdered because of it. Crossed identities of persons have their parallel in the switched cars at the crack-up. The names of Gatsby's house-guests that Nick records on the margins of a defunct railroad-timetable furnish, as it were, a forest-preserve of crossed identities. With the clan of Black*buck* (the Blackbucks flip up their noses like goats at whosoever approaches them) Cecil Roe*buck* – figuratively speaking – crossbreeds, and Roebuck shares what Frances Bull has in common with the *Horn*beams. Edgar Beaver with cotton-white hair suggests not beaver but rabbit, by whom Endive (Clarence Endive) is devoured, as it were, and Beaver is pursued by Rot-Gut Ferret – *ferret* being a weasel. Dr. Civet, the surgeon who is to operate on a star (the *star* is Miss Baedeker, named after the official Baedeker guidebook for travellers, travellers through space) suggests relationship with Catlip, as *civet* translates into cat; and Catlip in turn suggests kinship with Katspaugh, Gatsby's gangster-friend. Chester Becker has the same surname as one of the gangsters who murdered Rosy Rosenthal and got the Hot Seat. The gangster Becker (who got the Hot Seat), suggests relationship thus with a man named Bunsen, inasmuch as Bunsen was the inventor of the Original Burner! Nick describes Bunsen simply as a man he knew at Yale, but the connection that I detect here is not as fanciful as it may seem, for everything in the novel is punned upon, jokingly counterpointed or burlesqued, jazzed up – like Tostoff's '"Jazz History of the World"' (p. 41). Nick's timetable – outdated, outmoded, useless now – reflects the flaw in Nick's own time-sense: 'an old timetable now, disintegrating at its folds and headed "This schedule in effect July 5th, 1922"' (p. 49). Neither the timetable nor Nick is 'in effect' – In the meantime/In between time.

Nick's timetable is infested with violence and disruption: Beaver had his nose shot off in the war, Muldoon strangled his wife, the Quinns are now divorced, Civet was drowned, Endive boxed a man named Etty, an automobile ran over Snell's right hand, and Palmetto killed himself 'by jumping in front of a subway train in Times Square' (p. 50). Cannibalism, name devouring name, and violence link with confused identities: 'Benny McClenahan arrived always with four girls. They were never quite the same ones in physical person but they were so identical one with another that it inevitably seemed they had been there before' (p. 50). In contrast are the innocent plant-life names of Lilly, Orchid and Duckweed, and the Leeches, and bounding through the forest is Ewing Klipspringer, *klipspringer* being an antelope [an Afrikaans word for a small, agile South African antelope]. Another daisy-chain of puns, this one not furnished by Nick's timetable, is formed by Gatsby's first name, Jay, in rhyme with the last names of the two women who betray him, Fay and Kaye. So too Goddard couples with Stoddard, the one interchangeable with the other.

'Almost any exhibition of complete self sufficiency', as Nick remarks, 'draws a stunned tribute from me' (p. 11). Nothing in the book has self-sufficiency, not even Gatsby. Every person, place or thing exists in partnership with its opposite or with its double. Everybody borrows attributes of another and/or connects with somebody else. Gatsby, the Buchanans, Klipspringer, and Nick's girl out West, and Jordan, the golf champion – they are all sportsmen, at cricket [see p. 53, where Gatsby shows Nick a photograph of himself at Oxford, 'with a cricket bat in his hand'], or golf. They are all thus Dealers in Space.

The photographer McKee makes enlargements of things in space, Jordan jumps space by moving her golf-ball forward from a bad lie, and space is connoted by Miss Baedeker's name – the official guide-book for travelling about the globe. As Chester McKee fixes space, so Meyer Wolfsheim fixes time – he fixes the World Series! Fixing space and time provides thus analogy with the great Gatsby. Fitzgerald shows a marked predilection for doubling the identities of persons, places and things; fashioning them by two or pairs. Gatsby has two fathers (Mr. Gatz and his Heavenly Father, Owl Eyes); his life divides into two parts; he is tricked by two women. Nick has two girls (one in the East and one in the West); Myrtle plans to go West with Tom, and her husband plans to go West with Myrtle. Like Miss This-or-That and the Three Mr. Mumbles, it is all rather confusing. There are two timetables, two eggs, two necklaces, and so on. Two shining eyes look blankly at McKee, Tom demanding '"Two what?"'. McKee means his two photographs: "'Two studies. One of them I call 'Montauk Point – The Gulls', and the other I call 'Montauk Point – the Sea'''" (p. 28). They have the same bewildering difference as, say, East and West Egg. Gatsby's medieval mansion is at once a houseboat and a roadhouse – "'the world's fair'" (p. 64). "'I'll be the man smoking two cigarettes'", says Daisy (p. 98). Jordan Baker mannishly 'wore her evening dress, all her dresses, like sports clothes' (p. 42) (which are worn properly only in the daytime). All's confounded by mixed identity. Nothing is complete and whole as a thing in itself; nothing therefore is without imperfection. Nick reminds Daisy of an "'absolute rose'", but as Nick himself admits 'I am not even faintly like a rose' (p. 15). There are no absolutes in the book. Everything resides in what is outside itself. Epochs and places share the same fate as persons. Juxtaposed upon Versailles, scenes of which are tapestried in Myrtle's love-couch, there is a blood-spattered scandal sheet, *Town Tattle*. The great Voltaire sinks into Willie Voltaire, and by the same bathos the North and the South collapse into Mrs. Ulysses (Grant) *Swett* and Stonewall Jackson *Abrams* (p. 49).

Everybody is maimed, physically or spiritually. Not one woman is without some physical imperfection, not even Daisy is beautiful. The physically maimed include Daisy's butler whose nose was injured from polishing too much silverware; the motion picture director ['producer'] with his "'blue nose'" (p. 82); the Becker who had his nose shot off during the war; and Wolfsheim with his 'tragic nose' (p. 58) – a 'flat-nosed Jew' (p. 55) whistling "'the Rosary'" (p. 132).

Unfinished business and frustrated or muddled and broken-off relationships characterize the maimed action of the entire novel. Characters and scenes are undeveloped; nearly every scene is broken off – not finished but disrupted ("'[t]o be continued'" (p. 18)). The moralist Fitzgerald strikes out against the fragmented morality of his age by rendering his world thus: confused and fragmentary. When Nick turns to Gatsby he finds that Gatsby has vanished, and midway in his speech Gatsby's elegant sentences halt unfinished; Wolfsheim fills in unspoken words by a wave of his hand; Daisy's voice breaks off; and Tom's gibberish ends on a dash. "'[B]ut science –'" He paused. The immediate contingency overtook him, pulled him back from the edge of the theoretical abyss' (p. 95).[27] □

From the excitements of Stallman's essay, we can turn, once more, to a relatively sober account of *Gatsby* – but an account that, in contrast to the previous critics of the 1950s we have looked at, focuses not on theme and symbol, but on technique. This account comes from the first book-length critical study of Fitzgerald's fiction, James E. Miller, Jr's *The Fictional Technique of F. Scott Fitzgerald*, which came out in 1957. Miller sets his overall analysis in the context of the dispute between Henry James and H. G. Wells over the form and function of the novel. In particular, Miller looks at the tension between what James saw as the novel of 'saturation' – the novel that tries to get everything in – and the novel of 'selection', which works by selecting salient, significant details. Relating these terms to Fitzgerald, Miller classifies *This Side of Paradise* as a novel of 'saturation', *The Beautiful and Damned* as a novel of 'transition' that is moving from a 'saturated' to a more selective approach, and *The Great Gatsby* as a novel of 'selection'.

In the excerpt from his book that follows, Miller focuses first on Fitzgerald's use of the modified first person form in *Gatsby*, relating this to Conrad's use of a similar technique. Conradian echoes had been noted in *Gatsby* even on its first appearance; the *Times Literary Supplement* had seen *Gatsby* as a 'Conradian hero', akin to Almayer or Kurtz (see p. 34) and Gilbert Seldes's review had spoken, dismissively, of *Gatsby*'s 'cadences borrowed from Conrad' (see p. 31). In 1954, John W. Bicknell, in the essay we discussed earlier in this chapter, had also detected 'Conrad-like cadences'[28] in Fitzgerald's description of the valley of ashes (see p. 61). We may recall, however, that back in 1946, Arthur Mizener, in 'The Poet of Borrowed Time', had already suggested that it was more than a matter of cadences and that Fitzgerald took from Conrad what Mizener calls 'the modified first-person form' (see p. 47). Miller shows us in more detail what this means by identifying three methods that, combined together, enable Nick to reap the benefits and escape some of the drawbacks of the first-person viewpoint. One of these methods is Nick's eye-witness accounts. Another method is his reconstruction of events from several explicit or implied sources and/or from his own imagination (as in his account of Gatsby's death, which includes Nick's imaginative projection of how Gatsby 'must have' felt before he died (p. 126)). A third method is his reporting of another's narrative (as in Jordan Baker's recollections of Gatsby and Daisy in Chapter IV (pp. 59–62)).

Miller then goes on to analyse the way in which Fitzgerald alters the straightforward chronological events of the story so that the reader gets to know Gatsby in the way one might get to know someone in real life, moving from a first impression to a more detailed and complex kind of knowledge. We saw earlier that an early, anonymous review noticed this aspect of Fitzgerald's narrative technique (see p. 13), and Miller offers a developed account of how it works, relating it to the narrative techniques of Ford Madox Ford as well as Conrad.

■ In *The Great Gatsby*, Fitzgerald abandoned the omniscient point of view he had previously used in his novels and resorted to first-person narration, after the manner of Joseph Conrad. Until Conrad's special use of the first person, the method had been in disrepute among writers who thought of fiction primarily in terms of technique. Henry James, as Richard P. Blackmur has said, 'bore a little heavily against this most familiar of all narrative methods'.[29] James thought that the method led inevitably to irrelevance and saturation . . . But Conrad's use of the first person did not lead to the looseness which James so much feared . . . Conrad exploited the 'modified' first-person technique in a series of stories – 'Youth' (1902), 'Heart of Darkness' (1902), *Lord Jim* (1900), and *Chance* (1913) – in which Marlow acts as narrator, but not in the conventional first-person manner. By the use of a series of technical devices, Conrad avoided the usual pitfalls and limitations of first-person narration. . . .

In spite of his dislike for first-person narration because of its inevitable 'looseness', Henry James . . . cited Conrad's *Chance* as an example of the novel of selection. Conrad, James said, had multiplied 'his creators or . . . producers, as to make them almost more numerous and quite emphatically more material than the creatures and the production itself'.[30] By placing the narrator in the story and letting him reconstruct and interpret, by turning over all of his 'duties' as author to him, Conrad succeeded in effacing himself almost completely. The reader remains unconscious of the author behind the scenes but he becomes acutely conscious of the narrator as a character in the story.

Fitzgerald used the modified first-person in *The Great Gatsby* much as Conrad used it in the Marlow stories. Nick Carraway is charged with relating the story as he sees it, reconstructing by some means whatever he himself has been unable to witness. His qualification as a sympathetic listener is carefully established on the first page of the novel: 'I'm inclined to reserve all judgements, a habit that has opened up many curious natures to me and also made me the victim of not a few veteran bores . . . ' (p. 5). Such a characteristic is mandatory for an observer who must rely to a great extent on other people for information about those events which he himself is unable to witness.

There are three methods by which Nick Carraway informs the reader of what is happening or has happened in *The Great Gatsby*: most frequently he presents his own eye-witness account; often he presents the accounts of other people, sometimes in their words, sometimes in his own; occasionally, he reconstructs an event from several sources – the newspapers, servants, his own imagination – but presents his version as connected narrative. Nick is initially placed at the edge of the story: he rents a cottage next to Gatsby's mansion in West Egg, and he is remotely related to the Buchanans (he is 'second cousin once removed' to Daisy (p. 8), and he was at Yale with her husband, Tom), who live across the bay in East Egg. This slight relationship is gradually strengthened, particularly through Jordan Baker, whom he meets at the Buchanans, until Nick becomes, in spite of his reluctance, involved in Gatsby's pursuit of Daisy, the material symbol of his dream. Nick's position becomes such that he is naturally able to witness and report personally a maximum of the 'contemporary' action. Various devices are used to keep him on stage when Fitzgerald wishes to represent an event scenically through him. During the showdown scene between Tom and Gatsby, Nick informs the reader: 'At this point [after it is apparent that an argument between Tom and Gatsby is developing] Jordan and I tried to go but Tom and Gatsby insisted with competitive firmness that we remain – as though neither of them had anything to conceal and it would be a privilege to partake vicariously of their emotions' (p. 102). Nick's presence is carefully justified in order to enable him to present an eye-witness account of this important incident.

When Fitzgerald needs to inform the reader of material about which his narrator can have no firsthand knowledge, he sometimes permits Nick to listen extensively to an individual who has the information. Jordan Baker, one of the most technically useful characters in the book (like a Henry James *ficelle*, however, she is also granted a dramatic interest in the story)[31] informs Nick of the brief wartime love affair between Daisy and Gatsby, which had taken place some five years before. Her eye-witness account begins:

> One October day in nineteen-seventeen –
> (said Jordan Baker that afternoon, sitting up very straight on a straight chair in the tea-garden at the Plaza Hotel)
> – I was walking along from one place to another half on the sidewalks and half on the lawns. (p. 59)

By this simple device, a past event is represented fully from a point of view other than the narrator's.

Sometimes Fitzgerald permits his narrator to reconstruct in his own language what he has been told about some event he has not witnessed. Citing Gatsby as his source, Nick informs the reader of Gatsby's days with Dan Cody: 'James Gatz – that was really, or at least legally, his name. He had changed it at the age of seventeen and at the specific moment that witnessed the beginning of his career – when he saw Dan Cody's yacht drop anchor over the most insidious flat on Lake Superior' (p. 76). This method permits Nick to intersperse speculation and interpretation with the action: '[t]he truth was that Jay Gatsby, of West Egg, Long Island, sprang from his Platonic conception of himself. He was a son of God – a phrase which, if it means anything, means just that – and he must be about His Father's Business, the service of a vast, vulgar and meretricious beauty' (pp. 76–7). Had he simply 'overheard' Gatsby telling the story of his youth, the reader would have been deprived of Nick's imaginative conception of Gatsby's past.

In order to present as dramatically and connectedly as possible a scene at which there is no surviving observer, Fitzgerald occasionally allows the narrator to reconstruct an event rather freely from several sources, unstated but implied. In such a manner Nick describes the day on which Wilson tracks down and shoots Gatsby and then kills himself. Nick begins by saying, 'Now I want to go back a little and tell what happened at the garage after we left there the night before' (p. 122). There follows a dramatic representation of Wilson's eccentric behaviour, which Nick could have pieced together only from an account by Wilson's sole companion, Michaelis, who runs a coffee shop near the Wilson garage. But when Wilson sets out alone in the early morning on his mission of death, Nick's source of information becomes the newspapers or testimony at the inquest: 'His movements – he was on foot all the time – were afterward traced to Port Roosevelt and then to Gad's Hill where he bought a sandwich that he didn't eat and a cup of coffee . . . By half past two he was in West Egg where he asked someone the way to Gatsby's house. So by that time he knew Gatsby's name' (p. 125). Nick shifts next to an account of Gatsby's actions at about this time: 'At two o'clock Gatsby put on his bathing suit and left word with the butler that if anyone phoned word was to be brought to him at the pool' (p. 125). At this point and later in his account, Nick reconstructs Gatsby's actions from various servants – the butler, the chauffeur, and the gardener. But once Gatsby is alone, Nick's only resource is his imagination: 'He must have looked up at an unfamiliar sky through frightening leaves and shivered as he found what a grotesque thing a rose is and how raw the sunlight was upon the scarcely created grass. A new world, material without being real, where poor ghosts, breathing dreams like air, drifted fortuitously about . . . like that ashen, fantastic figure gliding toward him through the amorphous trees' (p. 126). This entire series of events is pieced together in proper order, placed in perspective, and presented by Nick as connected narrative. Whatever deficiencies in knowledge Nick has are made up for amply by his fertile imagination.

Fitzgerald's use of the modified first-person enables him to avoid 'the large false face peering around the corner of a character's head'.[32] By giving Nick logical connections with the people he is observing, by always making his presence or absence at the events probable, not accidental, and by allowing him several natural sources of information which he may use freely, Fitzgerald achieves a realism impossible to an 'omniscient' author or even to a limited third-person point of view: through Nick Carraway, Fitzgerald places the reader in direct touch with the action, eliminating himself, as author, entirely. What Fitzgerald says of Cecilia, in his notes to *The Last Tycoon* (1941), might well apply to Nick in *The Great Gatsby*: 'by making Cecilia, at the moment of her telling the story, an intelligent and observant woman, I shall grant myself the privilege, as Conrad did, of letting her imagine the actions of the characters. Thus, I hope to get the verisimilitude of a first person narrative, combined with a Godlike knowledge of all events that happen to my characters'.[33] Fitzgerald could have substituted his own name for Conrad's had he recalled Nick Carraway. *The Great Gatsby* is a minor masterpiece illustrating beautifully Conrad's governing literary intent 'to make you *see*'.[34]

The manner of the representation of events in *The Great Gatsby*, especially the order in which they are related, seems to follow a pattern derived (in part) also from Conrad. Ford Madox Ford, who collaborated with Conrad on a number of early novels, explained the theory behind the reordering of events to create a deliberate 'confusion':

> It became very early evident to us that what was the matter with the novel, and the British novel in particular, was that it went straight forward, whereas in your gradual making acquaintanceship with your fellows you never do go straight forward. You meet an English gentleman at your golf club. He is beefy, full of health, the moral of the boy from an English Public School of the finest type. You discover gradually that he is hopelessly neurasthenic, dishonest in matters of small change, but unexpectedly self-sacrificing, a dreadful liar . . . To get such a man in fiction you could not begin at his beginning and work his life chronologically to the end. You must first get him in with a strong impression, and then work backwards and forwards over his past . . . That theory at least we gradually evolved.[35]

In real life, the story of an acquaintance comes into focus only after apparently unrelated incidents from different periods of time are gradually pieced together; and, unless the individual makes 'a strong impression' in the beginning, there is little incentive for one to go to the trouble of discovering the incidents of his life. A story told in this manner gains not only in verisimilitude, however, but also in suspense: pieces of the protagonist's life can be so arranged and revealed as to create mystery, which is particularly effective if there is a sensitive observer to share the reader's bewilderment.

One of the best examples of Conrad's use of this device occurs in *Lord Jim*. Joseph Warren Beach has plotted graphically Conrad's rearrangement of the chronology in this novel:

The true chronological order would be:
A, B, C, D, E, F, G, H, I, J, K, L, M, N, O, P, Q, R, S, T, U, V, W, X, Y, Z
The order in the book is, by chapters:
KLMP, WA, E, B, E, E, H, GD, HJ, FE, E, E, F, F, F, FK, I, I, R, I, KL, MN, N, Q, QPO, OP, P, QP, P, P, P, QP, P, P, Q, Q, Q, R, ZV, YX, S, S, S, TY, U, U, U, WXY.[36]

This hopelessly scrambled alphabet shows to just what extent Conrad did depart from the traditional 'straight forward' method of the British novel. An undated passage in Fitzgerald's notebooks suggests that he was aware of Conrad's method and its purpose: 'Conrad's secret theory examined: He knew that things do transpire about people. Therefore he wrote the truth and transposed it to parallel to give that quality, adding confusion however to his structure. Nevertheless, there is in his scheme a desire to imitate life which is in all the big shots'.[37] Although this remark might well have been jotted down some time after 1925, Fitzgerald was probably, consciously or unconsciously, following Conrad's method in *The Great Gatsby*.

Fitzgerald does, certainly, get Gatsby in first with a strong impression. When, at the opening of the novel, Nick goes over to the Buchanans for dinner, all he knows about Gatsby is that a man by that name inhabits the fabulous mansion to the right of his cottage. During the course of the evening, Jordan Baker asks Nick if he knows Gatsby, and Nick feels that this 'would do for an introduction'(p. 20) when, later that evening after he has returned home, he sees Gatsby standing out on the lawn: 'But I didn't call to him for he gave a sudden intimation that he was content to be alone – he stretched out his arms toward the dark water in a curious way, and far as I was from him I could have sworn he was trembling. Involuntarily I glanced seaward – and distinguished nothing except a single green light, minute and far away, that might have been the end of a dock. When I looked once more for Gatsby he had vanished, and I was alone again in the unquiet darkness' (p. 20). After this brief but dramatically impressive first glimpse of Gatsby, Fitzgerald works 'backwards and forwards' over his past until the complete portrait finally emerges at the end of the book. Just how much Fitzgerald has rearranged the events of Gatsby's life can be seen by tracing events through the book chronologically; the only glimpse of Gatsby's boyhood is in the last chapter; the account of Gatsby, at the age of seventeen, joining Dan Cody's yacht comes in Chapter VI; the important love affair between Gatsby and Daisy, which took place five years before the action in the book when Gatsby, then in the army, first met Daisy, is related three separate times (Chapters IV, VI, and VII), but from various points of view and with various degrees of fullness; the account of Gatsby's war experiences and his trip, after discharge, back to Louisville to Daisy's home, is given in Chapter VIII; and Gatsby's entry into his present mysterious occupation through Wolfsheim is presented, briefly, in Chapter IX. The summer of 1922, the last summer of Gatsby's life, acts as a string on which these varicolored 'beads' of his past have been 'haphazardly' strung.

A simple diagram of the sequence of events in *The Great Gatsby* is, perhaps, helpful. Allowing X to stand for the straight chronological account of the summer of 1922, and A, B, C, D, and E to represent the significant events of Gatsby's past, the nine chapters of *The Great Gatsby* may be charted: X, X, X, XCX, X, XBXCX, X, XCXDX, XEXAX.[38] ☐

Miller's book confirmed that Fitzgerald's fiction could be the object of a full-length, serious critical study. But the literary and cultural status of the poet of the American Dream remained uncertain. Looking back in 1969, Matthew J. Bruccoli recalled the context in which he had founded the *Fitzgerald Newsletter* in 1958:

■ At that time American literature was moving into the second phase of the F. Scott Fitzgerald revival. The initial boom had peaked, and it seemed to me that the next ten years would determine whether Fitzgerald would become a cult figure or whether he would assume a position as 'one of the greatest writers [who have] ever lived'.[39] ☐

By 1958, Fitzgerald, and *Gatsby*, had been rescued from obscurity, and there seemed little doubt that they were here to stay. But as America approached the Sixties, the question arose: on what terms?

CHAPTER THREE

Precision Lenses and New Optics: Deeper Visions and Dissenting Views in the 1960s

IN 1961, the American journal *Modern Fiction Studies*, which had pub-lished R. W. Stallman's essay on *Gatsby* in 1955, brought out a special issue devoted to Fitzgerald – a further sign of his critical acceptance. This issue included a valuable checklist of selected Fitzgerald criticism to date,[1] and contributions ranging from Robert F. McDonnell's 'Eggs and Eyes in *The Great Gatsby*', which argued that the egg-shaped peninsulas in the novel and the eyes of Eckleburg were connected by multi-lingual puns,[2] to a paean of praise for *Gatsby* by the English critic A. E. Dyson. At that time, Dyson was co-editor, with Brian Cox, of *Critical Quarterly*, a journal they had founded in 1959 and which, in the Sixties, was to become influential in England, in higher education and in school sixth forms. This editorial position added a certain authority to Dyson's judgements, and his essay on *Gatsby* – '*The Great Gatsby*: Thirty-Six Years After' – was soon to be given wider circulation when it was included in Arthur Mizener's *F. Scott Fitzgerald: A Collection of Critical Essays* (1963). In the essay, Dyson, writing explicitly as an English rather than an American critic, affirmed that *Gatsby* belonged 'not only to American but to world literature' and that the end of the novel 'achieves a universal tragic vision'.[3]

Dyson's essay was evidence of an increasing acceptance in England of the stature of *The Great Gatsby*, at a time when the dismissive attitude to Fitzgerald epitomised by Leavis (see pp. 57–8) still had some currency, and when the whole notion of American literature, let alone 'great' American literature, continued to be viewed with some suspicion. The Bodley Head in London had begun to bring out an edition of Fitzgerald in 1958, starting with the publication of *The Great Gatsby* and *The Last Tycoon* in one volume, as in the Scribner's edition of 1941. The volume came with an introduction by the popular novelist and playwright J. B. Priestley, whose judgement of *Gatsby* was high, though qualified. He called it Fitzgerald's 'most perfectly planned and rounded piece of fiction' and 'one of the key novels of the 'twenties' but only '*perhaps* his master-piece' [my emphasis].[4] Partly in response to the Bodley Head edition, the novelist and critic Dan Jacobson wrote an essay on Fitzgerald in the London cultural and political journal *Encounter* in June 1960. Jacobson had some criticisms of *Gatsby* – for example, he agreed with Fitzgerald's own criticism that it lacked an account of Gatsby and Daisy's relationship between their reunion and his death; but he felt such points were of no great significance, finding the novel both pleasurably rereadable, and tragic – and its tragic nature, he argued, was due mainly to the way in which Gatsby was turned into a national and 'mythic' character at the end.

As Jacobson acknowledged, the term 'mythic' derived from Marius Bewley (see pp. 57–61), and Jacobson's use of the term demonstrates the influence of Bewley's interpretation of *Gatsby* outside the USA as well as within it. In fact, the 'American Dream' view of *Gatsby* proved more pervasive in England than Dyson's claim for the novel's 'universal' nature. We can see this in Walter Allen's critical history of the twentieth-century English and American novel, *Tradition and Dream*, which came out in 1964 (published as *The Modern Novel* in the USA, 1965). Like his earlier *The English Novel* (1954), *Tradition and Dream* was perceptive and accessible, and both reflected and helped to confirm the consensus view of the works it discussed. In his account of *The Great Gatsby*, Allen goes back beyond Bewley to Lionel Trilling's essay (see pp. 51–6) quoting Trilling's claim that 'Gatsby, divided between power and dream, comes inevitably to stand for America itself' and concurring in this, with only a slight qualification: the novel is 'about the nature of being an American' and 'Gatsby becomes the symbol *almost* of the United States itself at one moment in its history' [my emphasis].[5]

The growing agreement in both England and the USA as to the stature and nature of *The Great Gatsby* created a climate in which particular aspects of the novel could receive a fuller examination, without the need to make a more general case for its achievement. The first piece that we shall look at, J. S. Westbrook's 'Nature and Optics in *The Great Gatsby*', appeared in the journal *American Literature* in 1960–61 – *American Literature*, like *Modern Fiction Studies*, was, and remains, an important forum for discussions of Fitzgerald and of *Gatsby*. Westbrook focuses on an aspect of *Gatsby* that had attracted attention from the first reviews (see p. 13), and which had become a particular source of fascination in the 1950s: Fitzgerald's use of optical motifs in the novel, especially, of course, the eyes of Doctor T. J. Eckleburg. The use of such motifs, Westbrook argues, is one of the two 'patterns of reference' in *Gatsby* that combine to provide the organising principle of its poetic unity; the other pattern of reference is to the idea of nature. The essay also offers a useful discussion of colour symbolism and of flower symbolism in the novel.

Westbrook's discussion of 'seeing' makes no use of potentially fruitful psychoanalytic concepts such as scopophilia, and his notion of 'unadulterated nature' might now seem naive, given the prevalence of the post-structuralist claim that our perceptions and ideas of nature are always linguistically and socially constructed. On the other hand, we could detect today in his concern for nature an embryonic ecological awareness. His essay remains a suggestive one that could usefully inform readings that draw on more recent critical theory. We join the essay after an introductory paragraph in which Westbrook has argued that all attempts to adapt *Gatsby* for stage or screen have failed because the novel's unity fundamentally depends on its poetic organisation of language.

■ To understand the unity of *The Great Gatsby* we must first recognize that its primary subject is the growth of an awareness. The awareness belongs to the narrator, Nick Carraway, who not only enjoys the advantage of distance in time from the events he relates, but even at the scene of their unfolding has been more of a perceiver than a participant. It is significant that his retrospections are never so concerned with what he did as with what he saw. His freedom from crucial dramatic involvement enables the internalities of poetic vision to widen and deepen the implications of the ostensibly shallow world *The Great Gatsby* deals with. . . .

The lyricism, given such wide scope in the narrative, works rhetorically and visually to arrest qualities of setting, conduct and states of mind. At the heart of the excesses, the extravagant hopes and failures of the generation portrayed, has been its refusal to countenance limitation, the consequences of which are symbolized in two patterns of reference which combine to serve as the organizing principle for the poetic design of the novel. One revolves around the problem of seeing; the other around the idea of nature.

If with respect to other characters *The Great Gatsby* is a record of conduct, with respect to Carraway it is the record of an ocular initiation into the mysteries and wonders of a magical country, during which he is constantly absorbed in the process of adjusting his credulity to received visual data, and checking and rechecking to ascertain whether his eyes have played him false. The images that confront them are either blurred, or comprised of utterly improbable amalgams: the disconcerting alignment of Mrs. McKee's eyebrows; the vaguely familiar look of Meyer Wolfsheim's cufflinks, which turn out to have been constructed of human molars; the shirtless figure of

Gatsby's boarder, Klipspringer, doing 'liver exercises' (pp. 71–2) in a silk-lined bedchamber; the 'scarcely human orchid' sitting under a white plum tree at a Gatsby party who, upon closer scrutiny, turns into a 'hitherto ghostly celebrity of the movies' (p. 82); the whole ashen world of the dump with its ashen houses, chimneys, chimney smoke, and men; and finally the oddly frivolous corpse of Gatsby afloat on a rubber mattress in his swimming pool.

In all of these details there is a contention of elements and a striving of forms for a completion which the disparity of elements denies. Symbolically they reflect the abortive commitments of a generation whose sense of distinctions has been destroyed by the prodigious acceleration of a commercial and technical civilization. If we look at them closely, however, we find that they are bound together by another idea. In one way or another they all represent an assault upon nature, and as the tale unfolds the idea of nature insulted and abased is raised to the level of a general metaphor.

The people in *The Great Gatsby*, ironically enough, have not consciously renounced nature. They have only ceased to perceive its limits. They think continually in terms of fertility, but the forms of it that they wish upon the world are either altogether specious, or else 'forced'. When Carraway first arrives in West Egg, he finds 'great bursts of leaves growing on the trees', but these are special leaves to go with a special place. They remind him of the way things grow 'in fast movies' (p. 7). Whether they actually grow that way is beside the point; the atmosphere of West Egg makes them seem to. Its leaves are allied with the spirit of technology and fast money, and this sort of alliance is basic to a whole scheme of images and references that follow. So many and various are they that no convenient order of citation is possible. If the dump and the oculist's sign make up the all-encompassing symbol of the novel, it would seem unfair not to mention little touches like the wreath Myrtle Wilson wants to buy for her mother's grave, which will "'last all summer'" (p. 31). It is safe to say, however, that of all the devices whereby nature is 'crossed', the most frequent involve the use of colour; and in the majority of instances where colours are used it will be noted that the contexts in which they are presented deflect their primary meanings. The light on Daisy's dock is green – and electric. The 'golden arm[s]' (p. 36) of Jordan Baker are not simply those of a healthy girl who spends her afternoons on fairways, but of a girl whose wealth is linked with dishonesty. And the innocence of white suffers when that colour is employed to describe Manhattan rising in 'heaps and sugar lumps all built with a wish out of non-olfactory money' (pp. 54–5). But the colour which comes in for the most extensive manipulation is yellow. It figures prominently at Gatsby's parties – the 'yellow cocktail music'

(p. 34), and the stage twins in yellow dresses who do a baby act. Gatsby's cars, too, are yellow, the station wagon that transports guests to his parties and the "'death car'" (p. 107) with which Daisy runs down Myrtle Wilson. George Wilson's garage is yellow and, across the highway from it, the spectacles of [Doctor T. J.] Eckleburg. In general, the world of Gatsby may be said to abound in colours, all of the brighter varieties, but the most brilliant of them attends ironically upon its unhappiest events.

Yet although we are subjected at every turn to these cheapenings, vulgarizations, and distortions of the idea of fertility, the fact that that idea is kept in the forefront of our minds from one end of the book to the other is what accounts for its pathos. If *The Great Gatsby* can be interpreted as a study of an ethos in transition, the Americans it deals with retaining a certain innocence and vitality of desire we connect with a simpler, less deceptive phase of their history, but now confused as to values, mistaking losses for gains, and committing their hopes and beliefs to symbols that are shallow and inadequate, then the continual references to violated nature deepen our sense of what they have betrayed in themselves. Significantly enough, the ineffability of their dreams and the perishability of the things upon which they are founded are evoked in repeated references to flowers. Not only is Daisy Buchanan named after a flower but her whole history has been spelled out in orchids and roses. And Gatsby, for whom, five years prior to their reunion in West Egg, Daisy has 'blossomed . . . like a flower' (p. 87), cannot believe that that blossoming is irreclaimable, that indeed the world cannot be made to bloom perpetually. He, even more than she, is bent upon wringing from life impossible consummations, a fact which is symbolized by the prominence of his gardens in the novel's setting, the bales of cut flowers he imports by truck to Carraway's cottage for his first meeting with Daisy, not to mention his predilection for yellow autos and pink suits. The profusion of horticultural effects becomes, at last, oppressive. There is an overripeness, an unnatural plenitude in this new Eden, and its unwholesomeness is caught in such random details as Gatsby's garden paths clogged at the end of a party with 'fruit rinds . . . and crushed flowers' (p. 86), the flower-laden hearse Gatsby and Carraway pass on their way into New York, and the feeling expressed by Jordan Baker on a warm afternoon in the city that "'all sorts of funny fruits'" (p. 97) are going to drop from the sky.

No wonder, then, that in everything Carraway describes there is the suggestion of hallucination, and that he finds the problem of seeing such a challenge at every turn. Nor is he entirely alone in his optical adventures. They are comically shared by a minor character named Owl Eyes, whom we first encounter exclaiming over the fact that the books in Gatsby's library contain bona fide printed matter, and who later turns up unaccountably at Gatsby's funeral and keeps wiping his glasses 'outside and in' (p. 136). For Owl Eyes reality constitutes a phenomenon, reality is hallucination. The same, in a more tragic sense, is true of Gatsby. When he walks to his pool minutes before his demise, the world, now unyoked to his 'single dream', has become fantasy. The yellow leaves overhead are 'frightening', roses 'grotesque', the sunlight 'raw . . . upon the scarcely created grass' (p. 126).

For the most elaborate expression of the disparity between illusion and reality, however, we must turn finally to the image of the dump presided over by the yard-high retinas of [T. J.] Eckleburg. It is here that we get a synthesis of the whole constellation of ironies inherent in the theme of the novel, and it is here that the idea of violated nature and that of distorted vision are brought into the most striking conjunction. Eckleburg may be thought of as a commercial deity staring out upon a waste of his own creation.[6] But the enormous eyes behind yellow spectacles are diseased, 'faded' (p. 95), 'dimmed . . . by many paintless days' (p. 21). And the quality of dimness is carried over into the rendering of the 'ash-grey men' 'who move dimly and already crumbling through the powdery air'. Their shade-like forms, along with the 'small, foul river', where periodically a draw-bridge is raised to let barges through, lend the scene overtones of an inferno; but the dump is also described as a 'farm where ashes grow like wheat into ridges and hills and grotesque gardens', and what is implied is that a universal myopia has apprehended fertility in a 'valley of ashes' (p. 21) and mistaken a hell for a paradise.

The dump is introduced early in the novel, and is the scene of those ocular confusions that lead to its major dramatic climaxes. It is because Myrtle Wilson thinks the yellow car is Tom Buchanan's that she runs out to stop it. It is because George Wilson reads a portentous message in the eyes of Eckleburg ('"God sees everything"' (p. 125)) that he takes upon himself the role of avenger. When in the first days of the summer Gatsby's hopes of reclaiming Daisy have been at their highest, and the East has held a certain enchantment even for Carraway, it has been impossible to pass between New York and West Egg without passing the dump. And when the final event of a generally disastrous 'last day' has brought all paradisiacal illusions to an end, the dump is again the setting.

Carraway's Eastern adventure, as I have tried to show, is defined largely by references to a spurious and hallucinatory order of nature, the only kind acceptable or even recognizable to the people he is thrown in with. But in fleeting intervals throughout the story we are confronted with unadulterated nature. They happen late at night when the lights of the houses have gone out. The moon survives the glow of Gatsby's parties, the stars wheel in their courses; on the night that Carraway describes Gatsby genuflecting to the light on Daisy's dock, 'the full bellows of the earth' have blown 'the frogs full of life' and there is a sound of 'wings beating in the trees' (p. 20). At such intervals the intensity of nature's own utterances is a little eerie and inexplicable, like the crashing of surf on a deserted beach. These are adumbration of the forgotten, the 'unknown' (p. 141) island, which can now be summoned in its fullness only in visions. Carraway's vision of it, like a buried theme in music, struggles for articulation from the early pages of the novel to the moment near its terminus, with Gatsby dead and the houses in West Egg shut up, when it emerges in the famous 'ode' to a buried fertility, the 'green breast of the new world' (p. 140) that greeted Dutch sailors' eyes. Earlier in the tale we have been told that Gatsby has felt he could climb to 'a secret place above the trees [on Daisy's street] . . . and once there . . . suck on the pap of life, gulp down the incomparable milk of wonder' (p. 86). But one cannot live indefinitely on wonder, and the real fertility invoked in the vision of the old island which might have been commensurate with his 'sensitivity to the promises of life' (p. 6) is irrecoverable.

Even when Carraway resolves upon returning to the Middle West, it will be to a part where nature has been compromised by cities, granted that sleigh bells, holly wreaths, snow and lighted windows make for a more equable compromise than deep summer, gas pumps, and roadhouse roofs, or sunsets and the apartment houses of movie stars on the West 50's (p. 62). Carraway's resolve to settle for a mid-Western city – where, unlike the palaces of East Egg and West Egg, houses 'are still called through decades by a family's name' – signalizes the end of an era built on adventure and discovery, and the beginning of one built on consolidation. His reformation augurs the passing of a youthful culture into middle age, all of which accounts for the curiously affecting state of feeling communicated through the tone of his narration wherein renunciation of the Gatsby brand of sensibility is not unmixed with regrets that it has been lost to us for ever.[7] □

It is worth emphasising the way in which Westbrook, at the end of an essay that has focused closely on optics, colours, flowers and nature, moves into an observation on American history, and implies that the USA itself is now a 'middle-aged' culture. With historical hindsight, this has a certain irony in view of the explosion of youthful rebellion in the USA later on in the 1960s. Put back in the context of its time, however, Westbrook's remark perhaps reflects a wider feeling that the 1950s had become rather tranquil – or 'tranquillised', to use the adjective that the poet Robert Lowell applied to the decade. It could be said that this tranquillity had settled on literary criticism as well, despite the occasional excitements offered by a critic such as R. W. Stallman, and the tumults of the 1960s would not immediately change that, though they would have some impact. It was only in later decades that subversive intellectual movements that had begun in 1960s' Paris – most notably, post-structuralism and deconstruction – were to help to transform literary studies. For much of the 1960s, it was largely 'business as usual' – and expanding business – as far literary criticism, including Fitzgerald criticism, was concerned.

On this basis, much useful work was produced. In 1964, for example, James E. Miller, Jr, who had produced the first full-length study of Fitzgerald in 1957 (see pp. 65–72), brought out an enlarged version of that study, which added a chapter on *Tender is the Night* and *The Last Tycoon*. The second full-length study had appeared from Kenneth E. Eble the previous year, 1963, in Twayne's United States Authors series. Eble also published in 1964, in the journal *American Literature*, one of the first 'genetic' studies of *Gatsby*, which looked closely at its genesis and growth from the original pencil draft to its first publication, highlighting key changes Fitzgerald had made. These included the transfer of what was originally the long final sentence of Chapter One to the end of the novel, and the development of that sentence into *Gatsby*'s famous concluding passages; the compression of the story of Gatsby's past; and the elimination of a scene near the climax in which, instead of going directly to the Plaza Hotel, Nick and the others go to the Polo Grounds and sit through a ball game – a scene that, Eble argues, almost loses 'the undercurrent of passion and heat and boredom which sweeps all of them to the showdown in the Plaza'.[8] In 1965, two more general studies appeared, both devoting substantial discussions to *Gatsby*: Sergio Perosa's *The Art of F. Scott Fitzgerald*, translated from an Italian study that had first appeared in 1961, saw *Gatsby* as portraying 'an agonizing conflict of the moral and social order' and as enlarging its significance on the symbolic level 'by carrying to its tragic solution [*sic*] a conflict of characters which has a "universal" implication and a representative value'.[9] Henry Dan Piper's *F. Scott Fitzgerald: A Critical Portrait* combines biographical and 'genetic' approaches, drawing on Fitzgerald's life, his cultural and social context, and his drafts and revised galley proofs to offer an account of the evolution of the theme and the form of *Gatsby*. Richard Lehan's *F. Scott Fitzgerald and the Craft of Fiction* (1966) helpfully explored the development of Fitzgerald's fiction in relation to romanticism and the ideas of Oswald Spengler, while Robert Sklar's *F. Scott Fitzgerald: The Last Laocoön* (1967) saw that development as a criticism, adaptation and transformation of the genteel romantic ideals of late nineteenth-century American culture, a process in which Fitzgerald produced a new vision of moral order and beauty. Thus, in withdrawing to the West after Gatsby's death, Nick Carraway opts for order, but not before, in the final passages of the novel, he has assumed the mantle of a visionary seer – a role to which Sklar himself seems drawn, as he paraphrases Nick: 'The hope shall always be, its fulfilment shall never be. Men die, but their dreams are imperishable, renewed again and again at the fountain of nature – or of art'. Sklar affirms that *Gatsby* is a novel in which Fitzgerald 'created his own vision of national tragedy and of high art' and that every year it 'more clearly assumes a place among the imperishable works of American fiction';[10] he cannot resist drawing an analogy between Fitzgerald and his eponymous hero: 'With *The Great Gatsby* he found self-fulfilment and self-creation as an artist – and yet, as with Gatsby, a tragic fall was to follow closely upon his success'.[11] Sklar also exemplifies another tendency in some full-length books on Fitzgerald to put in a lot of padding, and, where *Gatsby* is concerned, simply to retell the story and to quote more copiously than is needed for the purpose of demonstrating points. Milton Hindus's *F. Scott Fitzgerald: An Introduction and Interpretation* (1968) is more concise, as befits its introductory function, and it is interesting to note that, like 'E. K.' in 1925, and Kenneth E. Eble in 1985 (see pp. 17–19), it praises the 'efficiency' of the novel.[12] But Hindus strains to try and offer something new, venturing but not expounding a comparison with Turgenev's *Fathers and Sons* (1862), and proposing what might now look like some rather sexist similarities between Fitzgerald and Proust – both writers, according to Hindus, 'observed the connection between unstable character in women'[13] and a meretricious way of holding the body (as in Jordan Baker!).

Much of the significant critical work on Fitzgerald in the 1960s was to be found, not in the full-length books that were appearing, but in essays. In 1967, for example, Robert Emmet Long produced a two-part essay in what was already becoming a subgenre of *Gatsby* criticism: the comparison of *Gatsby* to the fiction of Conrad (see p. 46). By 1967, this region had been partly mapped by R. W. Stallman,[14] James E. Miller, Jr (see pp. 65–72), and Henry Dan Piper, in the 1965 study we have just mentioned. Long, however, embarked on a more extensive exploration than these earlier travellers, and began by striking out into territory whose existence had been hinted at in the original *Times Literary Supplement* review of the novel (see p. 34) but had not been hitherto charted, comparing *Gatsby* with *Almayer's Folly*. He then moved on to *Lord Jim* before returning to the more familiar ground of *Gatsby* and 'Heart of Darkness'. Long's explorations fed into his book *The Achieving of The Great Gatsby*, which was published in 1979.

A particularly illuminating essay that focused on the internal structure of *Gatsby* appeared in the journal *Modern Fiction Studies* in 1969.

Victor A. Doyno's 'Patterns in *The Great Gatsby*' combines a 'genetic' approach, drawing on the manuscripts and galley proofs of the novel, with an exploration of some of the patterns in the novel. Doyno sees these patterns as being formed by means of the repetition of dialogue, gesture and detail, and by the way in which the final passages of some chapters echo each other. Doyno calls these passages 'codas', a metaphor derived from music: according to the *Concise Oxford Dictionary*, a coda is an 'independent or elaborate passage introduced after the end of the main part of a movement', or the 'concluding section' of a ballet.

Doyno's evaluative criteria are, in some respects, still very much those of realistic fiction and of the New Criticism: Fitzgerald's patterning is praised because it deepens characterisation, shapes the reader's attitude towards events and major themes, and creates and controls unity and emphasis. Unity was a particularly important notion for the New Critics, and Doyno expends some ingenuity in suggesting how the titles of the photographs that McKee shows to Nick after the party at Myrtle's flat – titles that Fitzgerald inserted while he was revising the scene – are not as irrelevant as they might at first seem. Indeed, he argues that they comprise an 'index' of 'leitmotifs' in the novel – like 'coda', 'leitmotif' is a musical term meaning 'leading motifs' or 'recurring themes', which in literature, as Chris Baldick points out, may be phrases, images, symbols or situations.[15]

While Doyno shares the New Criticism's concern for pattern and unity, he does not follow prominent New Critics such as W. K. Wimsatt and Monroe C. Beardsley in their rejection of the 'intentional fallacy'.[16] Wimsatt and Beardsley argued that it was wrong to take the author's expressed or inferred intention into account when interpreting or evaluating a literary work, since the text, once published, belonged in the public world and its significance and worth could no longer be governed by the author. Doyno, however, relates the patterns he finds in *Gatsby* to his study of Fitzgerald's revisions and concludes that Fitzgerald fulfilled his intention to produce, with *Gatsby*, 'a consciously artistic achievement'.[17] His essay thus seeks to confirm and enhance, not only the status of *Gatsby*, but also the stature of Fitzgerald as an author.

In its combination of genetic and formalist approaches, of a concern with the author and a concern with the text, Doyno exemplifies the major critical procedures still dominant in literary studies in the late 1960s. But his essay is no mere museum piece; his analysis still offers insights into the patterns of *Gatsby* that could feed into a structuralist, post-structuralist, or deconstructionist reading, and it is interesting to note how he seems to be hunting for an adequate critical vocabulary, drawing both on musical metaphors (coda, leitmotif) and on structural ones ('structural patterning', 'structural units'). And despite the ingenuity the essay sometimes displays, it remains accessible, perhaps because it arose out of a first-year undergraduate class on *Gatsby* that Doyno was teaching.[18] Doyno starts by raising the question of the relevance of the titles of McKee's photographs, and suggests that the answer lies in the intricate patterning of the novel – a patterning that can be illuminated by a study of the holograph manuscript and the galley proof revisions. He then moves on to explore the patterns themselves; our extract begins at this point.

■ Several patterns in the novel are obvious. The first three chapters present the different settings and social groupings of three evenings: dinner and strained conversation at Tom Buchanan's house, drinks and a violent argument at Myrtle's apartment, a party and loutish behaviour at Gatsby's mansion. Fitzgerald calls attention to this pattern when he has Nick say: 'Reading over what I have written so far I see I have given the impression that the events of three nights several weeks apart were all that absorbed me' (p. 46). Similarly, through Nick, Fitzgerald emphasizes the patterning of situation which presents two very different characters, George Wilson and Tom Buchanan, as cuckolded husbands. 'I stared at him and then at Tom, who had made a parallel discovery less than an hour before' (pp. 96–7). Clearly Fitzgerald is aware of these patterns and wishes the reader to share this awareness.

There are, moreover, numerous less obvious patterns in the novel which have the important functions of deepening characterization, shaping the reader's attitudes toward events and major themes, and creating and controlling unity and emphasis. Those patternings which affect characterization include the repetition of dialogue, gesture and detail. For example, Daisy's speech is used to characterize her in two comparable scenes which are far apart. Fitzgerald indicates the relation between the scenes by presenting the same tableau as Nick enters: Daisy and Jordan Baker, both in white, wind-blown dresses, lounge on a couch on a wine or crimson rug. The first scene (in Chapter I) occurs as Nick renews his acquaintance with Daisy; the second (in Chapter VII) when Gatsby intends to reclaim Daisy. In the latter scene Jordan and Daisy say together '"We can't move"' (p. 90), and the speech is perfectly appropriate to the hot weather. In the first scene Daisy says, as her first direct statement in the novel, '"I'm p-paralyzed with happiness"' (p. 11). This statement, however, was inserted after the second scene was written, since it first occurs in the galley proof. This inserted statement, besides presenting an apt characterization of Daisy, likens her feelings at the beginning to those which she has shortly before the argument about leaving Tom. Through this repetition Fitzgerald emphasizes Daisy's lack of growth within the novel.

Fitzgerald also deepens characterization by the repetition of gesture. Nick says that when he first saw Gatsby, 'he gave a sudden intimation that he was content to be alone – he stretched out his arms toward the dark water in a curious way, and far as I was from him I could have sworn he was trembling' (p. 20). This picture of Gatsby in the coda of Chapter I presents him with an air of mystery, and in the reader's memory he stands etched reaching for the green light. Gatsby's mysteriousness is transformed later in the novel when he tells Nick that as he was leaving Louisville he went to the open vestibule of the [railway] coach and 'stretched out his hand desperately as if to snatch only a wisp of air, to save a fragment of the spot that she had made lovely for him' (p. 119). This repetition of the reaching gesture explains the first picture of Gatsby, establishes the durability of his devotion, and thereby evokes sympathy for one who loves so fervently.

The characterization of Gatsby's rival, Tom Buchanan, is influenced by the repetition of details. Arthur Mizener has noted that Fitzgerald can 'sum up all he wants to say about Tom' in his last meeting with Nick.[19] An examination of the composition of this passage leads to a fuller explanation of Mizener's insight and an increased respect for Fitzgerald's craftsmanship. The manuscript version reads: 'Then he went into the jewellery store *for a* to buy a *pair of c* pearl necklace *and* or pair of cuff buttons' (MS. VIII, 42).[20] The evidence indicates that Fitzgerald probably planned for a moment simply to mention the cuff links, then decided to begin with the necklace. What is gained by the inclusion of a pearl necklace? Tom's wife, Daisy, already has the pearl necklace which was her wedding gift; the necklace is probably not for Daisy; perhaps Tom has found a replacement for his dead mistress. This meeting, which also associates Tom with cuff buttons, occurs directly after Nick's condemnation of the Buchanans for their callous inhumanity: 'they smashed up things and creatures and then retreated back into their money or their vast carelessness . . . ' (p. 139). Fitzgerald may have realized that the inhumanity of their attitude could be subtly reinforced by an unfavourable association with the cuff buttons. At any rate he decided to introduce an anterior reference to cuff buttons. Accordingly the galley proofs contain a passage not in the manuscript version in which Meyer Wolfsheim mentions his cuff buttons and calls them '"Finest specimens of human molars"' (p. 57). The attitude of gross inhumanity latent in this remark carries over to Tom. With the insertion of this unfavourable association for cuff buttons, Fitzgerald decided to alter the syntax of the later reference. The galley proof version is: 'Then he went into the jewellery store to buy a pearl necklace, or perhaps only a pair of cuff buttons'. This version, which created a deceptively casual tone while subordinating the cuff links, was modified when Fitzgerald, in revising the galleys, changed the commas to dashes and raised the importance of the alternative (Galley sheet 57). The final elaborated version conveys, in a devastatingly casual tone, oblique references of approximately equal emphasis to Tom's lust and to his inhumanity.

And this passage is not the only implicit character assassination of Tom brought about by a patterning of details. While leaving Gatsby's first party, Nick observes the aftermath of a car accident in which the vehicle is 'violently shorn of one wheel' (p. 44). The confusion and discordant noise of the scene create an unfavourable impression which is intensified when Nick tells of the driver's stupid, irresponsible drunkenness. With this scene in mind we can easily visualize an accident which Jordan Baker describes only briefly in the next chapter:

> A week after I left Santa Barbara Tom ran into a wagon on the Ventura road one night and ripped a front wheel off his car. The girl who was with him got into the papers too because her arm was broken – she was one of the chambermaids in the Santa Barbara Hotel. (p. 61)

The accident is primarily another indictment of Tom's lust, but the repetition of detail – the loss of a wheel in a night accident – associates Tom with the irresponsible drunken driver.

Besides adding depth to characterization, patterning also shapes the reader's attitudes toward events and themes in the novel. As it happens, this kind of repetition also includes a case of poor driving. Surprisingly few commentators have criticized Fitzgerald for the highly improbable plot manipulation whereby Daisy runs down her husband's mistress.[21] The reader's uncritical acceptance of the accident is influenced, I suggest, by something Nick says in the coda of Chapter III about his relationship with Jordan Baker: 'It was on that same house party that we had a curious conversation about driving a car. It started because she passed so close to some workmen that our fender flicked a button on one man's coat' (p. 48). This near-accident subliminally prepares the reader to think of Daisy's hitting Myrtle not as an unbelievable wrenching of probability but as a possible event. After all, Jordan nearly did a similar thing. Nick's ensuing conversation with Jordan reveals his attitude toward carelessness. This dialogue seems to be relevant only to Nick and Jordan's friendship, but the casual banter presents the same diction and attitude found in Nick's final condemnation of Daisy and Tom for their carelessness. In this case the patterning leads the reader to accept both an improbable event and the narrator's final judgement of it.

The reader's attitude is more frequently shaped by an ironic juxtaposition of such themes as romantic idealization and realistic dis-illusionment. For example, Nick learns from Myrtle of her first meeting with Tom Buchanan on the train to New York, and as she relates the story her limited word choice, additive syntax, and rushing narration establish both her character and her attitude toward the pickup:

> "It was on the two little seats facing each other that are always the last ones left on the train. I was going up to New York to see my sister and spend the night. He had on a dress suit and patent leather shoes and I couldn't keep my eyes off him but every time he looked at me I had to pretend to be looking at the advertise-ment over his head. When we came into the station he was next to me and his white shirt front pressed against my arm – and so I told him I'd have to call a policeman but he knew I lied. I was so excited that when I got into a taxi with him I didn't hardly know I wasn't getting into a subway train. All I kept thinking about over and over was 'You can't live forever, you can't live forever'". (p. 31)

The style and growing desperation of tone suggest that Myrtle is a socially and morally limited character who acted in an understandable way because of her romantic expectation. But her romantic opinion of her meeting with Tom contrasts with another version of the same situation which is told in a realistic style from a masculine and definitely un-romantic point of view when Nick tells this tale of the commuter train:

> The next day was broiling, almost the last, certainly the warmest, of the summer. As my train emerged from the tunnel into sunlight, only the hot whistles of the National Biscuit Company broke the simmering hush at noon. The straw seats of the car hovered on the edge of combustion; the woman next to me perspired delicately for a while into her white shirtwaist and then, as her newspaper dampened under her fingers, lapsed despairingly into deep heat with a desolate cry. Her pocket-book slapped to the floor.

> "Oh, my!" she gasped.

> I picked it up with a weary bend and handed it back to her hold-ing it at arm's length and by the extreme tip of the corners to indicate that I had no designs upon it – but every one near by, including the woman, suspected me just the same.

> "Hot!" said the conductor to familiar faces. "Some weather! . . . Hot! . . . Hot! . . . Hot! . . . Is it hot enough for you? Is it hot? Is it . . . ?"

My commutation ticket came back to me with a dark stain from his hand. That anyone should care in this heat whose flushed lips he kissed, whose head made damp the pajama pocket over his heart! (p. 89)

Nick's scornful attitude toward romance refers, in context, primarily to the love of Gatsby for Daisy, but the situation parallels Myrtle's first meeting with Tom and reflects a disillusioned view of such an event. Fitzgerald has controlled his material to make each of the attitudes – Myrtle's desperate romanticism and Nick's uncomfortable realism – valid in its own moment of presentation; but in the context of the novel each thematic attitude toward love is juxtaposed to and qualifies the other.

A similar attempt to influence the reader's attitudes occurs with the use of analogous scenes in the codas of Chapters V and VII. And, as shall later become clear, the positioning of the scenes lends them importance. In each case Nick sees a tableau of Daisy sitting and talking with a man who is holding her hand. In Chapter V, of course, the man is Gatsby, who has just re-won Daisy and is experiencing sublime happiness. Nick says:

As I watched him he adjusted himself a little, visibly. His hand took hold of hers and as she said something low in his ear he turned toward her with a rush of emotion. I think that voice held him most with its fluctuating, feverish warmth because it couldn't be over-dreamed – that voice was a deathless song.

They had forgotten me but Daisy glanced up and held out her hand; Gatsby didn't know me now at all. I looked once more at them and they looked back at me, remotely, possessed by intense life. Then I went out of the room and down the marble steps into the rain, leaving them there together. (p. 75)

However, Fitzgerald balances this moment of romantic bliss with a parallel but decidedly realistic description of Daisy after the auto accident:

Daisy and Tom were sitting opposite each other at the kitchen table with a plate of cold fried chicken between them and two bottles of ale. He was talking intently across the table at her and in his earnestness his hand had fallen upon and covered her own. Once in a while she looked up at him and nodded in agreement.

They weren't happy, and neither of them had touched the chicken or the ale – and yet they weren't unhappy either. There was an unmistakable air of natural intimacy about the picture and any-body would have said that they were conspiring together. (p. 113)

This second scene signals, of course, Gatsby's loss of Daisy. In addi-tion, the repetition destroys the uniqueness of Gatsby's moment of happiness and thereby makes the reader question the validity of his romantic idealization.

The reader's attitude toward romantic idealization and realistic disillusionment is also shaped by the elaborate patterning of a natural enough event – a man and woman kissing. In Chapter VI Nick tells of the movie director bending over his star, who had been described as a 'scarcely human orchid of a woman' (p. 82). 'They were still under the white plum tree and their faces were touching except for a pale thin ray of moonlight between. It occurred to me that he had been very slowly bending toward her all evening to attain this proximity, and even while I watched I saw him stoop one ultimate degree and kiss at her cheek' (p. 83). Although the setting is described romantically, the event itself is narrated with touches of sarcasm in the involved syntax, elevated diction ('attain this proximity') and precision of word choice ('kiss *at* her cheek [Doyno's emphasis]). The presentation of this kiss, which does not involve any of the major characters, prepares the reader to adopt a complex attitude toward the other kisses. In the coda of the same chapter, Nick relates Gatsby's description of kissing Daisy. Once more Nick's incongruous word choice, e.g. 'romp' (p. 86), helps give the passage a peculiar texture.[22] The dominant tone of the passage is, however, certainly one of romantic idealization, culminating in the flower simile:

> His heart beat faster and faster as Daisy's white face came up to his own. He knew that when he kissed this girl, and forever wed his unutterable visions to her perishable breath, his mind would never romp again like the mind of God. So he waited, listening for a moment longer to the tuning fork that had been struck upon a star. Then he kissed her. At his lips' touch she blossomed for him like a flower and the incarnation was complete. (pp. 86–7)

The idealization of Gatsby's description is touching, but Nick's sarcas-tic insertions are not the only means of qualifying the romantic point of view. The reader's attitude toward the kiss has already been influ-enced by the movie star's kiss and, more importantly, by a similar incident described from a less romantic point of view. In the coda of Chapter IV Nick says:

> We passed a barrier of dark trees, and then the façade of Fifty-

ninth Street, a block of delicate pale light, beamed down into the Park. Unlike Gatsby and Tom Buchanan I had no girl whose disembodied face floated along the dark cornices and blinding signs and so I drew up the girl beside me, tightening my arms. Her wan scornful mouth smiled and so I drew her up again, closer, this time to my face. (p. 63)

Throughout this sardonic description Nick has certainly reserved his emotional commitment; neither his motivation nor his choice of words, like 'scornful' conveys idealistic enthusiasm. As in the other passages the setting is described, and Nick even calls attention to the relation between the kisses by saying 'Unlike Gatsby . . . '. Furthermore the relationship between the kisses in the codas of Chapter IV and VI is subtly emphasized early in Chapter VII, when Tom goes out to make drinks and leaves Daisy alone with Gatsby in front of Nick and Jordan:

. . . she got up and went over to Gatsby, and pulled his face down kissing him on the mouth.
"You know I love you," she murmured.
"You forget there's a lady present," said Jordan.
Daisy looked around doubtfully.
"You kiss Nick too."
"What a low, vulgar girl!" (pp. 90–1)

In this patterning Fitzgerald has presented in order Nick's disenchanted personal account, his sarcastic third-person narration, and Gatsby's romantic, personal version of a kiss; in addition, Fitzgerald includes a scene which draws a parallel between the kisses involving major characters. The sheer idealization of Gatsby's love is qualified by this elaborate repetition, and the reader develops a complex attitude toward a major theme.

With all this evidence of patterning in mind, we may establish still a third function by [asking what is the possible relevance], [b]eyond combining the romantic and the mundane, [of the] titles [of the photographs which McKee shows to Nick at the end of Chapter Two], '"Beauty and the Beast . . . Loneliness . . . Old Grocery Horse . . . Brook'n Bridge"'? (p. 32). The first title, of course, refers to the well-known fairy-tale or folk tale in which a lowly creature regains his former princely condition by the transforming power of a beautiful girl's kiss.[23] Gatsby's background is analogous to this tale, since he was 'a son of God' (p. 77) whose imagination had never accepted his father and mother as his real parents. The transformation of James Gatz to Jay Gatsby was, of course, gradual, but when Gatsby kissed

Daisy 'the incarnation was complete' (p. 87); she embodied his dreams, and his princely status was confirmed by the love of 'the king's daughter' (p. 94). And Gatsby's casual remark that in Europe he '"lived like a young rajah"' (p. 52) seems quite appropriate to the prince motif.

The next title, 'Loneliness', calls to mind Nick's first sight of Gatsby, when 'he gave a sudden intimation that he was content to be alone' (p. 20). Several references to Gatsby's loneliness follow: he is 'standing alone on the marble steps' (p. 41) during his party, and Nick mentions the 'complete isolation' of the host (p. 46). The scenes of Gatsby's vigil outside the Buchanans' and of his body floating in the pool also reinforce the motif of loneliness. Gatsby, when alive, seems quite content with his isolation, but Nick, in a contrapuntal fashion, frequently refers to his own loneliness in terms of discomfort or unhappiness. Nick's dissatisfaction with loneliness makes Gatsby's satisfaction in isolation more striking, more mystic.

Since these motifs sufficiently account for the insertion, admittedly very tenuous suggestions about the last two titles may be offered. The word 'grocery' occurs twice in connection with financial necessity. Nick, when he is preparing to leave for the Midwest, sells his car to the grocer. And Tom Buchanan scoffs at Gatsby's financial and social inferiority when he first knew Daisy by saying '"and I'll be damned if I see how you got within a mile of her unless you brought the groceries to the back door"' (p. 102). The other two words of the title also possess some relevance to Gatsby's inferiority. Tom's wealth, of course, is old and established, while Gatsby's richness is quite *nouveau*. Tom's wealth and aristocratic background are indicated by his transportation of his string of polo ponies, and Gatsby's social ineptitude appears in Chapter VI when Tom and the haughty Mr. Sloane dispose of a dinner invitation Gatsby should have refused by riding away without him. There is, then, some evidence that the third title may be a complex and subtle reference to the financial and social differences between Tom and Gatsby.

The last of the titles, 'Brook'n Bridge', is even less obvious and has no relevance – unless we consider Fitzgerald's aural imagination and the context of the title within the novel. The brilliance of the catalogue of guests' names at the beginning of Chapter IV is a critical commonplace, but the person who reads these names silently misses a good bit. One must read aloud to appreciate names such as '[t]he Dancies', 'Gus Waize', 'young Brewer', 'Miss Haag' and 'Miss Claudia Hip' (pp. 50, 51). That Fitzgerald's imagination upon occasion worked aurally is beyond question. The title 'Brook'n Bridge' [which can be heard as 'Broken Bridge'] occurs just after Tom has broken Myrtle's nose and may be a punning reference to this incident and thus to the leitmotif of violence in the novel. Each chapter from the first, with Daisy's bruised finger, to the last, with Tom's story of Wilson's forced entry, includes some sort of violence. The only exception to this, of course, is the more or less idyllic Chapter V, in which Daisy and Gatsby are reunited.

Fitzgerald's decision to insert these picture titles into the version used for typesetting is quite significant. The titles serve as an index of leitmotifs within the novel. By picking these motifs from the many others in the book, Fitzgerald has singled them out for emphasis, and the presentation in one group subtly helps create unity in the novel.

In addition, the placing of this index in the coda of Chapter II contributes to the structural patterning for unity and emphasis. The conclusion of Chapter III, we remember, is also of particular importance, since by presenting Jordan's near accident with the discussion of carelessness it prepares us for what is to follow. Fitzgerald consciously uses this emphatic position at each chapter's end to call attention to major elements of the novel and frequently creates relations between the structural units.

For example, the codas of Chapters IV and VI present Nick's and Gatsby's versions of a kiss. Fitzgerald's awareness of this patterning is implied in the extensive revisions which brought Gatsby's story to its present parallel position. The story appears in manuscript in the beginning of an early version of Chapter VI and in galley proof at the beginning of Chapter VII (MS. VI. 3; Galley 35). In the galley version Fitzgerald has added a paragraph about a forgotten phrase in Nick's mind. This paragraph dealing with the forgotten phrase was originally written to follow Gatsby's singing of a song he composed in his youth, and Fitzgerald shifted the paragraph, with only a minor change, to its present position after Gatsby's kiss. This shift serves two purposes: it comments upon Gatsby's story, and it creates another analogy to Nick's narration of a kiss, because Nick also had a phrase in mind when he kissed Jordan. The similarities of the events and the phrases were then put into an unmistakable relationship when, in revising the galleys, Fitzgerald shifted Gatsby's narration and the paragraph about the forgotten phrase to a position parallel to Nick's. Thus the codas of [Chapters] IV and VI help unify the book by treating two similar events, and control thematic emphasis by presenting contrasting points of view toward romance. And, of course, the codas of [Chapters] V and VII, which picture first Gatsby and then Tom holding Daisy's hand, also function in this way.

The patterning of alternate codas is tightened to one of direct connection in the last three chapters. In VII and VIII, Gatsby is pictured as alone, first on his vigil and then in his pool. In the one chapter Gatsby is the faithful, devoted, vigilant protector of his lady. In the next he is dead. This contrast, a commentary on romantic idealization, works within the leitmotif of 'Loneliness'. A similar commentary also links the eighth with the ninth and final coda. At the novel's conclusion Nick likens the human struggle to 'boats against the current' (p. 141). And the previous coda presents the image of Gatsby, his struggle over, on a boat going against the current, as the faint wind and a cluster of leaves disturb the course of his mattress in the current of the pool.

The last coda must be discussed in conjunction with the first, since their composition is related. The conclusion of the first chapter was once very different. For example, the manuscript version does not mention that Gatsby was 'content to be alone' (p. 20), nor does it include the symbolic green light. Both these insertions were made, however, by the time the novel was ready for typesetting. The insertion of the green light picks up other uses of green as a symbol of romance which occur later in the novel, such as the '"green card"' (p. 82) which Daisy jokes about as entitling Nick to a kiss, the 'long green tickets' (p. 136) which carried young Nick to Midwestern parties, and the 'fresh, green breast of the new world' (p. 140) of the conclusion. The description of Gatsby reaching out was not, however, the original end of the chapter. The manuscript first chapter ends with a passage we now find at the novel's conclusion. Only by cutting away this material did Fitzgerald raise the importance of the picture of Gatsby on his lawn, reaching toward Daisy.

It is crucial to a complete understanding of the novel that we realize that this portion of the conclusion was composed early in the writing process:

> And as the moon rose higher the inessential houses began to melt away until gradually I became aware of the old island here that flowered once for Dutch sailors' eyes – a fresh, green breast of the new world. Its vanished trees, the trees that had made way for Gatsby's house, had once pandered in whispers to the last and greatest of all human dreams; for a transitory enchanted moment man must have held his breath in the presence of this continent, compelled into an aesthetic contemplation he neither understood nor desired, face to face for the last time in history with something commensurate to his capacity for wonder. (p. 140)

The references to the past in this section and in the remainder of the conclusion raise the thematic importance of Gatsby's '"Can't repeat the past? . . . Why of course you can!"' (p. 86) and of Tom's conversion of a garage into a stable. Both Gatsby and Tom are, each in his own way, borne back into the past. From the early composition of this section we can also surmise that several of the leitmotifs mentioned in the conclusion, such as the notion of pandering and the Edenic conception of America, may have been in Fitzgerald's mind from the beginning.

Similarly, the 'new world' (p. 140) seen by the Dutch sailors was already in Fitzgerald's mind when he wrote of the 'new world' (p. 126) which Gatsby had seen shortly before being killed by Wilson in the coda of Chapter VIII:

> . . . he must have felt that he had lost the old warm world, paid a high price for living too long with a single dream. He must have looked up at an unfamiliar sky through frightening leaves and shivered as he found what a grotesque thing a rose is and how raw the sunlight was upon the scarcely created grass. A new world, material without being real, where poor ghosts, breathing dreams like air, drifted fortuitously about . . . like that ashen, fantastic figure gliding toward him through the amorphous trees. (p. 126)

Fitzgerald's decision to present these radically different 'new worlds' – Nick's imputation of Gatsby's realistic disillusionment and the Dutch sailors' romantic idealization – in the codas to the last two chapters reveals once more his consummate use of patterning.

It is clear, I think, that Fitzgerald fulfilled his intention to write a 'consciously artistic achievement'. And a knowledge of the ways in which the novel is 'intricately patterned' from minor details up to large structural units, partially explains how Fitzgerald created a novel that is 'something extraordinary and beautiful and simple'.[24] □

Doyno's essay, like Westbrook's before it, belongs to the mainstream of *Gatsby* criticism in the 1960s. Both critics apply approved procedures, in interesting ways, that serve to enrich our understanding of the novel and to confirm Fitzgerald's status as a major author. But although the full impact of the 1960s was to take time to work through into literary criticism, there were already, in that decade, voices disturbing the critical consensus, raising uncomfortable questions. One of the major starting points of the 1960s had been the Civil Rights movement, and this had been followed by the rise of a challenging, affirmative African-American consciousness; in this climate, it is not surprising that the issue of Fitzgerald's representation of African-Americans should arise. In 1967, the magazine *Phylon: The Atalanta University Review of Race and Culture* published an essay by Robert Forrey called 'Negroes in the Fiction of F. Scott Fitzgerald'. Forrey, in his opening paragraph, charges that:

■ [d]arker skinned individuals, when they do appear in Fitzgerald's fiction, are generally relegated to clownish and inferior roles. The kind of social status he envied required not only money but the type of security that came from belonging to a very old and very white American family. To be at the top of society, in Fitzgerald's fiction, is axiomatically to be white and wealthy; to be at the bottom was, conversely, to be dark-skinned and poor. Nick, the narrator of *The Great Gatsby* tells us: 'a limousine passed us, driven by a white chauffeur, in which sat three modish Negroes, two bucks and a girl. I laughed aloud as the yolks of their eyeballs rolled toward us in haughty rivalry.' (p. 55)[25] □

Drawing both on Fitzgerald's fiction and on biographical evidence, Forrey suggests that 'Fitzgerald believed in the inherent inferiority of Negroes' and that in regard to race 'Fitzgerald does not belong in the liberal tradition in American letters'.[26] Forrey does find, however, that *The Last Tycoon* shows a change in attitude, not only towards African-Americans, but also towards other ethnic minorities. For example, in contrast to the criminal Wolfsheim, the 'small flat-nosed Jew' (p. 55) in *Gatsby*, Monroe Stahr in *The Last Tycoon* is Jewish, and the novel's hero.

Forrey does not apply the kind of analytic techniques used by Westbrook and Doyno in their essays, so it was easy for literary criticism in the 1960s to ignore the issues he raised. But it is possible today to see his essay as posing questions that readings of Fitzgerald in the 1990s and beyond will have to tackle more fully. Clearly it is not simply a matter of branding the Fitzgerald of *Gatsby* a racist: Tom, the explicit voice of racism in the novel, has never found a sympathetic defender,[27] and the monolithic racial identity he seeks to uphold is subverted in the novel by the presence of a range of characters of different ethnic origins: for example, Nick's unnamed Finnish servant, Michaelis, the young Greek, and perhaps even James Gatz himself, whose surname suggests German descent. The issue of ethnicity in *Gatsby* is taken up in the 1970s by Peter Gregg Slater, as we shall see.

If Forrey's challenge to Fitzgerald found little echo in the 1960s, that of Gary J. Scrimgeour resounded more loudly – partly because its note of brazen dissent was still struck on the accepted instruments of literary criticism. First published in 1966 in the journal *Criticism*, his essay quickly gained wider currency by its inclusion in 1968 in Ernest Lockridge's selection of *Twentieth Century Interpretations of 'The Great Gatsby'*. The title of that essay is unequivocal – 'Against *The Great Gatsby*' – and its opening remarks are provocative and polemical, damning with faint praise: '*Gatsby* is just good enough, just lyrical enough, just teachable-to-freshmen enough (and more than "American" enough) for unwary souls to call it a classic'.[28] Taking strong issue with what was by now a chorus of adulation for Fitzgerald's craftsmanship, he seizes on one of the swords that had been used by Fitzgerald's admirers such as James E. Miller, Jr – the comparison with Conrad's 'Heart of Darkness' – and turns it back on Fitzgerald himself. To set 'Heart of Darkness' against *Gatsby*, Scrimgeour contends, highlights Fitzgerald's failings. Like R. W. Stallman in '*Gatsby* and the Hole in Time', Scrimgeour assaults Nick's character, but, in contrast to Stallman, his ultimate target is Fitzgerald himself.

The excerpt below begins when, having made his general attack, and pointed out what he sees as flaws in Nick's character, Scrimgeour comes to the core of the matter:

■ . . . the key issue is undoubtedly [Nick's] honesty, because that provides the basis of the reader's reaction to the novel. It is here that he contrasts most strongly with Conrad's Marlow. For example, both Marlow and Carraway are reticent about many important matters, but when Marlow refuses to linger on a subject (such as the rites in which Kurtz participates) it is because enough has already been said; more would be too much. Carraway's reticences, however, verge on falsehood. Instead of stopping short with just the right impression, they often succeed in giving the wrong impression. The lie that Carraway acquiesces in at the inquest and the complaisance he reveals in finally shaking hands with Tom have as their motive no nobler desire than to let sleeping dogs lie, whereas Marlow, who finds himself pushed at the end of 'Heart of Darkness' into an agonizing untruth, lies because the truth would be infinitely more damaging and useless. The truth about Mrs. Wilson's death could be damaging, but it is more likely to be simply incommoding. We have, in any case, no sign from Carraway that he even considered the problem.

Honesty can in the end be based only on some kind of powerful drive, and this is something that Carraway does not possess. The real nature of his principles appears if we contrast his own estimate of his integrity with a similar statement by Marlow. Long after the events which wrapped him inextricably in falsehood, Carraway writes, 'Everyone suspects himself of at least one of the cardinal virtues, and this is mine: I am one of the few honest people that I have ever known' (p. 48). Marlow, on the occasion not of a falsehood but of a minor false impression, says:

You know I hate, detest, and can't bear a lie, not because I am straighter than the rest of us, but simply because it appals me. There is a taint of death, a flavour of mortality in lies – which is exactly what I hate and detest in the world – what I want to forget. It makes me miserable and sick, like biting something rotten would do. Temperament, I suppose.[29]

The difference between Marlow's and Carraway's words is the difference between a man who cannot deny reality and a man who cannot face it. Both men feel deeply, but Marlow, at the cost of real pain, has to push forward until he understands the meaning of what he feels, until he is honest with himself, whereas Carraway stops short with whatever feeling he can conveniently bear, dreading what further effort might uncover. Both men record as much as they understand, but Marlow's honesty forces him to a much deeper understanding than Carraway achieves. To Marlow, feeling is part of the process that creates understanding, and honesty is his strongest feeling; to Carraway, feeling is the end product of experience, and honesty a matter for self-congratulation.

If the reader cannot accept Carraway's statements at face value, then the integrity of the technique of the novel is called in question. Rather than accepting what Carraway claims to be the effect of the events on his nature, the reader must stand further off and examine Carraway's development as though he were any other character, in which case a second vital weakness becomes obvious. Again like Gatsby, he never realizes the truth about himself, and despite the lesson of Gatsby's fate he fails to come to self-knowledge. There is a curious use of the conditional in Carraway's introduction to his story. He writes, 'If personality is an unbroken series of successful gestures, then there was something gorgeous about [Gatsby], some heightened sensitivity to the promises of life' (p. 6). The reason for Carraway's hesitancy over a matter that should present no problem is that he himself is trying to construct a personality out of a series of gestures such as the 'clean break' with Jordan or the final handshake with Tom, behaviour which results from his inability to decide what he should be doing or why he should be doing it. He is a moral eunuch, ineffectual in any real human situation that involves more than a reflex action determined by social pattern or the desire to avoid trouble with '"*any*body"' (p. 36). At one stage Carraway senses that something is wrong and suggests that Tom, Gatsby, Daisy, Jordan and he all 'possessed some deficiency in common' (p. 137), but he fails to see that the deficiency is the hollowness in their moral natures that leaves them prey to self-deception and 'carelessness' (p. 139).

Consequently Carraway's distinctiveness as a character is that he fails to learn anything from his story, that he can continue to blind himself even after his privileged overview of Gatsby's fate. The defeat evident in his disillusionment is followed not by progress but by retreat. He returns not only to his safe environment in the Mid-West but also to the same attitudes from which he started. One cannot praise him for being disillusioned with the ashland life of the East. For him to be disillusioned with values that are, after all, transparently unworthy, is not as remarkable as the fact that he remains enamoured of the person who represents those values in their most brilliant and tempting form. He refuses to admit that his alliance with Gatsby, his admiration for the man, results from their sharing the same weakness. Writing when he has had time to deliberate on Gatsby's fate, he says 'Only Gatsby . . . was exempt from my reaction – Gatsby who represented everything for which I have an unaffected scorn' (pp. 5–6). This is precisely the attitude which he held long before, at the height of his infatuation with Gatsby's dream. He has learned nothing. His failure to come to any self-knowledge makes him like the person who blames the stone for stubbing his toe. It seems inevitable that he will repeat the same mistakes as soon as the feeling that 'temporarily closed out my interest in the abortive sorrows and short-winded elations of men' (p. 6) has departed. The world will not, despite his wishes, remain 'at a sort of moral attention forever' (p. 5).

Because of the weakness of Carraway's character, the meaning of *The Great Gatsby* is much blacker than that of 'Heart of Darkness'. In the latter Marlow progresses through his encounter with Kurtz to a greater self-knowledge; and even if we consider self-knowledge a pitiful reward to snatch from life, we must still admit that it has a positive value and that the gloom of the story is not unrelieved. Such cautious optimism is apparent only if we can see first that the narrator of 'Heart of Darkness' is a reliable purveyor of truth, and second that he has come to greater self-knowledge. It is to the end of emphasizing these qualities that Conrad fashions the structure of the novel. The beginning of the work and the interruptions in Marlow's narrative have the purpose of reminding us at key points that the story is being refracted through Marlow's mind and that he is a character whose reactions are as important as his tale. The most emphasized of Marlow's qualities are his self-knowledge (we recall his Buddha-like pose) and the stress of his desire to fight his way through the material of his experience to reveal the truth. We can accept Marlow's recounting of the events only if we believe that, both as narrator and as person, his judgement is to be respected, and Conrad takes some of the novel out of Marlow's hands for exactly this purpose.

But we have seen that it is just here that Fitzgerald makes a major change in the structure of *The Great Gatsby*. There is little doubt that we are intended to see Carraway both as a reliable narrator and as a character learning from experience, but because we see only his version of the events and of his character, an objective evaluation is difficult. When we do attempt to be objective, we find that we have to impugn Carraway's honesty as a narrator and his self-awareness as a person. In this way Fitzgerald's change in technique makes *The Great Gatsby* a much more pessimistic novel than 'Heart of Darkness'. If the story means (as Fitzgerald probably intended) that Gatsby's romantic dream is magnificent and Carraway's change a growth, then we have a sombre but reasonably constructive view of life. But if our narrator turns out to be corrupt, if our Adam is much less innocent than we suspected, then despair replaces elegy. Had Carraway been defeated by the impersonal forces of an evil world in which he was an ineffectual innocent, his very existence – temporary or not – would lighten the picture. But his defeat is caused by something that lies within himself: his own lack of fibre, his own willingness to deny reality, his own substitution of dreams for knowledge of self and the world, his own sharing in the very vices of which his fellow men stand accused.

The irony produced by a comparison with the superficially gloomier 'Heart of Darkness' is the realization that while Marlow sees the events as typical and Carraway as crucial, in effect they are crucial for Marlow and typical for Carraway. Where Marlow gains an expansiveness of outlook from his experiences, we find Carraway saying that 'life is much more successfully looked at from a single window, after all' (p. 7), surely a supreme expression of the ethical vacuity which brought about his sufferings in the first place. If the one person who had both the talent and the opportunity to realize his own weaknesses remains unchanged, then we have a world of despair. Perhaps in this light the final image of the novel gains a new felicitousness: 'So we beat on, boats against the current, borne back ceaselessly into the past' (p. 141).

It is usually considered that Fitzgerald intended *The Great Gatsby* to warn us against the attempt to deny reality. My interpretation of the novel goes further to suggest that unwittingly, through careless technique and cloudy thinking, Fitzgerald in fact created a novel which says that it is impossible for us to face reality. One would like to think that Fitzgerald knew what he was doing, that in the opening pages he intended Carraway's priggishness and enervation to warn the reader against the narrator. Certainly there is enough evidence in the novel to support such a view, which can no more be completely disproven than can similar readings of *Moll Flanders* and *Gulliver's Travels*, but before we accept it we have to answer two questions: was the young Fitzgerald capable of such ironic perception, which would involve an extraordinarily complex attitude not just to his characters but to his readers and to himself as writer and individual? and if so, why did he choose deliberately not to make the irony clearer to the reader, especially with the example of Conrad in front of him? My own belief is that Fitzgerald achieved something other than he intended. Knowing that he always had difficulty in distinguishing himself from his characters (and admitted to being even Gatsby!), we can legitimately suspect that Carraway's failure is Fitzgerald's failure, and that Fitzgerald himself was chronically unaware of the dangers of romanticism. If Daisy is Gatsby's dream, and Gatsby is Carraway's dream, one suspects that Carraway is Fitzgerald's dream.

Much of *The Great Gatsby* is of course brilliant, and its historical position as one of the earliest American novels to attempt twentieth-century techniques guarantees it a major position in our literary hierarchy. But it is usually praised for the wrong reasons, and we should take care that Fitzgerald does not become our dream, as the recent spate of biographies and articles might suggest. The character of Carraway as Fitzgerald saw it, the innocent Adam in the school of hard knocks, appeals to our liking for sentimental pessimism; critics and teachers can overvalue romanticism as much as authors, and thus damage our literary tradition by mistaking delicate perceptions for sound thinking. Unless we wish to teach what Fitzgerald intended rather than what he wrote, unless we prefer an attractive exterior to an honest interior, unless we cherish a novel because we think it says the things we want to hear, then we should be very precise about the value of what the novel actually says. Ultimately, to withdraw our sympathy from Carraway, even to lower our estimation of Fitzgerald's skill, is not to depreciate but to change the worth of *The Great Gatsby*. It may serve to teach both readers and writers that careful technique is worth more to a novel than verbal brilliance, and that honest, hard thinking is more profitable than the most sensitive evocation of sympathy. We may no longer be able to read it as a description of the fate that awaits American innocence, but we can see it as a record of the worse dangers that confront American sentimentality.[30] □

Scrimgeour's essay was a salutary reminder that the doubts about *Gatsby* that had been expressed in some of the reviews – such as the one by Isabel Paterson in the first chapter of this Guide (see pp. 14–17) – had not gone away and could be forcefully developed and defended in the context of academic literary criticism. But even such an attack could serve, in a sense, to enhance *Gatsby*'s status: it showed that the book remained controversial and provocative. The vehemence of Scrimgeour's assault on Nick could be taken as a sign that, in Nick, Fitzgerald had created a convincing, complex character, with whom you could get angry as you might get angry with someone in actual life. That *The Great Gatsby* could provoke fury proved that it was still alive.

The critic who most vividly demonstrated *Gatsby*'s aliveness in the 1960s was Leslie A. Fiedler. He did for *Gatsby* in the Sixties what R. W. Stallman had done for it in the Fifties, providing fresh, exciting perspectives on the novel. Fiedler was no ardent fan of Fitzgerald: way back in 1951, fifteen years before Scrimgeour, he had cast doubt on Fitzgerald's 'greatness': 'so a fictionist with a "second-rate sensitive mind" (the term is Tennyson's description of himself, and evokes the tradition of late Romanticism in which Fitzgerald worked) and a weak gift for construction is pushed into the very first rank of American novelists'.[31] He had then made a general criticism of Fitzgerald's fiction that Scrimgeour was to make with specific reference to Nick Carraway: that Fitzgerald 'never mastered' the devices of irony and detachment.[32] And although, in contrast to Scrimgeour, Fiedler seemed to regard *Gatsby* as a success, he did imply that a qualified estimate of Fitzgerald as a writer was in order: he should be seen as 'an imperfect good writer, who achieved just once a complete artistic success, but who in every book at some point breaks through his own intolerable resolve to be charming above all and touches the truth!'.[33]

In 1967, Fiedler returned to Fitzgerald in his rich and massive book *Love and Death in the American Novel*. His discussion of Fitzgerald occurs in a chapter called 'The Revenge on Women', in which he argues that '[a]ll through the history of our [the American] novel, there had appeared side by side with the Fair Maiden, the Dark Lady – sinister embodiment of the sexuality denied the snow maiden'.[34] Fiedler thus focuses, though in a distinctly pre-feminist way, on the representation of women, and he begins by invoking a figure also invoked by Carl Van Vechten (see pp. 26–8), in one of the first *Gatsby* reviews: Henry James's Daisy Miller. But whereas Van Vechten had likened Daisy Miller to Gatsby himself, Fiedler sees a different connection.

■ [Henry James's Daisy Miller is] a transitional figure, the hinge upon which the American adoration of pure womanhood swings over to reveal its underside of fear and contempt. The first notable anti-virgin of our [American] fiction, the prototype of the blasphemous portraits of the Fair Goddess as bitch in which our [American] twentieth-century fiction abounds, is quite deliberately called Daisy – after James's misunderstood American Girl. She is, of course, the Daisy Fay Buchanan of Scott Fitzgerald's *The Great Gatsby*, the girl who lures her lovers on, like America itself, with a '"voice . . . full of money"' (p. 94). More like James's Maggie Verver [in *The Golden Bowl* (1904)], perhaps, than Daisy Miller in the potency of her charm, she is yet another Heiress of All the Ages: great-great-granddaughter of that priceless Pearl [in Hawthorne's *The Scarlet Letter* (1850)], who got the best of the Old World and the New. She is an odd inversion of Clarissa-Charlotte Temple-Maggie Verver; no longer the abused woman, who only by her suffering and death castrates her betrayer, but the abusing woman, symbol of an imperialist rather than a colonial America. The phallic woman with a phallus of gold, she remains still somehow the magic princess James had imagined as the heroine of *The Golden Bowl*: 'High in a white palace the king's daughter, the golden girl' (p. 94). To Fitzgerald, however, her fairy glamour is illusory, and once approached the White Maiden is revealed as a White Witch, the golden girl as a golden idol. On his palette, white and gold make a

dirty colour; for wealth is no longer innocent, America no longer innocent, the Girl who is the soul of both turned destructive and corrupt.

There is only one story Fitzgerald knows how to tell, and no matter how he thrashes about, he must tell it over and over. The penniless
knight, poor stupid Hans, caddy or bootlegger or medical student,
goes out to seek his fortune and unluckily finds it. His reward is, just
as in the fairy tales, the golden girl in the white palace; but, quite dif-
ferently from the fairy tales, that is not a happy ending at all. He finds
in his bed not the white bride but the Dark Destroyer; indeed, there is
no White Bride, since Dark Lady and Fair, witch and redeemer have
fallen together. But it is more complicated even than this. Possessed of
the power of wealth, Fitzgerald's women, like their wealthy male
compeers, who seem their twins rather than their mates, are rapists
and aggressors. Of both Daisy and her husband Tom, Fitzgerald tells
us, 'they smashed up things and creatures and then retreated back into
their money' (p. 139). In a real sense, not Daisy but Jay Gatz, the Great
Gatsby, is the true descendant of Daisy Miller: the naïf out of the West
destined to shock the upholders of decorum and to die of a love for
which there is no worthy object.

In Fitzgerald's world the distinction between sexes is fluid and
shifting precisely because he has transposed the mythic roles and values of male and female, remaking Clarissa in Lovelace's image,
Lovelace in Clarissa's. With no difficulty at all and only a minimum of
rewriting, the boy Francis, who was to be a centre of vision in *The
World's Fair*, becomes the girl Rosemary as that proposed novel turned
into *Tender is the Night*. Thematically, archetypally even such chief male
protagonists as Gatsby and Dick Diver [in *Tender is the Night*] are
females; at least, they occupy in their stories the position of Henry
James's Nice American Girls. It is they who embody innocence and
the American dream, taking up the role the flapper had contemptu-
ously abandoned for what was called in the twenties 'freedom'; but
they do not know this, projecting the dream which survives only in
themselves upon the rich young ladies whom they desire . . .

[In *Tender is the Night*] Nicole, the goddess who failed, is postulated
. . . as a schizophrenic, in an attempt to explain her double role as Fair
Lady and Dark, her two faces, angelic and diabolic, the melting and
the grinning mask. But the schizophrenia is really in Diver, which is to
say, in Fitzgerald, which is finally to say, in the American mind itself.
There are not, in fact, two orders of women, good and bad, nor is there
even one which seems for a little while bad, only to prove in the end
utterly unravished and pure. There are only two sets of expectations
and a single imperfect kind of woman caught between them: only
actual incomplete females, looking in vain for a satisfactory definition
of their role in a land of artists who insist on treating them as

goddesses or bitches. The dream role and the nightmare role alike deny the humanity of women, who, baffled, switch from playing out one to acting out the other. Fitzgerald apparently never managed to accommodate to the fact that he lived at the moment of a great switch-over in roles, though he recorded that revolution in the body of his work. His outrage and self-pity constantly break through the pattern of his fiction, make even an ambitious attempt like *Tender is the Night* finally too sentimental and whining to endure.

Only in *The Great Gatsby* does Fitzgerald manage to transmute his pattern into an objective form, evade the self-pity which corrodes the significance and the very shape of his other work – and this is perhaps because Gatsby is the most distant of all his protagonists from his real self. To Gatsby, Daisy appears in the customary semblance of the Fair Maiden, however; he finds her quite simply 'the first "nice" girl he had ever known' (p. 116). It is [William Dean] Howells's genteel epi-thet which occurs to him, though by Fitzgerald's time the capital letters are gone and the apologetic quotation marks have insidiously intruded. Daisy, rich and elegant and clean and sweet-smelling, repre-sents to her status-hungry provincial lover, not the corruption and death she really embodies, but Success – which is to say, America itself. In Fitzgerald, the same fable that informs James is replayed, subtly transformed, for like James he has written an anti-Western, an 'Eastern': a drama in which back-trailers reverse their westward drive to seek in the world which their ancestors abandoned the dream of riches and glory that has somehow evaded them. Fitzgerald's young men go east even as far as Europe; though unlike James's young women, they are in quest not of art and experience and the shudder of guilt, but of an even more ultimate innocence, an absolute America: a happy ending complete with new car, big house, money, and the girl.

In the symbolic geography of *The Great Gatsby* the two halves of a nation are compressed into the two settlements on Long Island of West Egg and East Egg, from the first of which the not-quite arrived look yearningly across the water at those who are already *in*, Jay Gatsby at Daisy Buchanan. There is no need for a symbolic Europe to complete the scene; and indeed, even in *Tender is the Night*, Europe is only a place where the East Eggians go to play, a transatlantic extension of East Egg itself. In a concluding passage of great beauty and conviction, Fitzgerald manages to convey the whole world of aspiration which Daisy has represented to Gatsby, and transforms the book from a lament over the fall of the Fair Woman to an elegy for the lapsed American dream of innocent success:

> And as the moon rose higher the inessential houses began to melt
> away until gradually I became aware of the old island here that

flowered once for Dutch sailors' eyes – a fresh, green breast of the new world ... the trees that had made way for Gatsby's house, had once pandered in whispers to the last and greatest of all human dreams; for a transitory enchanted moment man must have held his breath in the presence of this continent ... face to face for the last time in history with something commensurate to his capacity for wonder.

And as I sat there, brooding on the old unknown world, I thought of Gatsby's wonder when he first picked out the green light at the end of Daisy's dock. He had come a long way to this blue lawn and his dream must have seemed so close that he could hardly fail to grasp it. He did not know that it was already behind him, somewhere back in that vast obscurity beyond the city, where the dark fields of the republic rolled on under the night. (pp. 140–141)

For Fitzgerald 'love' was essentially yearning and frustration; and there is consequently little consummated genital love in his novels, though he identified himself with that sexual revolution which the twenties thought of as their special subject. The adolescent's 'kiss' is the only climax his imagination can really encompass; and despite his occasionally telling us that one or another of his characters has 'taken' a woman, it is the only climax he ever realizes in a scene. In his insufferable early books, the American institution of *coitus interruptus*, from bundling to necking a favourite national pastime, finds at last a laureate; and even in his more mature works, his women move from the kiss to the kill with only the barest suggestion of copulation between. [35] □

Fiedler's provocative account opens up issues about the representation of women and of sexuality in *The Great Gatsby* that had previously been little discussed. In the following decades, which saw the development of feminism and of gender and gay studies, these issues were, as we shall see, to be taken up and explored further, though with rather different emphases from Fiedler's. But the start of the 1970s was also to see a renewed interest in Fitzgerald's treatment of American history.

CHAPTER FOUR

History, Herstory and Other Stories: From Political *Gatsby* to Gay *Gatsby* in the 1970s

THE TURBULENCE of the 1960s – the assassination of the Kennedys, the Vietnam War, the student and African-American protests – had forced the USA to engage in painful self-questioning, and it was not surprising that this should provoke a fresh look at a novelist who had seemed so memorably to express the promise, and the failure, of the American Dream. At the start of the 1970s, two books on Fitzgerald appeared that returned to the notion, encapsulated by Lionel Trilling and elaborated by Edwin Fussell and Marius Bewley, that Fitzgerald's work – and especially *The Great Gatsby* – was about America. Milton R. Stern's *The Golden Moment: The Novels of F. Scott Fitzgerald*, first published in 1970, contended that 'the centre of Fitzgerald's imagination' was 'the uses of history, the American identity, the moral reconstruction of the American past'[1] – all issues that, in the aftermath of the Sixties, had assumed a new urgency. For Stern, as the extract below shows, America is the 'golden moment' in the history of the human race that mirrors, on a grander scale, the 'golden moment' in each individual life, a moment that, briefly flowering in time, will also be destroyed by time, and which can never be experienced directly again but only relived in memory and imagination. In an argument that echoes in part that of R. W. Stallman (see pp. 61–5), Stern focuses on Gatsby's desire to escape from time, which exemplifies the desire of America to escape from 'the cold limitations of history'.

■ Gatsby sums us all up. He sums up our American desire to believe in a release from history, to believe that our early past did indeed establish redemption, to believe that in our founding the idea of our superb and hopeful heritage was actualized. He sums up the 'vast, vulgar and meretricious beauty' (p. 77) that our wealth has made and in which

we dress the romantic sense of self that the idea of American possibilities keeps whispering is at hand. He sums up, too, the fast-movietime
we have made of history, wiping out past, present and future in the
whirling certitude that the new, that our wealth and power, will make
time do our bidding. Nick, with his fourth decade opening before him,
repudiates finally the 'Younger Generation' that began as Isabelle and
ends up as the Buchanans and Jordan Baker. 'I'd had enough of all of
them for one day' (p. 111), he says, voicing once more Fitzgerald's
sense of the necessity for responsibility, for the 'fundamental decencies'
(p. 5), for work as meaning and as dignity, for all the ideologies, if not
the actualities, of an older America. This is not to say that Fitzgerald
prefers that amalgam of puritanism and gentility that went into the
Victorianism from which he grew. As his short stories, his letters, *This
Side of Paradise* and *The Beautiful and Damned* make clear, he was aware
that like all else in American history, those ideologies of work,
responsibility, politeness, respect, decency, had been perverted and
bastardized in actualities which were the grabbing of wealth and the
cloaking of the sweat and the 'marks' with gentility and the preten-
tious manner of a long-established identity. Yet, given the callousness
and disrespect of the younger generation, given the childish sense of
having the world on a string, given, in short, the existential alternative
of value in the intensity of the moment per se, Fitzgerald chooses community and history. In *The Great Gatsby*, he comes to a position in
which he says that though the Protestant ethic is to be scorned in its
Babbittry, scorn is neither the final nor the only judgement to be
offered. In what it could have meant it is the name for human responsibility and decency. Fitzgerald never resolved allegiance to a genteel
world whose hypocrisies he repudiated, but he had deep and lasting
connections with it. Yet the final choice is empty, too. Nick goes
'home', but he can never go 'Home', as Fitzgerald makes clear. And
like Nick, Fitzgerald repudiates reluctantly the gorgeousness of the
romantic sense of self. It was the highest point of human hope,
Fitzgerald mourns. How hard to grow up to be an American, enticed
by your nation, only to have to grow up at last and settle for the cold
limitations of history.

. . .

Gatsby never understood that he was trapped by time and human
history. Yet even in the only moment he ever had his future – in the
past, in his youthful imaginings – the dreamlight was punctuated by
the sounds of time. 'A universe of ineffable gaudiness spun itself out
in his brain while the clock ticked on the wash-stand and the moon
soaked with wet light his tangled clothes upon the floor' (p. 77). And
at the moment of his triumph, when he meets Daisy in Nick's bungalow, Gatsby is harassed by time, by dead time. He has troubles with a

clock whose time he can't control. He thinks he is turning time back, but the point is that the clock doesn't work.

> Gatsby, his hands still in his pockets, was reclining against the mantelpiece in a strained counterfeit of perfect ease, even of boredom. His head leaned back so far that it rested against the face of a defunct mantelpiece clock . . . the clock took this moment to tilt dangerously at the pressure of his head, whereupon he turned and caught it with trembling fingers and set it back in place. . .
> "I'm sorry about the clock," he said . . .
> "It's an old clock," I told them idiotically.
> I think we all believed for a moment that it had smashed in pieces on the floor. (p. 68)

It is inevitable that Nick's premonitory warning about time should be fulfilled in Daisy's final announcement of her inability to fulfil Gatsby's dream . . . Every tick of the clock had led up to the stroke that rang, 'time's up!' and foreshadowed – significantly at the moment of apparent triumph – what had to happen. When Gatsby had finally won Daisy into his house, he takes her to his bedroom window . . . Never missing a trick, Fitzgerald adjusts the imagery to 'time' when Gatsby, at the instant of the golden moment, begins to suspect that the comedown to actualities is all there is: Gatsby 'had passed visibly through two states and was entering upon a third. After his embarrassment and his unreasoning joy he was consumed with wonder at [Daisy's] presence. He had been full of the idea so long, dreamed it right through to the end, waited with his teeth set, so to speak, at an inconceivable pitch of intensity. Now, in the reaction, he was running down like an overwound clock' (p. 72).

Gatsby strikes a responsive chord in Nick, as in the reader, because the 'intensity in his conception of the affair' (p. 119) is the summation of all our unarticulated memories of a time when time was young. When Gatsby recounts to Nick what Daisy had meant to him through all the years, Nick's own memory is stirred by something 'unutterable', a ghost of a dream, an unarticulated remembrance of what might have been a dream of what might have been. 'Through all he said, even through his appalling sentimentality, I was reminded of something – an elusive rhythm, a fragment of lost words, that I had heard somewhere a long time ago. For a moment a phrase tried to take shape in my mouth and my lips parted like a dumb man's, as though there was more struggling upon them than a wisp of startled air. But they made no sound and what I had almost remembered was uncommunicable forever' (p. 87).

What is there to remember? The discovery of Columbus? The

Dutch sailors? The dream of the founding fathers, of great documents believed in by great men in small clothes? Buffalo Bill Cody and the great expansive spaces and the founding dream knocked into the cocked hats of the fathers? Fitzgerald leaves no doubt that the idea of America, what mankind and the self were supposed to have been in the actualization of that young nation now back there somewhere in the past, is sign and metaphor for human youth itself. The old America in memory's silent rictus is the young America of the past to which we ride on the thrilling returning trains of our youth. The old America is a snap of the mind that flashes us nostalgically back to the last, best hope of mankind when 'for a transitory enchanted moment man must have held his breath in the presence of this continent . . . face to face for the last time in history with something commensurate to his capacity for wonder' (p. 140). America is the golden moment in the history of the human race, and it is that instant of history that Gatsby's life re-enacts in modern dress and in all its complex modifications.[2] □

As Stern's last sentence suggests, his notion of 'history' tends to shade into myth: *Gatsby* re-enacts an instant of the history of the human race and that history is also re-enacted in each individual in the passage from youth to age, from innocence to experience. In contrast, the distinctions between myth, history and the individual life are kept very firmly in mind in John F. Callahan's 1972 book *The Illusions of a Nation: Myth and History in the Novels of F. Scott Fitzgerald*. Callahan reads Fitzgerald in the light of the question: 'What, in America, have been the relationships between complex human personality, history and those myths summoned to explain the facts of history?'[3]

The status of Callahan's study is a curious one. Kenneth E. Eble, in the revised edition of his 1964 study of Fitzgerald, which came out in 1977, calls Callahan's book 'academic' and charges that it 'does some limiting and distorting of Fitzgerald's work to make it fit the author's thesis'.[4] But Callahan's study is not 'academic' in the derogatory sense that Eble's comment might seem to imply; it is not dry and detached; indeed, it is very much concerned with the political implications of Fitzgerald's work for modern America – and not only twentieth-century America in general, but the America of the time in which Callahan was writing, the 1960s and early 1970s. Indeed, in Fitzgerald studies, Callahan's book is the one that demonstrates most explicitly how Fitzgerald might speak to the 1960s and to their aftermath. And it is this aspect that Richard Lehan, in his 1990 study of *Gatsby*, seizes on to make his own criticism of Callahan. Acknowledging that the book 'was certainly correct in connecting Fitzgerald's novels with themes in history', Lehan goes on to say that it 'has not worn well, perhaps because it connected Fitzgerald's fiction too facilely with the events of the 1960s'.[5]

It may be that the relatively explicit politics of Callahan's study makes critics of a less obviously political cast of mind uncomfortable. But Callahan's interpretation of *Gatsby* is provocative and powerful, and while some of his rhetoric indeed smacks of the Sixties, he recalls Fitzgerald criticism from myth to an interpretation of American history that highlights the atrocities and exclusions of that history. In this respect, his study is more rather than less relevant today, in the era of multiculturalism, where the dominant versions of American history are being fractured by the retrieval of the traces of those whom were pushed, or forced, to the margins. The extract from Callahan's book that follows focuses on the famous conclusion of the novel, and succeeds in bringing a new perspective to bear on those much-discussed passages.

■ [At the end of *Gatsby*], [w]hat Carraway does is to put a historical event in a metaphysical category. The polarity swings from man's imagination, his 'capacity for wonder', to the material of the universe, 'a fresh, green breast of the new world' (p. 140).

The word 'pandered' [in the passage], chosen to describe the qualitative relationship between man and matter, reveals Carraway's dualist, original-sin bias. The rhetoric itself gives him away. First, he alludes to the Dutch sailors, particular men who came to America in a particular cultural and historical context. Perhaps because of the colonial-mercantile nature of their journey, he shifts his paradigm to universal man, man enchanted outside time. 'Its vanished trees, the trees that had made way for Gatsby's house, had once pandered in whispers to the last and greatest of all human dreams; for a transitory enchanted moment man must have held his breath in the presence of this continent, compelled into an aesthetic contemplation he neither understood nor desired, face to face for the last time in history with something commensurate to his capacity for wonder' (p. 140).

Note the dichotomies between nature and history, beauty and labour, imagination and rationality. Implicit is the metaphysic that natural objects and the physical universe rarely provide realities worthy of human imagination. Yet Carraway puts the responsibility for despoiling America upon the perception and appetite of man: 'aesthetic contemplation he neither understood nor desired'. So the unknown beauty of pre-European America both 'pandered in whispers' (beckoned seductively) to man (Dutch sailors, possibly disassociated from Dutch merchants and owners) and compelled him into 'aesthetic contemplation'. Not consciousness but 'aesthetic contemplation'. Maybe what 'pandered' means historically is that the undefiled, unowned (America before property in a capitalist sense would have had a special appeal to landless Europeans) continent seemed to encourage 'the last and greatest of all human dreams'. Now

I think Carraway uses 'pandered' to suggest that by its overwhelming and original beauty America for a moment legitimized an essentially fraudulent (for him) dream. That dream I take to be the embodiment, simultaneously in and out of time and space, as we think of those concepts historically, changingly, the embodiment of man's 'unutterable visions' (p. 86), the aesthetic union of mind with all its Cartesian baggage of self-created, self-dependent systems and that which is perishable, subject to change, finally beyond the mind's control in the universe. Here history refers to a series of encounters during which man, in those rare moments when his imagination discovers a suitable object, himself lacks the sensibility necessary to 'aesthetic contemplation'. For this reason – not, in fact, man's disability but his failure – Carraway binds 'aesthetic contemplation' to the timeless but fragile 'transitory enchanted moment' and opposes aesthetic reality to history, a succession of particular actions, events and circumstances at distinct times and in distinct places.

The question has become: why this incompatibility between history and aesthetic sensibility? Why has man worn out the world? Previously, one has sensed the taint which for Carraway clings to matter. It is the incarnation myth and metaphor: the word or spirit descends to flesh or body. Earlier Carraway paradigmed Gatsby's choice of Daisy as a marriage between 'unutterable visions' and 'perishable breath' (p. 86). Involved in that union is recognition of otherness, mortality and history insofar as history conveys the stage on which individual men have brief lives and then depart forever. For no matter how far imagination's visions may seem to reach beyond physical territory, finally they must be acted out within bodies whose terrains are both limited and final. Gatsby, in the beginning, unconsciously feels these necessities, but after the experience, ironically, after the pressures of history, Daisy becomes for him more an 'unutterable vision' than a woman in a given context of a particular time and place, not to mention a particular history. So, contrary to Carraway's platonic rhetoric and metaphor, the real deceiver is male imagination insofar as it lulls man from awareness of the hardships which will confront him in the very otherness, the unknown of nature. Man then projects ideal perfection upon nature and other persons to conceal the possessive desires of his own dark heart.

When Carraway comes particularly to Gatsby, one feels him slip into allusions to Eden, primal myth of Western culture whose article of faith, at best, is that nature followed man into *essential* imperfection, corruption and evil; and, at worst, that evil found its original tangible presence in a temptation offered to man by nature or at least in nature's guise. In any case Carraway begs the question of historical analysis and explanation. He talks of 'the old unknown world' (again, why UNKNOWN?), then connects Gatsby to that first, mere projected moment of 'aesthetic contemplation': 'He had come a long way to this blue lawn and his dream must have seemed so close that he could hardly fail to grasp it. He did not know that it was already behind him, somewhere back in that vast obscurity beyond the city, where the dark fields of the republic rolled on under the night' (p. 141). Difficult to translate the metaphorical journey into history. Easy, however, to identify it with the Calvinist world view. Naive with his dream of election, Gatsby did not know that in America the issue had already closed in damnation. One must, I think, go from a Calvinist account of the Fall and its consequences to an analogously determinist version of history. Here the republic equals historical innocence and possibility – its place, nature beyond the urban pale, almost a pastoral myth. Empire yields to decadence and corruption: hopes washed out, possibility vanished, as with Rome its place the city, man's replacement of the natural world.

One senses in Carraway's evocation of the changing continent a loss of intensity between place and consciousness. '[V]ast obscurity', 'dark fields' (p. 141) summon an America unknown, unincorporated into any rational property system. But as there comes with ownership a certain death to the object, a dissolution, in the owner's view, of its independence and integrity, so the property system brought to the continent and its exploiters an end to aesthetic impulse. For property often makes the object an appendage of ego.

Not only did beauty become less real, less critical than wealth until wealth became beauty, but, worst of all, relation, in America, between property structure and the land went forth on an increasingly abstract level. Men rushed across the breadth of this continent plundering and acquiring, not discovering, certainly not contemplating. The Indians whose 'identity with this country' (p. 137) was as tangible as its geography were largely annihilated, always subjugated, dealt with as objects as they are dealt with to this moment. Men did not want to settle and live as human beings in relationship to a unique and particular place; their strongest impulse was to race to the last frontier of America. As if migration could somehow remove the blood from their hands, the horror from their souls. Unwilling to give justice and real citizenship to black and Indian Americans their descendants award democracy to Vietnamese and Thais: 'I cannot bear the truth' has become an American anthem. Its corollary in action: 'Love me or I'll kill you'.

Historically, Carraway's pastoral, Edenic allusions go back to the birth of this nation as republic, when it, in Jefferson's words, branded 'as cowardly the idea that the human mind is incapable of further advances'.[6] Now Carraway forgets or does not regard as central the fact that this republic owed its life as much to its institution of slavery and its colonial policy (really, a policy of extermination) toward the Indians as it did to the courage and democratic institutions of its citizens. The analogy implied with Rome also recalls the transition from republic to an empire largely incapable of re-examining historical process in relation to those past and present assumptions which determine the nation's course.[7] □

Although resonant of the 1960s in one sense, there is another sense in which Callahan's plea for a more historical and political reading of *Gatsby* was ahead of its time. In England and the USA in the later 1960s and in the earlier 1970s, the introduction of explicit political concerns into literary criticism, especially if they were related to contemporary issues as well as to the past, was still seen as an offence, an annoying diversion of attention both from the text itself, as enshrined in New Criticism, and from the more traditional concerns of textual and biographical scholarship. Moreover, the conceptual tools that have subsequently been developed for exploring the relationships between literary texts, culture and politics were not available as they are today. Nonetheless, Callahan's study succeeded in raising important questions in regard to *Gatsby*, and Fitzgerald's work in general, which have yet to be fully followed up.

Callahan's references to those who, in the first European conquest of America, already lived on the 'fresh, green breast of the new world' – the Native Americans – raises, once more, the issue of ethnicity in Fitzgerald, and this is taken up in the 1970s by Peter Gregg Slater. In his essay 'Ethnicity in *The Great Gatsby*', which appeared in *Twentieth Century Literature* in 1973, Slater proposes that 'a heightened awareness of ethnic differences does constitute a significant element in the book' and draws attention to the way that Nick as narrator, while distancing himself from Tom's blatant racism, 'tends to point out the ethnic affiliation of the individuals with whom he comes in contact whenever their ethnicity is not of an Old American type as is his own'.[8] In the extract below, Slater offers a penetrating criticism of what he calls 'Nick's rather limited version of [the American] dream' – although he does not turn this back to question Marius Bewley's version:

■ The last pages of [*Gatsby*] reveal at least three different interpretations of the American dream. There is the original version, the one forced upon the Dutch sailors as they gazed in enchanted wonder at the long, virginal island, 'fresh, green breast of the new world' (p. 140), a version now 'unknown' (p. 141), lost forever with the settlement and exploitation of the continent ('Its vanished trees . . . had made way for Gatsby's house' (p. 140)). There is Gatsby's interpretation of the dream as a romantic fairy tale in which a glamorous hero gains an inexpressible spiritual fulfilment through the winning of golden riches and a golden girl. [In a note in the original essay, Slater acknowledges that his interpretation of Gatsby's version of the American dream is partly based on Bewley's.] And there is Nick's version of the American dream which reduces the universal overtones of the original version ('greatest of all human dreams . . . man must have held his breath' (p. 140)), and the individualistic grandeur of Gatsby's interpretation to a Middle Western kind of community and stability. Recalling his 'thrilling' train trips home from prep school and college to a Middle West of bracing cold outside the dwellings and heartening warmth inside, 'street lamps and sleigh bells in the frosty dark and the shadows of holly wreaths thrown by lighted windows on the snow', Nick speaks of how he and his companions were 'unutterably aware of our identity with this country for one strange hour' (p. 137). Whereas the Dutch version of the American dream was available to any human who happened to come along at that moment in history, and Gatsby's version can be aspired to by anyone with the requisite imaginative potency, Nick's version is exclusive and provincial. It is basically limited to affluent Middle Western Americans who are white Anglo-Saxon Protestant, or willing and able to be acculturated to WASP modes. This is what Jay Gatsby has left behind 'in that vast obscurity beyond the city, where the dark fields of the republic rolled on under the night' (p. 141).

Though no proponent of the views of fervent ethnic baiters such as Tom Buchanan, Nick is presenting an ethnocentric interpretation of the American dream, excluding from it a whole section of the nation, the East, as well as those with intense ethnicity of a different sort than his own, such as unreconstructed Swedes ['the lost Swede towns' which are not part of Nick's Middle West (p. 137)] and the Jewish Meyer Wolfsheim.[9] □

As well as its ethnic exclusions, Nick's version of the American Dream might also seem to exclude women – and so, for that matter, might the versions of Gatsby and the Dutch sailors: '*man* must have held his breath' (p. 140 [my emphasis]). Questions about the women in Fitzgerald's texts began to be raised in the 1970s, and we shall look at two examples, both of which focus on the representation of Daisy, as Leslie A. Fiedler had done (see pp. 100–03). In the first essay, from the January 1975 issue of *American Literature*, Joan S. Korenman draws attention to two kinds of inconsistency with regard to what might seem, by some criteria, a minor matter: the colour of Daisy's hair. One inconsistency is within the novel itself: Daisy is described at different times as fair and dark.[10] A second inconsistency is between this textual variation and the assumption of most readers that Daisy is fair. Korenman suggests that the internal inconsistency relates to the way in which Daisy embodies both the fair and the dark women of romantic literature – to what Fiedler calls 'the Fair Maiden' and 'the Dark Lady', although Korenman herself does not refer to Fiedler.

■ In a 1972 newspaper article, Hollywood columnist and Fitzgerald intimate Sheilah Graham complained that Ali MacGraw was not an appropriate choice to play Daisy Buchanan in the forthcoming Paramount film of *The Great Gatsby* because the actress is 'dark, olive complexioned, and with the look of an Indian', while Fitzgerald's character is 'blonde, blue-eyed, feminine and frivolous'.[11] Interestingly, the novel both supports Miss Graham and refutes her; Fitzgerald describes Daisy in contradictory ways. This contradiction can be partially explained by an examination of Daisy's dual origin [she may be based both on an early love, the brunette Ginevra King, and on the golden-haired Zelda]. In part, too, the discrepancy reflects a fundamental duality in Daisy herself, her simultaneous embodiment of traits associated with the fair and the dark women of romantic literature.

Fitzgerald offers varying descriptions of Daisy's hair colour. When her three-year-old daughter makes a momentary appearance in the novel, Daisy holds her and asks, '"Did mother get powder on your old yellowy hair?"' (p. 91). Later in the same conversation, Daisy tells Nick Carraway: '"She looks like me. She's got my hair and shape of the face"' (p. 91). But while mother and daughter seem here to be unmistakably blonde, elsewhere in the novel Daisy is clearly a brunette. On the last afternoon before Gatsby goes off to the War, he and Daisy sit together silently; '[n]ow and then she moved and he changed his arm a little and once he kissed her dark shining hair' (p. 117). It is presumably this dark hair that several years later 'lay like a dash of blue paint across her cheek' (p. 67).

. . .

What is curious is that, although the dark and fair descriptions seem fairly well balanced, most readers come away from the novel convinced like Sheilah Graham that Daisy is blonde.[12] Obviously, they are responding not so much to the physical descriptions Fitzgerald provides as to the symbolic suggestiveness with which he endows Daisy, a suggestiveness achieved in part by extensive use of colour. From the 'hundred pairs of golden and silver slippers' (p. 118) among which she dances in Louisville to the '"little gold pencil"' (p. 83) she offers Tom at Gatsby's party, Daisy belongs in the realm of gold. Her voice is 'full of money'; she is 'the king's daughter, the golden girl' (p. 94). She is the pot of gold at the end of the rainbow, the fair-haired princess of the fairy tales.

The golden girl dwells '[h]igh in a white palace' (p. 94) and throughout the novel white rivals gold as the principal colour associated with Daisy.[13] The flower after which she is named is white with a gold centre. As scores of critics have noted, she almost always dresses in white. Even when Gatsby first meets her in Louisville, '[s]he dressed in white and had a little white roadster . . . ' (p. 59). Like gold, white undoubtedly reinforces the reader's impression of Daisy's being blonde. Considered most simply, white is much closer in appearance to light hair than to dark. More significantly, though, white has traditionally suggested purity and innocence, qualities that romantic convention has long attributed to fair rather than dark women: Scott's Rowena rather than Rebecca; Hawthorne's Priscilla and Hilda rather than Zenobia or Miriam; Cooper's Hetty Hutter and Alice Munro rather than their sisters Judith and Cora.[14] So strong is the hold such cultural conventions have on the imagination that it is difficult to envision a brunette Daisy all in white.

It would be a mistake, however, to think that colour symbolism alone gives rise to the impression that Daisy is a blonde. Much about her personality supports the image projected by Fitzgerald's use of gold and white. Daisy shares a number of traits in common with the fair-haired heroines of the romantic tradition. Like Alice Munro in [James Fenimore] Cooper's *The Last of the Mohicans* (1826) or Priscilla in Hawthorne's *The Blithedale Romance* (1852), Daisy is passive, security-minded and pragmatic. In love with the dashing Lieutenant Gatsby, she nonetheless chooses the course of 'unquestionable practicality' and marries the wealthy, solid Tom Buchanan, reassured by the 'wholesome bulkiness about his person and his position' (p. 118). She is flattered by Gatsby's monumental efforts to regain her, but, when pushed to act, she looks at Jordan and Nick 'with a sort of appeal, as though she realized at last what she was doing – and as though she had never, all along, intended doing anything at all' (p. 103). In the end, she elects to stay with her socially respectable husband; she and Tom close ranks and retreat 'back into their money or their vast carelessness or whatever it was that kept them together . . . ' (p. 139). Also like her blonde literary forebears, Daisy comes from acceptable Anglo-Saxon stock; the dark woman, by contrast, usually is descended from some exotic lineage that includes black, Jewish, Indian or simply 'foreign' blood. Finally, there are the purity and innocence that characterize the fair-haired heroine. In Daisy, though, these take the form of coldness and sterility of soul (which, interestingly, are also traditionally suggested by the colour white). Daisy is moved by Gatsby's romantic gestures on her behalf, but she finds offensive that which 'wasn't a gesture but an emotion' (p. 84). She and Jordan talk 'with a bantering inconsequence that was never quite chatter, that was as cool as their white dresses and their impersonal eyes in the absence of all desire' (p. 13).

But side by side with the sexually anaesthetic blonde is still the dark-haired Daisy. Fitzgerald's jaded, cynical young sophisticate who has '"been everywhere and seen everything and done everything"' (p. 17) certainly has spiritual affinities with the knowledgeable, experienced dark women of Cooper, Hawthorne, Scott and Melville. Less adventurous and independent than, say, Judith Hutter, Hester Prynne, Rebecca, Zenobia or Isobel, Daisy nonetheless shares with them their unsheltered exposure to life, including the sexual side of life. The dark woman exudes sexuality. Cora Munro's presence excites the young Indian warriors; Miles Coverdale conjures up visions of a naked Zenobia; Pierre Glendenning struggles in vain against the incestuous passion that drives him to abandon his golden-haired fiancée to follow his dark, mysterious half-sister. In some ways, Daisy seems out of place in such company. But if Daisy the blonde is a '"nice" girl' (p. 116) in a white dress, perhaps it is Daisy the brunette who sleeps with Gatsby before he leaves for the War and whose 'low, thrilling voice' (p. 11) offers a powerful sexual appeal. Jordan Baker knows of Daisy's 'absolutely perfect reputation' in Chicago, and yet she has her doubts about her friend's conduct. She confides to Nick: 'Perhaps Daisy never went in for amour at all – and yet there's something in that voice of hers . . . ' (p. 61). Nick, too, recognizes the voice's appeal and believes that it was this sultry voice, 'with its fluctuating, feverish warmth' (p. 75) that held Gatsby most. Significantly, in an early manuscript draft, Fitzgerald not only refers to Daisy as a 'dark lovely girl' but also uses the same terms to describe her seductive voice – 'the dark lovely voice of Daisy Fay'.[15]

. . .

. . . more is involved [in the question of the colour of Daisy's hair] than just a minor inconsistency in descriptive detail. Romantic tradition assigns diametrically opposed roles to fair and dark women. In his creation of Daisy, Fitzgerald reflects the influence of this tradition. The character that results is both cool innocent princess and sensual *femme fatale*, a combination that further enhances Daisy's enigmatic charm.[16] □

It is possibly the duality in the representation of Daisy to which Korenman draws attention that has contributed to the vituperative critical indictment she has received; the difficulty of categorising her as *either* a fair maiden *or* a dark seductress may make her more threatening to some critics and provoke a more vehement critical attempt to 'put her in her place' by means of severe condemnation – we saw an example from Marius Bewley earlier (see pp. 58–9). The second of our essays on the representation of women in *Gatsby*, Leland J. Person, Jr's essay '"Herstory" and Daisy Buchanan', which appeared in *American Literature* in 1978/9, takes these indictments as a starting point and suggests that they oversimplify the novel. Daisy's own story, which can be inferred from the novel, is more complex; if we try to listen to that story, Person proposes, we may come to see her as more victim than vixen; if she is corrupt, it is less a matter of something rotten in her character than a cumulative effect of the way she is treated by those around her. Gatsby converts her story to *his* story – even to *His* story, as a 'son of God' (p. 77) – and creates a platonic ideal no human being could ever live up to, while Nick converts Daisy's story to *his* story and to *history*, making her stand for the corruption of the American Dream. But the novel also allows us to see the limits of this male appropriation and to retrieve the traces of another story, Daisy's tale, *her* story, which speaks of her own desires, dreams and ideals, and which in some ways parallels Gatsby's story of disillusionment: indeed, Person argues, as we shall see in the excerpt that follows, that Daisy is Gatsby's 'female double'.

■ Few critics write about *The Great Gatsby* without discussing Daisy Fay Buchanan; and few, it seems, write about Daisy without entering the unofficial competition of maligning her character. Marius Bewley, for example, refers to Daisy's 'vicious emptiness' and her 'monstrous moral indifference'.[17] To Robert Ornstein she is 'criminally amoral'[18] and Alfred Kazin judges her 'vulgar and inhuman'.[19] Finally Leslie Fiedler sees Daisy as a 'Dark Destroyer', a purveyor of 'corruption and death' and the 'first notable anti-virgin of our fiction, the prototype of the blasphemous portraits of the Fair Goddess as bitch in which our twentieth-century fiction abounds' (see pp. 100, 102). A striking similarity in these negative views of Daisy is their attribution to her of tremendous power over Gatsby and his fate. Equating Daisy with the kind of Circean figures popular in the nineteenth century, the critics tend to accept Gatsby as an essential innocent who 'turn[s] out all right at the end'. Daisy, on the other hand, becomes the essence of 'what preyed on' Gatsby, a part of that 'foul dust [that] floated in the wake of his dreams' (p. 6).

Such an easy polarization of characters into Good Boy/Bad Girl, however, arises from a kind of critical double standard and simply belittles the complexity of the novel. Daisy, in fact, is more victim than victimizer; she is victim first of Tom Buchanan's 'cruel' (p. 9) power, but then of Gatsby's increasingly depersonalized vision of her. She becomes the unwitting 'grail' (p. 117) in Gatsby's adolescent quest to remain ever-faithful to his seventeen-year-old conception of self (p. 77), and even Nick admits that Daisy 'tumbled short of his dreams – not through her own fault but because of the colossal vitality of his illusion. It had gone beyond her, beyond everything' (p. 75). Thus, Daisy's reputed failure of Gatsby is inevitable; no woman, no human being, could ever approximate the platonic ideal he has invented. If she is corrupt by the end of the novel and part of a 'conspiratorial' coterie with Tom [the word 'conspiratorial' is not used in *Gatsby*, but Person's reference is to Nick's glimpse of Tom and Daisy and his sense that 'anybody would have said that they were conspiring together' (p. 113)], that corruption is not so much inherent in her character as it is the progressive result of her treatment by the other characters.

In addition to being a symbol of Gatsby's illusions, Daisy has her own story, her own spokesman in Jordan Baker, even her own dream. Nick, for example, senses a similar 'romantic readiness' (p. 6) in Daisy as in Gatsby, and during the famous scene in Gatsby's mansion, Daisy herself expresses the same desire to escape the temporal world. '"I'd like to just get one of those pink clouds"', she tells Gatsby, '"and put you in it and push you around"' (p. 74). If Daisy fails to measure up to Gatsby's fantasy, therefore, he for his part clearly fails to measure up to hers. At the same time that she exists as the ideal object of Gatsby's quest, in other words, Daisy becomes his female double. She is both anima and *Doppelgänger*, and *The Great Gatsby* is finally the story of the failure of a mutual dream. The novel describes the death of a romantic vision of America and embodies that theme in the accelerated dissociation – the mutual alienation – of men and women before the materialistic values of modern society. Rather than rewriting the novel according to contemporary desires, such a reading of Daisy's role merely adds a complementary dimension to our understanding and appreciation of a classic American novel.

A persistent problem for the contemporary critic of *The Great Gatsby* is the reliability of Nick Carraway as narrator, and certainly any effort to revise current opinion of Daisy's role must begin with Nick. Without rehearsing that familiar argument in detail, we can safely suggest that Nick's judgement of Daisy (like his judgement of Gatsby) proceeds from the same desire to have his broken world 'in uniform and at a sort of moral attention forever' (p. 5). Returning to a Middle West which has remained as pure as the driven snow he remembers from his college days, Nick flees an Eastern landscape and a cast of characters which have become irrevocably 'distorted beyond [his] eyes' power of correction' (p. 137). Life, he concludes, is 'more successfully looked at from a single window, after all' (p. 7), and the same tendency to avoid the complexity of experience becomes evident in Nick's relationship to women.[20]

While he is far more circumspect and pragmatic than Gatsby, in his own way Nick maintains a similarly fabulous (and safely distanced) relation to women. In effect, he represents another version of that persistent impulse among Fitzgerald's early protagonists (for example, Amory Blaine, Anthony Patch, Dexter Green [of 'Winter Dreams'], Merlin Grainger of '"O Russet Witch!"') to abstract women into objects of selfish wish-fulfillment. Nick, after all, has moved East at least in part to escape a 'tangle back home' (p. 48) involving a girl from Minnesota to whom he is supposedly engaged. And in New York he has had a 'short affair' with a girl in the bond office but has 'let it blow quietly away' because her brother threw him 'mean looks' (p.46). In both cases Nick seems desperate to escape the consequences of his actions; he prefers unentangled relationships. Indeed, he seems to prefer a fantasy life with Jordan and even with nameless girls he sees on the streets of New York: 'I liked to walk up Fifth Avenue', he admits, 'and pick out romantic women from the crowd and imagine that in a few minutes I was going to enter into their lives, and no one would ever know or disapprove. Sometimes, in my mind, I followed them to their apartments on the corners of hidden streets, and they turned and smiled back at me before they faded through a door into warm darkness (pp. 46–7). Even with Jordan, Nick manifests the sort of attraction to uncomplicated little girls that will seem almost pathological in Dick Diver of *Tender is the Night*. Jordan, he enjoys thinking, rests childlike 'just within the circle of [his] arm' and because he has no 'girl whose disembodied face floated along the dark cornices and blinding signs' (p. 63), Nick tightens his grip on Jordan, trying to make of her what Gatsby has made of Daisy.

Despite the tendency of critics to view her as a 'monster of bitchery,'[21] Daisy has her own complex story, her own desires and needs. '"I'm p-paralyzed with happiness"' (p. 11), she says to Nick when he meets her for the first time, and even though there is a certain insincerity in her manner, Daisy's words do perfectly express the quality of her present life. In choosing Tom Buchanan over the absent Gatsby, Daisy has allowed her life to be shaped forever by the crude force of Tom's money. According to Nick's hypothesis, 'all the time [Gatsby was overseas] something within her was crying for a decision. She wanted her life shaped now, immediately – and the decision must be made by some force – of love, of money, of unquestionable practicality – that was close at hand' (p. 118). Yet Daisy discovers as early as her honeymoon that Tom's world is hopelessly corrupt; in fact, Daisy's lyric energy (which so attracts Gatsby) must be frozen before she will marry Buchanan.

In a scene which has attracted remarkably little critical attention, Jordan tells Nick of Daisy's relationship with Gatsby in Louisville and of her marriage to Tom. Despite the $350,000-dollar string of pearls around her neck, when Daisy receives a letter from Gatsby the night before the wedding, she is ready to call the whole thing off. Gatsby's appeal far surpasses Tom's, and the pearls quickly end up in the wastebasket. The important point to recognize is that Gatsby is as much an ideal to Daisy as she is to him. Only Gatsby looks at her – creates her, makes her come to herself – 'in a way that every young girl wants to be looked at sometime' (p. 60). Thus, it is only after she is forced into an ice-cold bath and the letter which she clutches has crumbled 'like snow' that Daisy can marry Tom 'without so much as a shiver' (p. 61). She has been baptized in ice, and with her romantic impulses effectively frozen, Daisy Fay becomes 'paralyzed' with conventional happiness as Mrs. Tom Buchanan. Her present ideal, transmitted to her daughter, is to be a '"beautiful little fool"' because that is the '"best thing a girl can be in this world"' (p. 17).

Although Fitzgerald certainly depicts Daisy as a traditionally mysterious source of inspiration, even here he dramatizes the limitations of the male imagination at least as much as Daisy's failure to live up to Gatsby's ideal. Gatsby's world is founded on a fairy's wing (p. 77), and as the discrepancy between the real Daisy and Gatsby's dream image becomes apparent, Nick observes, Gatsby's count of 'enchanted objects' is diminished by one (p. 73). In effect, Gatsby scarcely apprehended or loved the real Daisy; she was always an 'enchanted object': initially as the 'first "nice" girl he had ever known' (p. 116), and then as the Golden Girl, 'gleaming like silver, safe and proud above the hot struggles of the poor' (p. 117). The essence of Daisy's promise, of course, is best represented by the magical properties of her voice; yet the process by which Nick and Gatsby research the meaning of that essentially nonverbal sound progressively demystifies the archetype. When Gatsby weds his unutterable vision to Daisy's mortal breath, he immediately restricts the scope of her potential meaning. Much like Hawthorne in *The Scarlet Letter*, Fitzgerald demonstrates the recovery and loss of symbolic vision in *The Great Gatsby*.

Early in the novel, for example, Nick only faintly apprehends the uniqueness of Daisy's voice. Like a fine musical instrument, Daisy's voice produces a sound so impalpable and suggestive that it seems purely formal. 'It was the kind of voice', Nick says, 'that the ear follows up and down as if each speech is an arrangement of notes that will never be played again' (p. 11). Full of creative promise, the voice seems to beckon the imagination into a new world of sensation, for 'there was an excitement in her voice that men who had cared for her found difficult to forget: a singing compulsion, a whispered "Listen," a promise that she had done gay, exciting things just a while since and that there were gay, exciting things hovering in the next hour' (p. 11). Here, in short, Daisy's voice seems full of unrealized possibility.

A vivid expression of an archetype which is fluid in form yet suggests nearly infinite designs, her voice inspires both Nick and Gatsby to wild imaginings. Nick, in fact, hears a quality in Daisy's voice which seems at first to transcend the meaning of words. 'I had to follow the sound of it for a moment, up and down, with my ear alone', he says, 'before any words came through' (p. 67). Daisy's effect is thus linked explicitly to the kind of auroral effect that a truly symbolic object produces on an artist's mind, 'bringing out a meaning in each word that it had never had before and would never have again' (p. 84). She seems able to transform the material world into some ephemeral dreamland in which objects suddenly glow with symbolic meaning. Thus, Gatsby 'literally glowed' in Daisy's presence 'like an ecstatic patron of recurrent light' (p. 70), and the objects he immediately revalues 'according to the measure of response [they] drew from her well-loved eyes' (p. 72) suddenly seem no longer real. Existing within a realm of as yet uncreated possibility, Daisy's essential meaning, in short, suggests a psychic impulse too fleeting to be articulated or brought across the threshold of conscious thought. Frantically trying to comprehend the impulse within himself which Daisy's voice evokes, Nick concludes: 'I was reminded of something – an elusive rhythm, a fragment of lost words, that I had heard somewhere a long time ago. For a moment a phrase tried to take shape in my mouth and my lips parted like a dumb man's, as though there was more struggling upon them than a wisp of startled air. But they made no sound and what I had almost remembered was uncommunicable forever'(p. 87).

Like Gatsby with his 'unutterable vision', then, Nick admits his failure to realize (and communicate) the essence of Daisy's meaning. Together, both men effectively conspire to reduce that meaning to a 'single window' (p. 7) perspective. As successfully as the townspeople of *The Scarlet Letter* in their efforts to confine the punitive meaning of Hester's 'A', Nick and Gatsby progressively devitalize Daisy's symbolic meaning until she exists as a vulgar emblem of the money values which dominate their world. Her voice was 'full of money', Nick agrees; 'that was the inexhaustible charm that rose and fell in it, the jingle of it, the cymbals' song of it . . . High in a white palace the king's daughter, the golden girl . . . ' (p. 94). Paralleling Fitzgerald's sense of America's diminishing possibilities, Gatsby's action has the added effect of forfeiting forever his capacity to reclaim Daisy from Tom's influence. When he tries to become a *nouveau riche* version of Tom, Gatsby ceases to have the power to take Daisy back to her beautiful white girlhood. No longer does he look at her with the creative look the 'way that every young girl wants to be looked at' (p. 60); instead, Daisy becomes the victim of what has become Gatsby's irrevocably meretricious look.

Because she, too, seeks a lost moment from the past, Gatsby

succeeds momentarily in liberating Daisy from Tom's world. However, just as the shirts in his closet 'piled like bricks in stacks a dozen high' (p. 72) signal the disintegration of Gatsby's obsessively constructed kingdom of illusion, Daisy's uncontrollable sobbing with her magical voice 'muffled in the thick folds' (pp. 72–3) represents the end of her dream as well. Even as Nick apologizes for its simplicity, Daisy is simply 'offended' by the vulgarity of Gatsby's world (p. 84). Thus, although both characters do enjoy the moment '[i]n between time' possessed of 'intense life' (p. 75) which they have sought, Gatsby and Daisy inevitably split apart. When Tom reveals the real Gatsby as a '"common swindler"' (p. 104), Daisy's own count of 'enchanted objects' (p. 73) also diminishes by one. She cries out at first that she '"won't stand this"' (p. 104), but as the truth of Tom's accusation sinks in, she withdraws herself from Gatsby forever. For the second time, Tom's crude, yet palpable force disillusions Daisy about Gatsby, and in spite of the latter's desperate attempts to defend himself, 'with every word she was drawing further and further into herself, so he gave that up and only the dead dream fought on as the afternoon slipped away, trying to touch what was no longer tangible, struggling unhappily, undespairingly, toward that lost voice across the room' (p. 105). Because she cannot exist in the nether world of a 'dead dream' which has eclipsed everything about her except the money in her voice, Daisy moves back toward Tom and his world of 'unquestionable practicality' (p. 118). Reduced to a golden statute [sic. Editor's Note: should this be 'statue'?], a collector's item which crowns Gatsby's material success, Daisy destroys even the possibility of illusion when she runs down Myrtle Wilson in Gatsby's car.

Not only does she kill her husband's mistress, thus easing her reentry into his life, but she climaxes the symbolic process by which she herself has been reduced from archetype to stereotype. At the moment of impact – the final crash of the dead dream into the disillusioning body of reality – it is surely no accident in a novel of mutual alienation that Daisy and Gatsby are both gripping the steering wheel. Daisy loses her nerve to hit the other car and commit a double suicide (thus preserving their dream in the changelessness of death); instead she chooses life and the seemingly inevitable workings of history. She forces the story to be played out to its logical conclusion: Gatsby's purgative death and her own estrangement from love. Despite Nick's judgement of her carelessness and 'basic insincerity' (p. 17), her conspiratorial relationship with Tom, Daisy is victimized by a male tendency to project a self-satisfying, yet ultimately dehumanizing, image on woman. If Gatsby had 'wanted to recover something, some idea of himself perhaps, that had gone into loving Daisy' (p. 86); if Nick had nearly recovered a 'fragment of lost words' (p. 87) through the inspiring magic of her voice, then Daisy's potential selfhood is finally betrayed by the world of the novel. Hers remains a 'lost voice' (p. 105), and its words and meaning seem 'uncommunicable forever' (p. 87).[22] □

The essays by Person and Korenman are evidence of the new questioning of the roles and representations of women in literary texts that arose in the 1970s. The decade also witnessed a revival of interest in the relationship of psychoanalysis to literature. While any literary text, from any era, is open to a psychoanalytic reading, it may be particularly interesting to apply one to a text – such as *The Great Gatsby* – that was written during the period in which psychoanalytic ideas and techniques were being developed and circulated. This is not only because such a text may have been influenced in some explicit way by psychoanalysis; even if there is no evidence of such an influence, such a text can be linked with psychoanalysis because both emerged in the same cultural and historical moment – which is not to play down the many differences between, say, Freud's Vienna, and Fitzgerald's USA in the late nineteenth and early twentieth century.

Fitzgerald was born in 1896, four years before Freud published one of the founding texts of psychoanalysis, *The Interpretation of Dreams*, and he grew up in the era in which psychoanalytic notions were starting to spread in the USA; in 1909, for example, Freud gave his famous 'Five Lectures on Psycho-Analysis' at Clark University in Worcester, Massachusetts. The most explicit influence of psychoanalysis in Fitzgerald's fiction is in *Tender is the Night*, with its psychiatrist protagonist married to a woman traumatised by an incestuous relationship with her father. But *The Great Gatsby* was published only five years after Freud's *Beyond the Pleasure Principle*, and both texts are haunted by desire and death in ways that might be distinctively related to the cultural situation after the First World War (allowing, once again, for the many differences at this time between the USA and Europe).

A psychoanalytic approach to *Gatsby* need not, however, make specific links between Fitzgerald's novel and those texts of Freud that emerged in the same era. *Gatsby* is open to many other kinds of psychoanalytic interpretation, and an especially powerful one was produced in the later 1970s, A. B. Paulson's 'Oral Aggression and Splitting', which appeared in the Fall 1978 issue of the journal *American Imago*, and was later collected in Harold Bloom's 1986 volume of *Modern Critical Interpretations* of *Gatsby*. Paulson is careful not to claim that a psychoanalytic approach can determine the final meaning of *Gatsby*, and he is aware that such readings may be reductive. But they may also, he suggests, enhance our appreciation of the intricate patterning that Fitzgerald himself wanted *Gatsby* to have.

In his essay, Paulson employs two psychoanalytic notions of splitting: 'splitting of the object' and 'splitting of the ego'. 'Splitting of the object' means the splitting, in phantasy, of the object of love, and it is a notion especially associated with the psychoanalyst Melanie Klein. Klein saw 'splitting of the object' as 'the most primitive kind of defence against anxiety' in which 'the object, with both erotic and destructive instincts directed towards it, splits into a '"good" and a "bad" object'.[23] Thus a mother may, in phantasy, split into a 'good' and 'bad' mother. The 'object' that is split may also be what Klein calls a 'part-object'; a 'part-object' is not the whole person, but a part of the person, usually a part of the body – such as a breast – or its symbolic equivalent – for example, the 'old island' envisioned by Nick Carraway that he calls 'a fresh, green breast of the new world' (p. 140). Applying these ideas to *Gatsby*, Paulson suggests that the good/bad split is figured in the novel in Daisy, on the one hand, who is the good object, the good mother, the object of love, and Myrtle, on the other hand, who is the bad object, the bad mother, the object of aggression – and who is aggressively mutilated in death and provides an almost literal 'part-object' in her torn, loose breast.

The second concept of 'splitting' that Paulson employs is Freud's concept of 'splitting of the ego', in which a component of external reality that prevents the realisation of a desire is, simultaneously, affirmed and denied. Nick Carraway is the most obviously divided character in the novel, and he himself acknowledges that division, at least in some respects. His self-division has, of course, been noted before by critics, but Paulson offers a psychoanalytic interpretation of this split with particular reference to Nick's relationship with Jordan. Jordan, he suggests, is the reassuring (rather than threatening) 'phallic woman', endowed in phantasy with an imaginary phallus. And the way in which Fitzgerald associates Jordan with Daisy at key moments in the novel implies that Daisy may have phallic attributes as well.

Paulson also proposes, drawing on Jeanne Lampl-de Groot, that Myrtle and Daisy can be seen as 'pre-Oedipal' and 'Oedipal' mothers. In the 'pre-Oedipal' phase, the small son may feel intense hostility for the mother; in the 'Oedipal' phase, he loves and admires the mother. In later life, the hostility towards the 'pre-Oedipal mother' may be redirected on to the woman who is regarded as a degraded sexual object – as Myrtle is, in part, in *Gatsby*. Daisy, the revered female object, is the Oedipal mother. But, as Paulson suggests, if Daisy is the Oedipal mother for Gatsby, this is, in psychoanalytic law, his death sentence: like Oedipus, 'he has possessed the mother'.

As we can see, Paulson's argument turns much on mothers; and it may be objected that mothers are not, in fact, prominent in *Gatsby* and that fathers and father-figures feature more strongly – Carraway senior, Dan Cody, Henry Gatz. Paulson acknowledges this, but goes on to suggest that the absent mothers are partly figured by 'three prominent breasts in the text': the 'fresh, green breast of the new world' (p. 140); the 'pap of life' holding the 'milk of wonder' to which Gatsby, before he kisses Daisy for the first time in Louisville, imagines he could climb, 'if he climbed *alone*' (p. 86, [my emphasis]); and the 'left breast . . . swinging loose like a flap' (p. 107) of the dead, mutilated Myrtle Wilson. The first breast is ambiguous in its evocation of both immense promise and irrevocable loss; the second breast is that sucked by the infant as he merges with the mother in a bliss that excludes all else; the third breast is the object of oral aggression, torn and disconnected. We join Paulson's essay at the point at which he focuses on Myrtle's death.

■ [The] malign oral theme in [*Gatsby*] is embodied in a third image of the breast. I have in mind, of course, the breast of Myrtle Wilson as Fitzgerald imagined it after the accident:

> Michaelis and this man reached her first but when they had torn open her shirtwaist still damp with perspiration they saw that her left breast was swinging loose like a flap and there was no need to listen for the heart beneath. The mouth was wide open and ripped at the corners as though she had choked a little in giving up the tremendous vitality she had stored so long. (p. 107)

The emphasis on her mouth is odd here, although it runs parallel to the earlier pairing of 'pap of life' (p. 86) with '[a]t his lips' touch' (p. 87). To my mind, the 'tearing open of the shirtwaist', the mouth that is 'wide open and ripped', and the mutilation itself – which reduces Myrtle's ample flesh to a kind of empty shell: 'swinging loose like a flap' – all this suggests an extremely primitive act of aggression.
. . .

One of the novel's first and most famous readers – Fitzgerald's editor at Scribner's, Maxwell Perkins – also singled out this passage, apparently objecting to it. When Fitzgerald wrote back to defend the scene, he underlined the feeling of desire that I sense in the passage, associating the verb 'ripped' not with the mouth but with the torn breast. He wrote, 'I *want* Myrtle Wilson's breast ripped off – it's exactly the thing, I think, and I don't want to chop up the good scenes by too much tinkering'.[24]

Fitzgerald's phrase 'I don't want to chop up the good scenes' indicates how the specific image of the torn breast underlies a more general theme of destruction in the novel. He claims that he won't 'chop up', yet the scenes whose form he is anxious to preserve and order have as their content a predominant pattern of chopping, breaking, smashing, and falling to pieces. As Ernest H. Lockridge has pointed out, the novel is strewn with dismembered bodies, discon-nected objects, and fragments against whose background Nick Carraway, along with his drive to make connections between things and events, appears as an ordering force.[25]

If one surveys the mass of critical literature devoted to the novel, one is apt to encounter a larger symptom of this 'splitting' and conse-quent doubling in the text. At this more general level, the terms critics most often employ are 'polarity', 'doubles', 'divided', 'ambivalence', with 'duplicity' being a special favourite. R. W. Stallman's list of doubling is a good example of Fitzgerald's technique in the novel [see pp. 64–5] . . .

. . .

If we look back at the scene of [Myrtle's] death, there are details which render it disturbing in other ways. First, what strikes us is how degrading – really dirty – her death is. ' . . . Myrtle Wilson, her life vio-lently extinguished, knelt in the road and mingled her thick, dark blood with the dust' (p. 107). Again, there is something vaguely erotic about the manner in which the two men who reach her body tear open her shirtwaist, as if the occasion were really a sexual assault. Even the description of the car striking her ('"the one comin' from N'York knock right into her"' (p. 109)) has an erotic ring to it. Partly this is a function of the phallic role the automobile plays in the fantasy life of Americans – compare Gatsby's magnificent vehicle. But more impor-tant, it is a function of Fitzgerald's earlier description of adult sexuality in the novel. Especially in the relationship between Myrtle and Tom Buchanan, sexuality is rendered in terms of aggression, dom-inance, and victimization.

Tom first appears in the novel described in phallic terms. There is a moment in that passage when Fitzgerald teasingly moves our atten-tion from his open legs, to his eyes, then down to his boots, up to the boot lacings, then up again, as if he was about to describe the phallus itself:

> Tom Buchanan in riding clothes was standing with his legs apart on the front porch . . . Two shining, arrogant eyes had established dominance over his face and gave him the appearance of always leaning aggressively forward. Not even the effeminate swank of his riding clothes could hide the enormous power of that body – he seemed to fill those glistening boots until he strained the top lac-ing *and you could see a great pack of muscle shifting* when his shoulder moved under his thin coat. It was a body capable of enormous leverage – a cruel body. (p. 9, Paulson's emphasis)

Fitzgerald's little joke here – he betrays it with the phrase 'effeminate swank' – is that for all his power Tom is the sort of man who can exercise his potency only if he is with a certain kind of woman. Myrtle Wilson is such a woman; Tom's chambermaid in Santa Barbara is another. Daisy describes such girls as '"common but pretty"' (p. 83). And it is the aggressive pursuit of such 'common' women that Freud called a 'psychical debasement of the sexual object'. A man like Tom conceives of the sexual act as something degrading and potentially violent; therefore, he seeks out 'a woman who is ethically inferior, to whom he need attribute no aesthetic scruples, who does not know him in his other social relations and cannot judge him in them'. But this figure of the woman as prostitute only exists in tension with another sort of woman to whom such men remain devoted. This, explained Freud, is a woman of 'a higher kind', respected, even over-valued, but who is sexually forbidden.[26] Both, however, taken together, actually comprise the mother who – because she has been split as an object – can be simultaneously preserved as an unreachable, respected woman, at the same time as she is possessed and degraded as a sexual object.

If Myrtle Wilson stands as the degraded half of this split image of the mother, then Daisy Buchanan – especially from the narrator's point of view – represents her counterpart: the unreachable, idealized mother. Indeed, Daisy is the only biological mother in the novel, while the emotional distance she places between herself and her daughter as she retreats from the business of childrearing only empha-sizes how aloof and unreachable she is as a maternal figure. Fitzgerald pictures her '[h]igh in a white palace the king's daughter, the golden girl' (p. 94). But Daisy's ostensible 'girlishness' only betrays the unconscious fantasy that Gatsby projects out of early adolescence and then internally pursues with outstretched arms. For Daisy is really a 'first love' to which he remains so intensely faithful that we wonder if it is not some earlier woman – that *first* 'first love' of all little boys – to whom he is so fanatically devoted.

. . .

If we sort Daisy and Myrtle into the categories of Oedipal and pre-Oedipal mothers, then several things become clear. First, it explains an odd vacuum placed just at the point where Gatsby finally reaches and possesses the unreachable woman. 'The worst fault in it', Fitzgerald wrote after the novel was published, 'I think it is a BIG FAULT: I gave no account (and had no feeling about or knowledge of) the emotional relations between Gatsby and Daisy from the time of their reunion to the catastrophe'.[27] I would argue that Fitzgerald 'had no feeling about or knowledge of' this relationship because, as the for-bidden possession of a forbidden object, it is simply 'unimaginable'.

Seeing the '"nice" girl' (p. 116), Daisy, as an Oedipal mother also makes clear our response to Gatsby's death, which in the novel is called 'accidental' (p. 126) yet which nevertheless has a kind of tragic inevitability to it. Gatsby must die because his offence is severe: he has possessed the mother. And he is killed by two of the several father figures scattered throughout the novel; that is, by Wilson in collusion with Tom. Tom is particularly good as a pivotal character in the novel (one who will play the role of 'bad boy' who pursues Myrtle as a 'bad mother', as well as the role of threatening Oedipal father), because he is chronologically about the same age as Nick Carraway, yet his wealth and power make him superior as a 'man', yet who still functions emotionally and intellectually as a child. Again, Wilson in the early part of the novel is characterized as a child until the point at which he dominates and possesses Myrtle by locking her in her room. Throughout the novel, one might say, the male characters struggle towards manhood – and fatherhood – by fighting for possession of women. It is, for example, just when Wilson locks Myrtle up that [Nick] pays him an ambiguous compliment; he says Wilson looked 'as if he had just got some poor girl with child' (p. 97). Thus it is Wilson, as weak father magically become potent, inspiring moral strength from the Wasteland God Dr. Eckleburg, and guided by Tom's directions, that finally – gun in hand – takes revenge on Gatsby for his Oedipal crime.

There is another elaboration of Freud's notion (splits in object choice) that will take us one step closer to understanding the manner in which Daisy and Myrtle function as Oedipal and pre-Oedipal mothers. First, we can add that unworthy, degraded women are seen as castrated in the unconscious. This is one dimension of that abrupt nightmarish moment when Tom, at the end of the raucous party, breaks Myrtle's nose. More important, it is, I think, the final reason why Myrtle's death makes us so uncomfortable. The breast 'swinging loose like a flap' (p. 107) is also a kind of symbolic castration that stamps her as debased. Now, the correlative notion, that the Oedipal mother (and here I mean Daisy) is not castrated, requires some explanation. For here we cross over the realm of objects that are split to a second meaning of Freud's term: splits within the ego.

Briefly, to fill in the theory, there is a class of neurotic disorders activated by castration anxiety (that is, homosexuality, exhibitionism, transvestism, and fetishism) which all revolve around the dream of the hermaphrodite; that is, the woman with a penis. Freud traced this idea back to a common misconception in children's ideas about sexuality. Most children, he argued, discard this belief under the pressure of reality. But others, for a number of reasons, cling to this old vision because they cannot tolerate the notion – again a mistaken one – of castrated beings in the world. This fear is the source of terror that so-called 'phallic women' (the Medusas and witches riding broomsticks) hold for men. Such women are perceived as castrated in spite of the symbolic phalluses they exhibit. Now there is another sort of 'phallic woman' whose effect is somewhat different. That is to say, the woman reassuringly endowed – at the unconscious level – with an imaginary phallus which then makes her tolerable as a sexual partner. Individuals who entertain this fantasy in order to make their sexual objects acceptable must at once affirm and deny that women possess such an organ. This is, they must have that ability prized by Fitzgerald 'to hold two opposed ideas in the mind at the same time, and still retain the ability to function'.[28] To do this, in Freud's terms, there must occur a split in the ego. I shall argue, then, that the unconscious dynamics which underlie genital perversions, if applied to imagery, events, and characters in the text, make sense of much that otherwise remains inexplicable . . .

In *The Great Gatsby*, the one character who seems to have this ability to split himself into two halves, to be 'simultaneously enchanted and repelled' (p. 30), is the narrator, Nick Carraway. It is appropriate, then, that Nick will choose for 'his girl' the hermaphroditic Jordan Baker. Lionel Trilling was the first to note that Jordan was 'vaguely homosexual' (see pp. 54, 55). It is partly her disinterest in men that gives this impression, partly the punning symbolic resonance of her golf clubs and balls, but mostly – as with Tom Buchanan – it is a matter of posture, of her whole body really. Recall Nick's first careful look at her: he says, 'I enjoyed looking at her. She was a slender, small-breasted girl with an erect carriage which she accentuated by throwing her body backward at the shoulders like a young cadet' (p. 12). This motif of 'the soldierly girl' is one which Otto Fenichel has linked to a fantasy in which the 'girl' plays the unconscious role of phallus.

. . .

But if Jordan is in some sense a phallic woman in the novel, Fitzgerald twins her with Daisy so many times that it is tempting to search for phallic characteristics in her as well. As the 'golden girl' (p. 94) for example, she is the perfect woman; that is, as Oedipal mother, unmutilated, uncastrated. But unlike Jordan, it is not posture that Fitzgerald employs to characterize Daisy, rather it is the mysterious quality of her voice. Now it happens that there are a number of psychoanalytic case histories in which the voice of a woman played the unconscious role of 'female phallus'. If this unconscious equation between the voice and the hermaphroditic ideal seems farfetched, one need only recall the fascination with which eighteenth-century Western Europe regarded the castrati in Italian opera. Appropriately, in Daisy's case, her voice has the power to subdue men, to make them lean toward her. The repeated imagery which Nick employs is that '[i]t was the kind of voice that the ear follows up and down' (p. 11). If this up and down rhythm in the voice, along with the similarities to Jordan Baker, as well as some of the less than 'fresh' associations to the name of Daisy itself (one thinks of homosexual slang . . .) – if all these indicate that Daisy at some level functions as a girl-phallus, then it may make clear one of the most enigmatic scenes in the novel. I have in mind the one scene set in Gatsby's bedroom to which Nick is again an enchanted and repelled observer. Here Gatsby flings out his many-coloured shirts into a 'soft rich heap' that mounts higher with a kind of erotic but uncomfortably fetish-like intensity, until a climax is reached:

> Suddenly with a strained sound Daisy bent her head into the shirts and began to cry stormily.
>
> "They're such beautiful shirts," she sobbed, her voice muffled in the thick folds. "It makes me sad because I've never seen such – such beautiful shirts before." (pp. 72–3)

I've never been able to make much sense out of what Daisy says in this scene. But the significance may all lie in the dramatization (the 'strained sound', the 'bent head', the 'crying', 'sobbing' and 'voice muffled in the thick folds') in which Gatsby, uniting fetish with his girl-phallus, provokes what amounts to an ejaculation. After a morning of anxious doubt, Gatsby has found a triumphant means for at once possessing and preserving the unreachable woman.[29] □

Paulson's essay concludes with an analysis of Nick as an 'anal character' – the kind of character whom Freud, in his essay 'Character and Anal Erotism [sic]' (1908) defined as 'orderly, parsimonious and obstinate'.[30] Nick's retreat to the Middle West is a retreat to order and away from the complications of adult sexuality. His final vision of the 'fresh, green breast' (p. 140) signifies, on one level, the breast that is to be – which historically has been – the object of aggression: the land that will be ravaged by the American colonists. On another level, however, Nick's extended description of the 'fresh, green breast', with its blending of feminine and masculine features ('flowered'/'trees'), is an androgynous, reassuring image, 'in the face of vexing fears about gender and sexual identity'.[31]

There is another aspect of the 'vexing fears about gender and sexual identity' in *Gatsby* that began to be publicly addressed in the late 1970s. As Paulson recalls, Lionel Trilling, back in 1945, had called Jordan Baker 'vaguely homosexual'; but what of the sexual orientation of Nick himself? For example, is Jordan Baker, as Paulson argues, the kind of 'phallic woman' with whom Nick feels safe, or is she a substitute man? And what of Nick's feelings for Gatsby?

The idea that there was a gay subtext to *Gatsby* had been around for some time. In Ken Kolb's novel *Getting Straight* (1967), the protagonist, Harry, has to attend an oral exam for his Literature MA. One of his interrogators, Dr Lysander, 'seeker of ids and egos beneath the lush verbiage'[32] draws attention to the masculine qualities of Jordan Baker and observes that she was '"not attractive enough for the romance to overshadow the primary repressed love – that of Carraway for Gatsby!"'. Harry reacts inwardly with disgust, only able to stare silently. 'It was like something you'd find written in a public toilet in a bad neighbourhood. Nick Carraway is queer for Jay Gatsby.' He dismisses Lysander to himself as 'a raving maniac'.[33] But the very vehemence of Harry's dismissal could suggest that the issue is not so easily disposed of. And so it was to prove.

The first essay that extensively explored the gay subtext of *Gatsby* appeared in 1979 in the journal *English Studies in Canada*. Its author was Keath Fraser, and it was innocuously entitled 'Another Reading of *The Great Gatsby*'. Fraser starts by suggesting that the famous phrase about Gatsby's 'Platonic conception of himself' (p. 77) could allude to Plato's parable in the *Symposium* in which there were originally three circular sexes, hermaphrodite, male and female. An angry Zeus cut them in half like eggs, and the halves now seek to be reunited with each other: the hermaphrodite halves became heterosexual men and women, the female halves became lesbians, and the male halves became homosexuals. Fraser proposes that *Gatsby* is 'a love story . . . aware of this complex sexuality of antiquity'.[34]

Fraser then points to the possible sexual innuendoes in the scenes near the end of Chapter Two where, after the party in Myrtle's apartment, Nick and Mr McKee – 'a pale feminine man' (p. 26) – go home together. As Nick and McKee go down in the lift, the elevator boy snaps '"Keep your hands off the lever"' and Mr McKee apologises for this unconscious transgression – '"I didn't know I was touching it"' (p. 32). The 'lever' can be read as a phallic symbol, as can the 'great portfolio' that McKee, 'sitting up between the sheets, clad in his underwear' shows to Nick, who is 'standing beside his bed' (p. 32). Fraser does not claim that this scene can be definitively interpreted as a homosexual encounter, but he does see it as an example of the 'ambiguity' of the 'treatment of sex in the novel' – an ambiguity that may be read as a 'cultivated'[35] ambiguity on the part of Nick to hide '[a]n uncertain sexuality'.[36] And an understanding of his 'disingenuous sexuality'[37] may help to explain why Nick feels, at the end of the novel, that the *'orgastic* future . . . year by year recedes before us' (p. 141, [my emphasis]).

The extract from Fraser's essay that follows starts by referring to Leslie A. Fiedler's 1967 interpretation of *Gatsby* in *Love and Death in the*

American Novel (see pp. 99–103), goes on to explore Nick's interest in Tom's masculinity, and suggests how Tom and Wilson are contrasted in terms of images that relate to sexual potency.

■ Still of little interest to scholars is the way Fitzgerald handles sexuality in his writings. The truly great artists, according to Virginia Woolf, are androgynous in mind, and Leslie Fiedler, in passing, has noted this interesting quality in Fitzgerald (it is a quality Fiedler is reluctant to admire) . . . Fitzgerald himself, of course, acknowledged that 'I am half feminine – at least my mind is . . . Even my feminine characters are feminine Scott Fitzgeralds'.[38] [(see also p. 158)] This last sentence could be put another way: his masculine characters are masculine Scott Fitzgeralds, which is to say they are no less feminine than his own 'half feminine' mind. At the party in Myrtle Wilson's flat, for example, Nick, looking out the window, makes an admission which is generally read as a comment on the tension created by the technique which critics have admired in the novel: Fitzgerald's ability to observe as well as to participate: 'I was within and without, simultaneously enchanted and repelled by the inexhaustible variety of life' (p. 30). It has never been read as a suggestion of the narrator's epicene nature.

Writing to Maxwell Perkins before the publication of his novel, Fitzgerald confessed that 'it may hurt the book's popularity that it's *a man's book*'.[39] By this he meant that his best characters were men and that his women faded out of the novel. In the same letter Fitzgerald had to agree with his editor that until now he had not revealed enough about Gatsby – which would allow Gatsby, and not Tom Buchanan, to dominate his story. Throughout the novel Nick holds the masculine forms of Gatsby and Tom in sharp contrast. For him, Gatsby's form seems preferable to Tom's, yet it is Tom's masculinity which captures Nick's attention in so convincing a manner that critics of the novel, in identifying the grander theme of the American dream, have perceived in Tom the cruel and palpable foil to Gatsby's idealism and illusion. For Nick the 'gorgeous' (p. 6) Gatsby fails to come 'alive' until Jordan Baker explains to him that Gatsby's house was deliberately chosen by its owner to be across the bay from Daisy's own house in East Egg. Then, says Nick, '[h]e came alive to me, delivered suddenly from the womb of his purposeless splendour' (p. 62). In contrast to the insuperably *physical* purpose in the novel of Tom Buchanan, Gatsby and his purpose seem clearly metaphysical, springing agilely from that 'Platonic conception of himself' (p. 77). Imagery associated with Gatsby suggests solipsism, sexlessness. It is otherwise with Tom: 'Not even the effeminate swank of his riding clothes', Nick observes, 'could hide the enormous power of that body – he seemed to fill those glistening boots until he strained the top lacing and you could see a great pack of muscle shifting when his shoulder moved under his thin coat. It was a body capable of enormous leverage – a cruel body' (p. 9).

Here is a body of rather more interest to Nick than the one he courts in Jordan Baker. In fact, it fascinates him. As the novel progresses Tom's body comes to represent, far more than Gatsby's corruption and criminal associates do, the threat and evil force of the book. 'Making a short deft movement Tom Buchanan broke her nose with his open hand' (p. 31). The nose, of course, is Myrtle's. Myrtle's husband, on the other hand, suffers Tom's cruelty in a more subtle and central way, reaching its culmination on the fatal day Nick lunches with the Buchanans. The day is blisteringly hot. On his way to lunch Nick comments to himself, 'That anyone should care in this heat whose flushed lips he kissed, whose head made damp the pajama pocket over his heart!'. Upon entering Tom's house he records what he overhears: '"The master's body!" roared the butler into the mouthpiece. "I'm sorry Madame but we can't furnish it – it's far too hot to touch this noon!"' Nick then adds: 'What he really said was "Yes . . . Yes . . . I'll see"' (p. 89). In fact the caller is Myrtle's husband, hard up for cash, hoping that Tom will sell him the car on which Wilson hopes to make enough profit to take his wife away. What Nick purports to hear first is an illusion, yet it is an illusion artistically contrived to make the scene which follows between Tom and Wilson at the garage all the more adroit with respect to the underlying competition between the two rivals for Myrtle Wilson's favours. More particularly, it causes us to examine Nick's own narration of the scene.

> "Let's have some gas!" cried Tom roughly. "What do you think we stopped for – to admire the view?"
> "I'm sick," said Wilson without moving. "I been sick all day."
> "What's the matter?"
> "I'm all run down."
> "Well, shall I help myself?" Tom demanded. "You sounded well enough on the phone."
> With an effort Wilson left the shade and support of the doorway and, breathing hard, unscrewed the cap of the tank. In the sunlight his face was green.
> "I didn't mean to interrupt your lunch," he said. "But I need money pretty bad and I was wondering what you were going to do with your old car."
> "How do you like this one?" inquired Tom. "I bought it last week."
> "It's a nice yellow one," said Wilson, as he strained at the handle.
> "Like to buy it?"
> "Big chance," Wilson smiled faintly. "No, but I could make some money on the other."

"What do you want money for all of a sudden?"
"I've been here too long. I want to get away. My wife and I want to go west." (pp. 95–6)

I want to suggest that this scene, like the McKee scene, is easily passed over, and that the sexual undertow adrift in the particular images which link Wilson and Tom has been carefully set up by Fitzgerald to contrast the two male rivals. We recall that three chapters earlier Nick has admired the incomparable form of Gatsby's car – the one Tom now is driving – 'swollen here and there,' observes Nick, 'in its monstrous length' (p. 51). In *The Great Gatsby* it is worth remembering that the car is a symbol of masculinity, and the women (Jordan and Daisy) who drive cars do so badly, upsetting, even killing people. In the same chapter that Nick draws our attention to Gatsby's proud possession, he also glimpses 'Mrs. Wilson straining at the garage pump with panting vitality as we went by' (p. 54). The scene above, with Tom and Wilson, seems therefore suggestive in the images it chooses to repeat. There is the elongated car driven by the potent Tom; and in the pump yet another phallic image, at which Wilson strains with rather less vitality than his wife, who has thrown him over for Tom.

At this point the afternoon sun continues to play chimerically with Nick's perception – this time of Wilson: '[t]he relentless beating heat was beginning to confuse me and I had a bad moment there before I realized that so far his suspicions hadn't alighted on Tom' (p. 96). What follows is a curious generalization by Nick 'that there was no difference between men, in intelligence or race, so profound as the difference between the sick and the well' (p. 97). It is precisely this difference one feels tempted to rephrase (without necessarily replacing one chimera with another), in order to suggest that in sexual terms what Fitzgerald is implying is that there is no difference so great as the difference between the normal and the abnormal. For Nick goes on to equate Wilson's sickness with guilt – and the simile he uses to illustrate this guilt is, it will have to be agreed, ambivalent: 'Wilson was so sick that he looked guilty, unforgivably guilty – as if he had just got some poor girl with child' (p. 97).

For Wilson (about whom we recall his wife having earlier said he knows nothing about '"breeding"' (p. 30)), such a potent act might indeed be upsetting, indeed abnormal. (Our sense of Wilson's guilt is made the more ambivalent perhaps by our recollection of Tom's earlier joke that Wilson would make quite a suitable study for the effeminate photographer McKee – '"'George B. Wilson at the Gasoline Pump'"' (p. 28).) Naturally what Wilson looks guilty about is having had to lock up his wife – upstairs in the garage. This act is the reality Nick cannot foresee in Chapter II, when he and Tom first visit the garage, and Nick observes only half correctly, 'It had occurred to me that this shadow of a garage must be a blind and that sumptuous and romantic apartments were concealed overhead' (p. 22). There Nick's perception is illusory, but such perception has continued to bear upon what is normal and abnormal. On the day Myrtle is to die, Nick has overheard Tom telling Gatsby, '"I've heard of making a garage out of a stable . . . but I'm the first man who ever made a stable out of a garage"' (p. 92). As a stud, Tom clearly has what Wilson does not, though he, as much as Wilson, has made a mess of his relationship with Myrtle. The curious conjunction of these two men is the inevitable result of Nick's apparently random association of garages, cars, pumps, and cameras; for in spite of the romantic ideals normally associated with Nick, the reality of sex through his eyes is both a shifty and a mechanical proposition.

After Myrtle's death it is the 'enormous leverage' (p. 9) of Tom's body (earlier observed by Nick in the same, apparently irrelevant way as the 'lever' (p. 32) in the elevator with McKee) which seems to pry its way into the garage where Wilson has begun to come apart, gripping the doorposts of his office. 'His eyes would drop slowly from the swinging light to the laden table by the wall and then jerk back to the light again and he gave out incessantly his high horrible call. "O my Ga-od! O my Ga-od! O Ga-od! O my Ga-od!"' (p. 108). This orgastic call emitted in mechanical jerks, seems complemented in the next sentence by Tom when he lifts his head with a 'jerk' (the word repeated). Tom proceeds to extricate himself from the death for which he is, in effect, responsible (though of course, ironically, it is his wife who has driven over Myrtle, in Gatsby's car), by seizing Wilson 'firmly by the upper arms', telling him with 'soothing gruffness' (p. 109) to pull himself together. The narrator tells us Tom keeps 'his hands firm on Wilson's body', insisting to the investigating policeman that Wilson is a friend of his, and claiming that car which '"did it"' was yellow; the colour of his car, he says, is blue. Then he picks up Wilson 'like a doll' (p. 110), deposits him in a chair, and escapes with Nick in tow. Worth noting, I think, is that Tom has no more perceived his cruelty to Wilson than he has his cruelty to Daisy, when much earlier she accuses him of injuring her little finger. '"You did it, Tom . . . I know you didn't mean to but you *did* do it. That's what I get for marrying a brute of a man, a great big hulking physical specimen of a – "' (p. 13). If it is the lover which intrigues Nick in Gatsby, it is the man which intrigues him in Tom; our failure to notice the delicate way in which Fitzgerald allows Nick to perceive Tom's relationship with Wilson has limited our response to the full play of sexuality in the story. Fitzgerald, by letting Nick have the kind of reverberating observations he does – observations increasingly integral to the way his narrator comes to look at the world – creates a kind of sexual anarchy in *The Great Gatsby*. It is a narrative of potency and impotency, of jealous sex and Platonic love, of sexuality, in fact, owing more to the simultaneity of withinness and withoutness than the narrator appears to be aware of confessing.[40] □

Fraser's essay, along with the essays of Person, Korenman and Slater, and John L. Callahan's book, comprised, in the 1970s, a provocative series of challenges to the accepted readings of *Gatsby* that had emerged in the Fifties. Moreover, as the 1980s approached, a more general transformation of literary studies was taking place, under the impact of post-structuralism, deconstruction, feminism and post-modernism. The consequences for *Gatsby* criticism are explored in our final chapter.

CHAPTER FIVE

New Roads To West Egg

Brecht, Bakhtin and Baudrillard at Gatsby's party; postmodernism, popular culture and gender in *Gatsby* criticism in the 1980s and 1990s

THE CHALLENGES in the 1970s to accepted interpretations of *The Great Gatsby* were not, in fact, widely taken up in the following decade. Of course, much attention continued to be devoted to the novel, and the Fitzgerald industry in general kept on expanding. But a sign of the comparative critical inertia of *Gatsby* studies in the Eighties is provided by a volume called *New Essays on 'The Great Gatsby'*, which appeared in 1985, sixty years after the novel's first publication. Edited by the godfather of Fitzgerald biography and bibliography, Matthew J. Bruccoli, the book is most notable for a fascinating essay called '*Gatsby's* Long Shadow', about the immense cultural influence of *Gatsby* and the way in which the book, and the character, have been echoed in American culture, in film and in fiction by other writers, in novels that range from J. D. Salinger's *The Catcher in the Rye* (1951) to John Irving's *The Hotel New Hampshire* (1981). But, insofar as the title of Bruccoli's collection might imply that we are being offered new *critical* approaches to *Gatsby*, it is misleading: the more strictly critical essays in the book are perfectly competent but have little new to offer. Susan Resneck Parr's 'The Idea of Order at West Egg', for example, fails to live up to the promise of its brilliant title, offering a fairly orthodox reading of *Gatsby* whose concluding paragraph reaffirms familiar, unexceptionable sentiments: 'The dilemma that Nick, Daisy, and Gatsby face is, of course, a human one as well as an American one: whether to embrace the dreams of youth and keep alive the hopes bred in innocence or to face the reality that such dreams are inevitably elusive and illusory because they are part of the past'.[1] As the inclusion of Daisy with Nick and Gatsby in this quotation suggests, however, Resneck is notably more sympathetic to Daisy than critics of previous decades, comparing her to Gatsby as a character who '[a]t crucial moments in her life . . . deliberately chooses to embrace certain illusions and play certain roles as a way of creating for herself a sense of meaning and purpose and as a way of coping with "the pressure of the world outside" (p. 118)'.[2]

The collections of essays edited by Scott Donaldson (1984) and by Harold Bloom (1986) are more adventurous. Bloom reprints full versions of the essays by Paulson and Fraser from which extracts were given in the last chapter of this Guide, although these two essays were, of course, first published in the 1970s. Fraser's essay also features in Donaldson's volume, which is generally more substantial, interesting and useful than Bloom's. Donaldson gathers a range of critical material from past decades and also offers a section called 'Fresh Approaches' that includes seven essays, one of them Keath Fraser's. Fraser's essay provides the freshest approach, but two other essays start to open up new perspectives, even if they do so with rather old tools. In 'Beneath the Mask: The Plight of Daisy Buchanan', Sarah Beebe Fryer – acknowledging, at the outset of her argument, the essays by Korenman and Person at which we looked in the previous chapter of this Guide – offers a sensitive and thoughtful defence of Daisy, seeing her as torn between a desire for personal freedom (represented by her love for Gatsby), and her fear of emotions and need for stability. This essay later formed part of Fryer's book *Fitzgerald's New Women: Harbingers of Change* (1988). It is a valuable defence of Daisy, but it is conducted very much in terms of traditional character analysis, treating Daisy as if she were a real person: it does not seek to locate her within wider fictional and non-fictional systems of the representation of gender. Ross Posnock's essay aligns Fitzgerald with Marx and, more particularly, with the Hungarian Marxist critic and theorist Georg Lukács, whose *History and Class Consciousness* was published two years before *Gatsby*: Posnock sees Fitzgerald in *Gatsby* as concerned, like Lukács, with commodity fetishism and the contradictions of capitalism and as able to grasp them, in the novel, as a totality, an antagonistic whole. But Posnock's Marxism, like Fryer's character analysis, is of a rather old-fashioned kind, and his literary criticism is not especially penetrating or nuanced.

One essay of the 1980s that does draw partly on Marxism, but which offers a more sophisticated and more original analysis of *Gatsby* than Posnock's account, had, in fact, appeared two years before the publication of Donaldson's volume, in the *Journal of American Studies*. Richard Godden's '*The Great Gatsby*: Glamour on the Turn' highlights those points in the novel at which Gatsby's self-projection seems to falter. There is, for example, the moment when Gatsby says to Nick '"I'll tell you God's truth"', declares that he is '"the son of some wealthy people in the middle-west"', and then, when Nick asks him in what part of the Middle West his people lived, replies: '"San Francisco"' (p. 52). Godden observes: '[t]he creator of a criminal network operating bond-fraud on a national scale can surely manage better lies than the one about San Francisco?'[3] Such apparent slips, Godden suggests, can be read as operating like deliberate mistakes; it could be that Gatsby, in such moments, is functioning like a Brechtian actor who draws attention to the fact that he is playing a role, not through incompetence, but in order to jolt the audience out of their consoling illusions and make them aware of an uncomfortable reality. Rather than Gatsby's personality being, as Nick claims at the outset of his narrative, 'an unbroken series of successful gestures', (p. 6), it is, as indeed Nick cannot help recording, full of what could be regarded as calculatedly broken, unsuccessful gestures – although, Godden provocatively suggests, it may be difficult to see them in this way when those for whom they are performed 'wish to see glamour and to prefix Gatsby with "Great"' – a category that, it is implied, clearly includes a high proportion of *Gatsby*'s readers and critics.

The extract that follows attacks those many readings of *Gatsby* that talk of the novel in such terms as love, dream, tragedy and romance, and draws attention to its references to money, which Nick both records and which, sometimes, he also tries to elide. Godden alights, for example, on the hitherto little-noticed detail that Gatsby, while he is waiting for Daisy in Nick's bungalow, 'look[s] with vacant eyes' (p. 66) through a copy of Henry Clay's book *Economics: An Introduction for the General Reader* (1918).[4] Godden constructs a Gatsby who 'responds to the vibrancy of market emotions', very much a Gatsby for the 1980s, for a decade when market forces seemed very sexy. Whereas many critics tend to run together Gatsby's famous comment that Daisy's '"voice is full of money"' and Nick's elaborations and displacements of that idea – 'High in a white palace the king's daughter, the golden girl' (p. 94) – Godden opens the gap between the two registers of language, sharpens the difference between an economic and a fairy-tale discourse, brings out the way in which Nick's romantic mellifluousness obscures but cannot wholly repress the dialogue he would, at this point, rather not hear: a dialogue in which 'love meets money and adultery speaks to class'.

■ . . . readers have alleged the 'eternally human' in Gatsby's life and have called up a vocabulary of timeless verities, 'love', 'dream', 'tragedy'. In Gatsby and Daisy Buchanan a 'universal situation' is discovered, if the 'American Dream' can be spoken of so generically. As Brecht said of 'bourgeois theatre':

> [i]ts story is arranged in such a way . . . that . . . Man with a capital M . . . express[es] himself: a man of every period and every colour. All its incidents are just one enormous cue and this cue is followed by the 'eternal' response: the inevitable, usual, natural, purely human response.[5]

The cues that emanate from Gatsby are, however, cues from a different theatre:

"Her voice is full of money," he said suddenly.

That was it. I'd never understood before. It was full of money – that was the inexhaustible charm that rose and fell in it, the jingle of it, the cymbals' song of it . . . High in a white palace the king's daughter, the golden girl . . . (p. 94)

Nick has heard and chosen not to listen: his rhythm is melodious, his phrasing assonant, his reference literary – an orchestration of the cash nexus. As a commentary on Gatsby's observation the whole statement is liable to fall to pieces, with fault lines developing along the ellipses: in the gaps, love meets money and adultery speaks to class – a dialogue in which Nick would rather not participate.

The failure is doubly disappointing in that it is a dialogue that Gatsby wants heard and that Nick is elsewhere capable of hearing. Reporting later on the early courtship he notes:

She had caught a cold and it made her voice huskier and more charming than ever and Gatsby was overwhelmingly aware of the youth and mystery that wealth imprisons and preserves, of the freshness of many clothes and of Daisy, gleaming like silver, safe and proud above the hot struggles of the poor. (p. 117)

The passage is not without its evasions. To whom does the pun belong and is its economic force muted by its alliteration? 'Safe' may be rendered so, as [Thorstein] Veblen's assertion that 'the leisure class live by the industrial community rather than in it'[6] is deflected into an aesthetic niceness that matches 'cold' with 'hot'. Nonetheless, Nick hears 'silver' as a synonym for 'coinage'. Like 'safe', the word is 'double-voiced', uncomfortably aware of another voice alongside, attempting an alternative social inflexion.[7] Nick's lyricism gives way to its own inner polemic and releases Gatsby's resistant voice, reporting directly the surprise of one from the lower orders on being invited into the 'white palace' by 'the golden girl' (p. 94) – '"She thought I knew a lot because I knew different things from her . . ."' (p. 117).

By 1922 Gatsby is less shockable: in asking Nick to set up a meeting that will preface the affair, and in requesting the use of Nick's bungalow for his purpose, Gatsby is hiring a pimp to make a 'gonnegtion'. There is a pay-off:

"You're selling bonds, aren't you, old sport?"
"Trying to."
"Well, this would interest you. It wouldn't take up much of your time and you might pick up a nice bit of money. It happens to be a rather confidential sort of thing."

> I realize now that under different circumstances that conversation might have been one of the crises of my life. But, because the offer was obviously and tactlessly for a service to be rendered, I had no choice except to cut him off there. (p. 65)

By implication, a tactfully phrased offer would have proved acceptable. Why then does Gatsby abjure subtlety? With Cody, Daisy, Wolfsheim, he has his subtleties; with Nick he is obvious, risking 'crisis' in order to juxtapose crime and adultery: to what end? Jay Gatz plays and is the lover – we remember the cut grass, the white flowers, the dripping lilac; do we remember that just before the liaison he reads 'a copy of Clay's "Economics"' (p. 66). The choice is apt in that Gatsby is engaged in economic subversion. He is a thief who steals the 'badge', 'prize', or 'trophy' of a group – in the language of Veblen's *The Theory of the Leisure Class* (1899). As the leisure class female, Daisy's task is to display manifest consumption and manifest leisure; as Veblen has it, '[t]he pervading principle and abiding test of good breeding is the requirement of a substantial and patent waste of time'. She does it rather well, and her capacity for display attracted Gatsby from the first:

> He found her excitingly desirable. He went to her house, at first with other officers from Camp Taylor, then alone. It amazed him – he had never been in such a beautiful house before. But what gave it an air of breathless intensity was that Daisy lived there – . . . There was a ripe mystery about it, a hint of bedrooms upstairs more beautiful and cool than other bedrooms, of gay and radiant activities taking place through its corridors and of romances that were not musty and laid away already in lavender but fresh and breathing and redolent of this year's shining motor cars and of dances whose flowers were scarcely withered. It excited him too that many men had already loved Daisy – it increased her value in his eyes. (p. 116)

Gatsby responds to the vibrancy of market emotions: the *frisson* that he undoubtedly feels exists somewhere between mystery and inventory, between emotional and monetary 'value', between sensuous and economic 'appreciation'. Daisy's quality has a tendency to became a quantity: how many bedrooms, how many men, what brand of car? Even as the object of Gatsby's desire is translated into 'commodity' so Gatsby's desire is commodified:

> [T]his is to say that in the commodity age, need as a purely material and physical impulse (as something 'natural') has given way to a structure of artificial stimuli, artificial longings, such that it is no

longer possible to separate the true from the false, the primary from the luxury-satisfaction, in them.[8]

This does not deny Gatsby his 'romance' – it would be inappropriate to deny the very quality that sells the novel – it sets his 'romance' within a social context, and argues that Gatsby is aware of the contradictions inherent in his adultery. For him Daisy's glamour is glamour on the turn, and he would have Nick know it, but Nick will not be distracted from his simple identification with 'love': he tells us that Gatsby reads Clay's *Economics* with suitably 'vacant eyes' (p. 66). Rather, Gatsby loves Daisy because she is his point of access to a dominant class. Marriage would allow him to harden his liquid assets, but would separate him from his origins and more importantly from those among whom he works – the Wolfsheim milieu. Further, his love ties him to a woman formed to display merchandise, who consequently has repressed her body and cashed in her voice.[9] □

Godden achieves a different perspective on *Gatsby* by inviting Bertolt Brecht to the mystery man's mansion; but, when he describes the words 'safe' and 'silver' as being 'double-voiced', he is summoning from the shadows another unexpected guest, from further afield: the Russian critic and theorist Mikhail Bakhtin, whose work was only rediscovered in Europe in the 1970s and 1980s. It is the thought of Bakhtin that his American translator and expositor Michael Holquist brings to bear on *Gatsby* in his essay 'Stereotyping in Autobiography and Historiography', published in *Poetics Today* in 1988. In a complex argument that approaches Fitzgerald's novel from an unusual angle, Holquist first of all takes issue with the view of the post-colonial theorist Homi Bhabha that the stereotype is to be understood primarily as a quasi-pathological feature of colonial and racist discourse. He argues that, in the light of Bakhtin's account of the way that perception and language work, 'stereotyping is a global activity', 'a universal strategy for seizing the other' and 'perception's normal mode of operation'.[10] It is the way the linguistic sign itself operates. Language constitutes an attempt to fix meaning that is inevitably always unsuccessful. Meaning, in Bakhtin's view, can never be fully frozen; it is always 'double voiced', open to more than one interpretation, and 'dialogic', engaging in exchange and contestation with other voices. Both linguistic sign and stereotype are characterised by ambivalence, since they can never pin down meaning unequivocally, and by lack, since they can never incorporate the full, substantial presence of that which they seek to represent. But stereotyping, like the operation of the sign, cannot be eliminated. Holquist suggests, however, that it may be possible to mitigate the harm that it can do by attending to its effects in particular circumstances.

For Holquist, *Gatsby* is interesting because it offers an example of the operations of stereotyping, not in an obviously colonial situation, but in a largely white and upper class milieu. Moreover, it is a novel that, in a sense, is 'about' stereotyping: the characters stereotype themselves and each other – Gatsby stereotypes Daisy, Daisy stereotypes Gatsby – and the text offers, implicitly throughout and explicitly at the end, a stereotype of 'America'. *Gatsby* also, by means of oxymoron, dramatises the ambivalence and lack that characterise the stereotype, which constantly undermine its attempt to fix meaning.

As a trope or figure of speech, 'oxymoron' is a phrase that brings two contradictory ideas together (for example, 'bitter-sweet'). Holquist points to some oxymoronic phrasing of this kind in the text of *Gatsby* – for instance, 'the rock of the world was founded securely on a fairy's wing' (p. 77); but he also sees oxymoronic-like contradictions and incongruities manifesting themselves on a larger scale throughout the novel – for example, the contradiction between Gatsby's image, or stereotype, of Daisy, and Daisy as she controverts, escapes from, or falls outside that image. For Holquist, it is Gatsby above all who exemplifies the process of stereotyping – a process that, paradoxically, tries to escape from process. Stereotyping involves, Holquist contends, a neo-Platonic perspective that sees the static as more real than the changeable: and Gatsby, born 'from his Platonic conception of himself' (p. 77) and seeking to arrest the flow of time, is a neo-Platonist *par excellence*. We join Holquist's essay at the point at which he starts to develop his analysis of Gatsby:

■ Unlike Jimmy Gatz, the self that chance has assigned him and which is prey to every contingency, 'Jay Gatsby' (p. 115), the self he lusts to produce for himself, is one that will be improved in the sense that it will be liberated from chance, free of intervention from the other, characterized by the absolute stasis of identity that guarantees the higher reality of a god. . . . What is particular about the way Gatsby goes about this task is determined by American history, not only in the apparent features of frontier, dreams of success, invention, etc. but by the very temporality that governs all its major moves. I have argued that, if I am at all right about the nature of stereotyping, its mode of activity must be understood as neo-platonic. A major reason why *The Great Gatsby* is so paradigmatic a text for any attempt to understand the relation of stereotyping to history is that it works out not only the surface features of stereotyping as they are particularized in a specific history, but at the more basic level of temporality as well.

Gatsby, remember, is someone who is seeking to erect his own selfhood, an identity that is whole, immaculate and lasting; bluntly stated, what he needs is a biography free of changes, thus a narrative without time. This is, like the sign or the stereotype, an absurd condition, one that is literally oxymoronic; which is why, at the level of text, the oxymoron dominates *The Great Gatsby*. The Americanness of Gatsby's dilemma is caught in the general term for what he seeks to become: a self-made man. Thus, like Henry Ford, he must believe that 'history is bunk'. America is the sort of place where you can get a 'Jazz History of the World' with no discrepancy felt between the improvisatory nature of jazz and the linear nature of history – the irony being compounded by the composer's name 'Tostoff' (p. 41). The chronotope [Bakhtin's term for an intersection of time and space] of 'self-made' men is one that must be split-level: it requires change and radical change, very rapid change, to move from the contingent space of rags into which such men are thrust by the accident of birth to the absolute space of riches that is all invested with their intention, and thus must be free for contingency and change. Thus they need time at one stage and must deny it at another stage. This double bind determines the dual asymmetry organizing the narrative shape of biographies appropriate to self-made men . . .

It should come as no surprise that Gatsby has great trouble with time. This is especially true as time relates to Daisy, the icon of his individual appropriation of his American dream. As he is about to meet her for the first time after his return from the Army and her marriage, he becomes anxious and says to Nick, who is hosting the meeting, '"[i]t's too late!"'. But Nick points out that it is in fact early for the meeting: '"it's just two minutes to four"' (p. 67). He is out of synchrony with the time of his dream, a point reinforced when he almost knocks over the clock on Nick's mantle. Even at this first meeting, there are hints of a rupture between Gatsby's stereotype of Daisy and Daisy's capacity to be adequate to the stereotype, a problem expressed in temporal terms: 'He had been full of the idea so long, dreamed it right through to the end, waited with his teeth set, so to speak, at an inconceivable pitch of intensity. Now, in the reaction, he was running down like an overwound clock' (p. 72).

Gatsby has trouble with clocks because of his need to deny time. When Nick tells him not to expect too much of Daisy, because you cannot repeat the past, Gatsby, as a good American neo-platonist, is outraged: '"Can't repeat the past?" he cried incredulously. "Why of course you can!"' (p. 86). And of course, as someone who gave birth to himself in the past, he must take such a position. It is the American version of stereotyping, captured as well in the careers of other self-made men, like the brewer who originally built the great mansion Gatsby has bought, a monument to the proposition that you can repeat the past, at least architecturally: it 'was a colossal affair by any standard – it was a factual imitation of some Hôtel de Ville in Normandy'

(p. 8). But it is an eclectic repetition of the past: it has 'Marie Antoinette music rooms and Restoration salons', and its books are kept in '"the Merton College Library"' (p. 71), a location the text gives, like Gatsby's name (p. 115), in quotation marks. But such radical attempts to repeat the past, to make time stop, have consequences for the future. The brewer who built Gatsby's house had wanted to imitate the past so badly he had 'agreed to pay five years' taxes on all the neighbouring cottages if the owners would have their roofs thatched with straw'. But men who spring from themselves, who resist continuity, pay the price in their own genealogies: the brewer goes into decline and '[h]is children sold his house with the black wreath still on the door' (p. 69). Stereotyping history, relating to the past as if it could be packaged and bought and then rearranged not in time but in the fixed space of 'period rooms', has the effect of catapulting Americans back into flux and change so rapid, that 'historical' houses are sold 'with the black wreath still on the door'. The symbol of ultimate stasis, death, is transformed by such haste into a sign of change and movement: new owners come, as Gatsby does, to repeat the dream of fashioning history with a fixed identity, only to fall back into a transience beyond the power of human categories to arrest.

In conclusion, we may say that the house where Gatsby's corpse lies at the end of the novel is his true home insofar as it is an architectural monument to the architectonics of his place in existence, the place at which he has been addressed by the dual mandate of language's requirement for a fixity that always fails. It is a situation in which history in America has been stereotyped into the American dream.[11] □

Bakhtin and Brecht might seem improbable guests at Gatsby's party. But it would not be impossible to imagine such names on Nick's famous list; and, as Godden and Holquist show, those two exotic theorists have something to add to the conversation. Meanwhile, the conversation of the more established critical party-goers continued. The year 1990 saw the publication in the 'Twayne's Masterwork Studies' series of Richard Lehan's *The Great Gatsby: The Limits of Wonder*, an excellent summation that sets *Gatsby* in its historical context and offers clear and perceptive discussion of themes, characters, narrative technique and style. Lehan had, however, first published a book on Fitzgerald in 1967, and his study of *Gatsby* breaks little fresh critical ground. He is not oblivious to new readings of the novel, but he is not especially open to them either, as he shows when he refers to Keath Fraser's interpretation only to dismiss it: '[t]o argue that Nick is a homosexual . . . overparticularizes the scene at the end of Myrtle's party' where Nick finds himself in McKee's apartment with McKee clad in his underwear . . . '[t]o read this scene as other than a comic counterpart to a later tragic blurriness, to see something sinister going on between Nick and McKee, is to distort narrative unfolding, the way language works in this novel, and to impute motives to Nick that otherwise have no bearing – no other connection – in the novel at all'.[12] It is correct to object to any attempt to fix the meaning of the McKee scene – or of any other scene in *Gatsby* – too literally and definitively. But Lehan has fixed Fraser's meaning too definitely. Fraser says, not that Nick is a homosexual, but that his sexuality is 'uncertain'[13] – and it is significant that Edward Wasiolek, in his 1991 essay 'The Sexual Drama of Nick and Gatsby', attacks Fraser for being 'too timid . . . in making firm and definite Nick's homosexual proclivities'.[14] Nor is it the case, as Lehan affirms, that the homosexual implications of the McKee scene have 'no other connection' in the novel: as the extract from his essay printed in the previous chapter of this Guide demonstrates, Fraser suggests 'connections' between the McKee scene and the way Nick responds to Tom Buchanan's body.

But Lehan's study may mark the end of an era. In the 1990s, we are starting to see a range of fresh approaches to *Gatsby*, and we shall look at three important examples of these in this final chapter. We begin with an extract from Patti White's remarkable book of 1992, *Gatsby's Party: The System and the List in Contemporary Narrative*. White's approach is a heady combination of structuralism, post-structuralism, deconstruction, post-modernism, and information and chaos theory. She not only discusses *Gatsby* – she looks also at Don DeLillo's *White Noise* (1985), Thomas Pynchon's *Gravity's Rainbow* (1973), John Barth's *The Sot-Weed Factor* (1960) and Julian Barnes's *Flaubert's Parrot* (1984) – but her analysis of these novels takes the famous list of Gatsby's guests (pp. 49–51) as a model of narrative. White defines narrative as 'a system of systems' or a 'supersystem, a union of relatively autonomous systems that interact in the creation of the conceptual construct "narrative"'.[15] The Gatsby guest list is a paradigm of this, a form of structuring that orders information and produces meaning through a combination of systems – for example, the system of naming, the system of gender division, the system of professional accreditation (*Doctor* Webster Civet), the kinship system ('a whole clan of Blackbucks'), the commercial entertainment system ('connected with the movies'). The link between this guest list and narrative in the more usual sense perhaps becomes clearer if we think of how Fitzgerald's list is rich in incipient stories; the connotations of the names themselves, or the anecdotes attached to the names, could generate much longer narratives.

The extract that follows is the commentary on *Gatsby* that concludes White's book. In this commentary, which draws partly on the work of the post-modernist theorist Jean Baudrillard, White sees Gatsby's West Egg world as a kind of hyperspace, removed from reality, and suggests that Gatsby himself, created from a concept, is a replicant, or what Baudrillard calls a 'simulacrum', a copy that has no original. To the many interpretations of Nick Carraway that critics have made over the years, White adds a new and ingenious one: she compares Nick, in the Gatsby hyperworld, to an anthropologist trying to understand, record and classify an alien culture, but losing the reality of what he seeks to grasp as he turns it into data that can be passed on. White also provides another interpretation of the Nick/McKee scenes. In contrast to Fraser (see p. 130) and to Frances Kerr (see p. 158), she does not raise the issue of homosexuality, but, like Victor A. Doyno in 1969 (see pp. 82–3, 89–91), she focuses on the titles of McKee's pictures. Whereas Doyno, however, in his concern with the patterning of *Gatsby*, interpreted these titles as referring to the overall themes of the novel (such as isolation), White, in her concern with listing, characterises them as a failed list, which cannot hold together or sum up the vision that it seeks to classify and allows that vision, a potentially disturbing 'nightmare' vision of the city, to slip away. Finally, White, like so many critics before her, goes to Gatsby's funeral, a funeral in relation to which, as she points out, the list of guests functions as an absent presence, naming all those who are *not* there.

■ When he moves to West Egg, Jay Gatsby vacates his past and enters a Baudrillardian hyperspace where everything stands at right angles to reality. Distanced from the originary Jimmy Gatz, removed from context and exhibiting no content, the man who inhabits the mansion is essentially a replicant, a facsimile of a Gatsby who can never be accurately stated.

The owl-eyed (nameless) man who admires Gatsby's library understands that a process of replication has taken place; when he sees that Gatsby's books are real (in a way that Gatsby himself is not) Owl-eyes exclaims to Carraway:

"It's a triumph. What thoroughness! What realism! Knew when to stop too – didn't cut the pages. But what do you want? What do you expect?" (p. 38)

Focusing on Gatsby's skilled representation of himself as a man of taste and education, he comprehends the targeted position as one that requires only a limited realism and not the thing itself. However, his tribute ironically marks Gatsby's failure; his perception confirms that Gatsby has not occupied the position of the projected 'genuine' Gatsby, and that the statement of the mansion has therefore been garbled in transmission.

The exchange in the library identifies the mansion as a locus of alterity, as a space inhabited by unstable objects whose relation to context must be suspect. Gatsby, of course, is one of those objects: a token in his own museum, a self objectified both by his own introspection and the distanced gaze of his party guests. The exchange also mimics Carraway's own analytic project when it calls for a set of expectations against which the realistic library can be measured. Carraway, like the other guests, measures Gatsby against the public conception of the man as well as Gatsby's own claims to successful replication; in the end, he participates in Gatsby's complete abandonment of subjectivity by recreating him in narrative.

Baudrillard notes that we are all the subject of ethnological reconstruction, for we live under the glare of examination in a world 'completely catalogued and analyzed and then *artificially revived as though real,* in a world of simulation . . . '[16] Carraway approaches Gatsby as if he were an alien culture, codifying his relationships, recording the reports of informants, tracing and translating his creation myths. In the process, Gatsby as subject disappears; instead, he becomes a body of knowledge, a transmissible information structure with a name twice removed from the original man.

Gatsby's position at the centre of the guest list enacts a cultural statement about the way objects (even human objects) can be known. In Gatsby's world, things are already denatured, distanced by observer evaluations and extracontextual or imaginary relations. Carraway, for instance, envisions Gatsby in Louisville excited by the many men who had loved Daisy before him (p. 116). Gatsby retains his quantitative nature in this vision, but even accurate recreation voids objective presence. Thus, the Carraway version displaces the West Egg Gatsby representation, modulating a replication and thereby threatening an infinite serial regression of hyperreal simulacra.

Gatsby himself is deeply involved in similar projects. Having renovated and recreated his own identity, he dreams of reproducing earlier relations with Daisy, telling Carraway that the past can certainly be repeated if he can only '"fix everything just the way it was before"' (p. 86). He looks to simulation to locate and fix a Daisy who has been removed by time and experience from the position she occupied in Louisville and to recreate a set of relations that have naturally altered over time. His investment in simulation prevents an accommodation with the present and troubles an already unstable subjectivity.

An unstable subject position provides opportunities for objective intrusion and occupation. In the Gatsby hyperworld, groups of tokens enter into subject sites and even replace isolable objects. The green light on the dock is one among a number of 'enchanted objects' (p. 73) that substitute for Daisy, occupying her relational position until her presence finally dismantles the category. An overdetermined pile of shirts pushes Daisy into tears (p. 72), erasing an important Gatsby statement under sensory signals directed at colour, line, and texture. And, when Mr. McKee's set of city scenes rises like a nightmare into a drunken space between Myrtle's apartment and Carraway's cold bench at Pennsylvania Station (p. 32), McKee's vision of the city disappears under a series of mumbled titles, leaving Carraway with another list that fails either to encapsulate or to cohere. In each case, a collection of tokens substitutes for a single object or statement and permits the elision of a potentially disturbing presence.

Indeed, ordering processes on Long Island are noticeably incoherent, severing information from purpose, space from position, and self from subjectivity. On the morning of Gatsby's death, Carraway kills time by making lists of stock quotations (p. 120). This nondirected task models but does not constitute a purposive information construction process. The structure that results is an empty one, with no message that can be forwarded to any receiver. In her New York apartment, Myrtle Wilson makes lists of things to acquire or do (p. 31), but these lists are only relevant within that isolated city space; she cannot transfer her plans to her alternative systemic position without revealing her duality and introducing chaos into the Valley of Ashes. And young Gatsby in Minnesota orders his day around a self-improvement schedule and a set of resolutions (pp. 134–35). As early evidence of a split subjectivity, this project shows a Gatsby already distanced from himself and straddling an internal gap which will subsequently extend itself across his external world. As the sign of a man eventually encircled and effaced by systematization, young Gatsby's list is dismally prophetic.

Human positions within this strange and inordinate system are based upon possession and destruction; relations fracture and shatter in response to turbulence, and reintegration comes from external impositions of order rather than interactive reconfiguration. Nick's narrative accuses Daisy and Tom of seeing others as objects to be smashed and left for still others to clean up (p. 139). This suggests that Gatsby's disintegration can be attributed primarily to the Buchanans, that it results from outside (and identifiable) pressure. Carraway's accusation further indicates his belief that the fragmented Gatsby can be rectified by narrative – again, a completely external operation.

In the end, Gatsby cannot be reintegrated. He remains forever fragmented by Carraway's analysis, separated into his component parts, measured and named, replicated as a character and repositioned within a series of relational systems. Carraway's rage for order, and for knowledge, creates a chaotic monster: 'Gatsby' animates an endlessly replicable and reducible object, one that forms in response and relation to variant concepts and then instantly reveals a disruptive capacity for misstatement and incongruity.

However, the Gatsby system, the Long Island hyperworld, does constitute an integrated and coherent entity. Gatsby, Carraway, the Buchanans, the guests – these are all component positions within an operating information system, one which states itself in its continual reconfiguration of intercomponent relations and contrives a cultural message about order and information in the process. The Gatsby system is finally about analysis and construction rather than Gatsby himself, and Carraway's inability completely to reintegrate his subject keeps the lines of communication open, powering the system through self-statement functions and enabling it successfully to absorb even the chaos of critical debate.

The Great Gatsby thus maintains an interactive relationship with the cultural hypersystem that contains it, participating in the construction of literary discourse and offering itself as a perturberant element in discourses about knowledge and information. Within those discourses, it insists upon the necessity of analytical explanation as it simultaneously proclaims the inadequacy of all explanatory projects. Further, it suggests that temporary collections and systematizations of information are ultimately our only connection with each other and our sole defence against chaos. It derides and feeds our desire for order.

Early in the novel, Carraway spies on Gatsby's silent communion with the night sky and the distant green light and then turns away. When he looks back towards Gatsby's position, he finds that Gatsby has vanished into the darkness (p. 20). This seems to me to represent, elegantly and concisely, the analytic paradox: in this brief scene, the object of observation is fixed, evaluated, defined – and then escapes into chaos as soon as the gaze is lifted.

. . .

None of the named party guests attends Gatsby's funeral. Gatsby goes into the ground surrounded by people whose names appear on no list: Carraway, Owl-eyes, Mr. Gatz, a few servants, and the West Egg postman. And even though the procession is delayed for half an hour, no one else appears from East Egg, West Egg, or New York to swell the pitiful number of Gatsby mourners.

The party guests overwhelm the funeral by virtue of their absence; they crowd the cemetery with conspicuous neglect. In a manifestation of severed social relations, they refuse Gatsby's last act of hospitality and thereby transform their categorical position from one of presence to absence. The party guest list now registers absent mourners – containing identical names in a symmetrical structure that encodes a violently reversed significance. The cohesion of the list tightens under this alteration: the guests enact a unanimous similarity here, and not one of them abandons the confines of the category. Even Klipspringer the boarder declines to attend – in spite of Carraway's concerted efforts to convince him.

Indeed, a disturbing and comprehensive sense of vacancy pervades the occasion: the mourners who do attend the funeral also suggest untenanted positions. Mr. Gatz appears on Long Island bearing tokens of Gatsby's long absence from name and home, young Jimmy's self-improvement schedule and a photograph of the mansion. Though supported 'generously' by his son over the past years, he has nevertheless missed the party and has had no real contact with the replicant being buried under the name of Gatsby. Gatz and Gatsby are systemically non-congruent: each suggests an empty node occupied only by an imaginary other.

The second mourner, the man who once admired Gatsby's library, carries a similar suggestion of vacancy. Although Owl-eyes has a legitimate claim to inclusion in the party guest list, Carraway as narrator refuses acknowledgement of his status. Even his appearance at the funeral does not gain the owl-eyed man a name. Thus he is twice excluded from the record – and his position, though physically tenanted, has no denomination. Since his presence cannot therefore be fully expressed, he must eventually slip away into the abyss of the anonymous.

Finally, Carraway absents himself from the funeral by inhabiting multiscalar modes. Since he occupies an external component as observer/narrator and an internal one as participant in the funeral, he is simultaneously present and absent from the graveside. The resultant turbulence destabilizes both positions – narrator and mourner – and calls into question the entire system of relations, hinting that relations with Gatsby are necessarily those of vacancy with void.

In the end, the problematics of the funeral foreground an essential emptiness, an absence initially defined by the transformed guest list and extended towards inscriptions of name and narrative function. This absence perhaps suggests a fundamental similarity which informs the entire system, a likeness of node to node in which subject and object positions are finally vacated. It is a problematics of chaos, and one which deconstructs the system which encounters it: as everyone becomes relationally invisible, it becomes clear that no one was ever at the party at all.[17] □

As White's reading suggests, there is much in *Gatsby* that relates to postmodernism; but her final evocation of void and vacancy echoes an earlier, high-modernist melancholy – the melancholy, indeed, of *The Waste Land* or of *Gatsby*'s valley of ashes. *Gatsby*, like postmodernism itself, emerged from the modernist moment, and there is much to be learnt by returning the novel to that moment from the perspectives of the 1990s. The last two extracts in this Guide make that return in different ways. Ronald Berman's 1994 book *The Great Gatsby and Modern Times* combines the most enduring aspect of traditional critical practice – close attention to textual detail – with a contextual awareness that takes account of high modernism but also, in a spirit akin to that of modern cultural studies, opens up to the popular culture of early twentieth-century consumer capitalism – which was not by any means wholly melancholy. Berman explores the ways in which the language of the marketplace, the desire for and possession of commodities, pervade the text of *Gatsby*; how its characters draw their models of identity and behaviour from the larger cultural text around them – from childhood reading, from advertising, from consumer commodities, from Broadway theatre, from the movies; how the rhythm of Fitzgerald's prose relates to industrial production; how his images and descriptions are informed by the geometry of industry, of the modern city, and of modernist art; and how his representational techniques resemble those of moving-picture technology, especially of silent films and the cinema. The extract from Berman that follows is from the introduction to his book and provides a concise, clear and fascinating summary of the topics he explores further in subsequent chapters.

■ *The Great Gatsby* devotes much of its narration to the description of industrial things and forms – for example, an apartment [Myrtle's] loaded with the spoils of production. Its own prose rhythm is interrupted by counterpoint: the beat of engines and the metronomic, empty sound of an unanswered telephone. The story takes place within a geometric grid of streets and avenues. When she first meets Tom Buchanan, Myrtle Wilson is on her way to '"a subway train"' (p. 31). Chapter VII is about the life of first-class hotels – and the rest of the text is alive with the mention of places to rent and sell and stay. There are dance halls, rooms that 'always . . . throbbed incessantly' (p. 118) with the sound of the blues. There are those big, cool movies around Fiftieth Street, and also the reiterated presence of movie images in magazines; of movie selves imitated by personality. As for billboards, windows, and luminous signs, they overlook much of the novel's action and provide certain meanings.

Fitzgerald is, however, preoccupied with more than the rendition of objective content. The death scenes of Myrtle and Gatsby are problems in the statement of form, not in the statement of affectiveness. In Myrtle's case, a road is intersected by her line of flight. The car moves along a curved line and leaves her kneeling in parabolic form with her left breast 'swinging loose like a flap' and her mouth open and 'ripped at the corners' (p. 107). Gatsby is last seen moving in circles like those drawn by a compass. Both are studies in stillness and motion.

Description is intensely geometrical. It seeks comparison with artefact and mechanism. And if this novel comes from a home-made world, then many parts have been disassembled, strewn through the pages of the text.

The perception of things in the novel reinforces and eventually redefines our perception of relationships. Few other novels insist so continuously on the difficulty of seeing, judging, even of describing what is seen. Although extremely visual, *The Great Gatsby* is full of barriers to sight and insight. It may be that the dimness of perception of people and things corresponds to the ambiguity of human relationship.

Two of the most important aspects of perception are time and place. But in *The Great Gatsby* their invocation is more than realistic. We are instructed that there are 'at least 450 time words in the novel',[18] yet many of them do the opposite of what we expect. They do not locate us in a chronology of act and experience. Instead, they imply a kind of double vision. It is easy to see that for Gatsby past and present are dangerously undifferentiated – but the reader's sense of time and place is affected also by the way that Nick states his own perceptions and restates the dialogue he remembers. He will do for place what Gatsby does for time: impose upon its specificity the consciousness of what it was – and often what it is not. The text is full of alterations of time and place, reminding us that Eden is on the other side of the Queensboro Bridge, and the abounding blessed isles beyond Long Island Sound.

Fitzgerald's intricate statement of time and place calls our attention to some possible meanings of his text. Throughout the narrative, he alludes to both in interlocking ways. One way is realistic, serving to locate the action in a given chronological sequence over the summer of 1922. We see events, cultural issues, styles, and ideas of this brief period and also of the quarter-century in which it is set. The second kind of time in this novel is connected to an idea of its imbalance like that so recently brought to consciousness by T. S. Eliot in the same year that the novel's events take place. There is a historical world in this text with its own exact chronology, but it subsists within a much deeper temporality.

The historical world is decisively implied, as when the text insists on context. For example, it connects one date, July 5, 1922, with certain events and also with the endless permutations of class and style and self-chosen character in America. The date is just after Independence Day, linked (even being written on the self-expressive form of a timetable) with the progression of names of those who went to Gatsby's. These names suggest social change and personal change and ethnic change; the irresistible forces of social mobility; the alchemy of self-designation; and the 'blurring and loss of identity'[19] of

American democracy. The combination of dating and naming translates listing into something more complex. The same kind of reasoning ought to be applied to another date established by the text, September 12, 1906. That is the date of Jimmy Gatz's SCHEDULE, with its resolution to study 'needed' inventions, that is, those that are conceptually related to a public sense of self; and to read 'improving' books or magazines or those that relate the development of the self to models of excellence (pp. 134–35). The word *improving* has an American history much as the word *earnest* has an English history. One date suggests the dangerously heterogeneous present, the other calls to mind a vanished world of moral certainties and public obligations, the world of Teddy Roosevelt. There are connections throughout Fitzgerald's work between the two worlds.

But in this novel each character has a different sense of time and the text itself differentiates between many ways of locating ourselves in the moving present. We know the timetables for the summer solstice and the commuter train and the escaping years of our lives. Time is connected not only to history but to space. The more Nick Carraway tries to locate himself through the named and known quantities of West Egg on Long Island in North America in the Western Hemisphere the more he finds that he is somewhere he scarcely knows at all. We realize the disparities of time and place when we see the Merton College Library on West Egg; or San Francisco somewhere between Denver and Detroit; or Monte Carlo and Versailles on 158th Street on the West Side. Confusions of time and place impose relativity, affect the co-ordinates of logic as well as geography. We progress (within a very few pages) from New Haven and Westchester and Louisville and Maine and Georgia and Times Square and Oxford and Paris, Venice and Rome, and the Argonne Forest and 'Little Montenegro' (p. 53) to the Pisgah view from the Queensboro Bridge, where all of the above are cancelled out in order to see the created world for the first time. Very little is simply descriptive: we are asked to see a sidewalk in Louisville become Jacob's Ladder; and to lift our eyes from the Buchanan's lawn – or from the printed page – is to see something and some place that is not there.

In addition to chronology and sequence, the dating of particulars, and the temporality of being, time in this text means the dating of ideas. Because so much of the information that is released by the text is connected to serial publication, to what its characters read, we are forced to recognize the momentary quality of that information and of the thought it occasionally inspires. Fitzgerald emphasizes the way that ideas already shaped are distorted through dissemination. Ideas are rarely originated in the text. They are communicated and often translated into their dimmest forms. The text identifies the acquisition of ideas, as when Nick recognizes that Gatsby's 'biography' is an imitation. He tells Nick about living the life of '"a young rajah"' (p. 52) in all the capitals of Europe, collecting jewels, hunting big game, and trying to forget a painful love affair of his past. The facts of his life are fictions put together from other fictions. Hugh Kenner writes that even when Gatsby's words are wrong, 'the music is right; the cadence of "painting a little, things for myself only" – cuddling self-deprecation – or of "trying to forget something very sad that had happened to me long ago" (p. 52). That is the authentic music, the cello throb of *Collier's* and the *Post*, purveying with slick effrontery the dreams Horatio Alger could never quite realize to himself'.[20] Myrtle gets her identity, in part, out of the generically named *Town Tattle* and the scandal magazines of Broadway and moving-picture magazines that redouble the effect of the new medium. They connect entertainment with consumerism, and consumerism with the acquisition of character. Tom gets his ideas from books with long words in them, books that dissipate ideas under the impression that they are radiating them. In this narrative, ideas are bought and paid for. We measure time in many ways, but one of the most interesting is through reliance on 'news'. Gatsby scans the dailies to find out what has happened to Daisy after her marriage; Nick recognizes Jordan from 'a picture' (p. 12) he has seen in the weekly rotogravure (p. 18); Jordan reads soothingly to Tom from the *Saturday Evening Post*.

. . .

We recall that Jordan Baker's name implies one kind of technology,[21] and we may conclude that her appearance suggests another: 'Flattened, impossibly elongated figures attest to Cubist influence as well as that of Marie Laurencin and Modigliani. The asymmetry, geometrically precise pleats and tubular forms of dresses and figures relate directly to painting'.[22] . . . The ultimate product of technique was the self. There were by the early twenties vast numbers of examples of self-construction through commodities . . .

The marketplace of *The Great Gatsby* is located on Broadway, and the geography of the narrative encircles it, going south on Fifth Avenue to the borders of Murray Hill, then west to Pennsylvania Station, north to those big movies in the fifties, then east again to the Plaza. This area serves not only as the location for Nick's meeting with Wolfsheim, the beginning of his affair with Jordan, and the break-up of Gatsby's own affair with Daisy: Broadway contains the news-stands, movies, and theatres that offer ideas as commodities. The movies are probably most important. Movies sell not only styles but identities; and their effect is redoubled by the magazines and rotogravures and dailies that are the matrix of allusion in the text.

The language of the marketplace infiltrates everywhere. Wilson can't tell the difference between God and an advertisement; Nick sees Jordan for the last time, 'thinking she looked like a good illustration' (p. 138). The tactic of placing the description so firmly in marketplace terms states silently the nature of relationship. Feelings and perceptions may even be provided by the marketplace. Marketplace relations dominate relations in the text. Myrtle buys her dog and Tom buys Myrtle. Nick rents, Gatsby buys, the Buchanans inherit. McKee, the idiot photographer who represents so much of the salesmanship in the narrative, lives to peddle his work on the North Shore. One moment in the text reverses the Jamesian theme of Americans abroad: 'I was immediately struck by the number of young Englishmen dotted about; all well dressed, all looking a little hungry and all talking in low, earnest voices to solid and prosperous Americans. I was sure that they were all selling something: bonds or insurance or automobiles' (p. 35). Commodities are definitions: Wilson knows that Tom's car is the equivalent of his own going west to start a new life; Gatsby knows that his gorgeous and melodic car establishes his status.

Especially when Myrtle Wilson is involved in the action, we can see what Fitzgerald has learned about the American marketplace. When Myrtle assembles herself, complete to dress, dog, apartment, and dialogue ('"My dear"' (p. 27)), we see not only her own vast energies but those of the economy and the new consumer culture. Through Myrtle we become aware of the realm of imitation, hence of the human dynamics of the story. The party at Myrtle's apartment is one of the great messes in literature. Yet everywhere among the fallen are contravening images: 'to move about was to stumble continually over scenes of ladies swinging in the gardens of Versailles' (p. 25). These scenes of the aristocracy of Fragonard, Boucher, Watteau, and Le Brun belong now to manufactured interior decoration. They have been stamped out in their thousands. The subject may be French, but the technique is Hogarthian: the apartment is itself an economy, full of objects and commodities that have been duplicated. As his biographer says of Hogarth, 'the real, feigned (acted), carved, and painted are all related within a single picture. The richness of literary content cannot be dissociated from the effect of the purely formal elements'.[23] In this case there are 'scenes' within the scene that both parody and describe. The assembly-line tapestries state high life as Myrtle imagines it, fully clothed, richly at leisure, always dressed for a part. And they remind us, as objects and commodities and replications do throughout the text, that ideas are things.

The characters of *The Great Gatsby* see ideal forms of themselves in film and in magazines. They are conscious, sometimes deeply and emotionally so, of advertisements. The narrative uses a highly intentional language of replication: 'picture', 'illustration', 'advertisement', 'photograph', 'newspaper reports', 'copy' and other things which continually argue that they are as 'true' as Gatsby's photograph of Trinity Quad, and as 'real' as his father's photograph of the great house on West Egg. But this language prepares us to understand also that how we do everything is theatrical. There is hardly a character in the novel who does not have an ideal self in mind, a self which is constructed or achieved. But the sense of self – even dreams of selfhood – in this story are the products of ideology or market enterprise. The idea of self is often specifically related to magazines and movies. People play at roles and sometimes even seem to have scripts in mind: there is Myrtle, who shows us in her apartment the way she looks after she has become what she thinks she is. We see Tom self-consciously wrapped in the robes of Native Americanism, ready, according to Nick Carraway, to pose for a painting of Civilization on the Barricades. There is Daisy playing always to an audience and, in one startling moment that links the rhetoric of film to text, viewed in front of the gorgeous, empty actress who is her simulacrum. But theatricality is not only a way of expressing desires but of concealing them. We are accustomed to think of *The Great Gatsby* as a story of mobility and change, but it is also a story of disguise, that is to say, of appearing to change while remaining the same.

One of the most powerful oppositions in the book is that between Broadway and Hollywood. Both stand for artifice, but the former stands also for emotional authenticity. Gatsby may be '"a regular Belasco"' (p. 38) or producer of his own life's theatre, but the 'act' he puts on is considerably preferable to other kinds of acting and enactment. Daisy is drawn to the distancing, aesthetic and moral, of Hollywood – her genre, so to speak, is film, or at least film romance. Gatsby is a figure of Broadway, a place and an idea with an overwhelming presence in the text. Broadway sells dreams – and even ideologies – but it expresses real desires, calls on real feelings. It is where Gatsby comes back to life as Wolfsheim lifts him out of the street. It is where his guests come from in their 'simplicity of heart' (p. 34) that corresponds to his own combination of vulgarity and emotional authenticity. It is Gatsby's milieu, and it becomes Nick's. Very little is emotionally or sexually disguised on Broadway . . . at Gatsby's second party Nick feels 'many-coloured, many-keyed commotion . . . a pervading harshness' (p. 81) that Daisy plainly does not want to understand.

In terms of technique, we will often [in *Gatsby*,] see things, landscape and human objects, through the momentary glimpse of film and lens. The text will direct our attention to certain 'scenes' by looking at them through the 'flicker' of film movement – on Broadway, or crossing the Queensboro Bridge we see a mechanical world through mechanical means. When we look at Tom Buchanan, on our first assessment of him, he becomes for the moment a kind of machine in himself, and our perception of his bodily structure is in fact the perception by a moving-picture lens of an object in front of it. Nothing could be more appropriate than the inspection of one machine, calculated in terms of its force and leverage, by another.

The text is permeated with references to still photography; film development, prints, copies, illustrations, etc. But some of its longest scenes depend on the audience's familiarity with 'moving-picture' technique and technology. Possibly the most noticeable thing about such scenes is their silence. Part of Fitzgerald's experiment in this novel is the rendition of gesture that takes the place of speech. There is what seems to be intentional correspondence to the perception of the silent lens. There are certain silent scenes in *The Great Gatsby* that are, I think, openly cinematic, as in the theatre view that we get of Tom and Daisy through the pantry window in which they are on stage in the light and we see them from the dark. Such scenes can be reminiscent of film staging, with special kinds of lighting and even props. Or they can suggest the perspective (and even the operation) of lenses. They will at times invoke the idiom of photography, as when expressions of Myrtle's face appear as if they were 'objects' in 'a slowly developing picture' (p. 97). In addition to film technique there is film allusion. At certain moments in the narrative we are intended to see Daisy and Myrtle through the new mythology (and vocabulary) of social character: Daisy loves to act out the script of the Poor Little Rich Girl while Myrtle echoes many of the social-climbing themes of movies about 'working girls' who marry rich and Rise to the Top.

. . .

The characters of *The Great Gatsby* absorb ideas and feelings from what is communicated to them. It might be said that their closest relationships are not with each other – and certainly not with family or community or tradition – but with published, advertised, and perceived images and print. As the narrative begins Nick Carraway tells us how far we are from family, tradition, and clan; on the last page of most editions he states our irretrievable distance from historical beginnings. Much of the narrative in between registers the advent of ideas and values from other kinds of sources.[24] □

Where Berman sets *Gatsby* in the context not only of high modernism but also of the broad popular culture of the earlier twentieth century, Frances Kerr, in the last extract in this Guide, explores how Fitzgerald and *Gatsby* relate to one very significant strand of high modernism: its strongly gendered aesthetic discourse, which – in the polemics of Ezra Pound, for instance – opposed a masculine hardness to a feminine softness. In her essay 'Feeling "Half Feminine": Modernism and the Politics of Emotion in *The Great Gatsby*', which appeared in the journal *American Literature* in 1996, Kerr gives an example of this gendered discourse at the outset of her argument by quoting remarks from the review of *Gatsby* by H. L. Mencken that is printed in the first chapter of this Guide: Mencken calls Gatsby a 'clown' with 'the simple sentimentality of a somewhat sclerotic fat woman' (see p. 20). Kerr sees Fitzgerald as strongly influenced by, and sometimes liable to indulge in, this kind of rhetoric, but also aware of a 'femininity' in himself in the act of writing; according to Andrew Turnbull's biography, Fitzgerald said to his secretary Laurie Guthrie in 1935: '"I don't know what it is in me or that comes to me when I start to write. I am half feminine – at least my mind is"' – a statement that Keath Fraser had earlier seized on (see p. 131).[25] And in *Gatsby*, Kerr argues, Fitzgerald produced a subtle questioning of *macho* modernist aesthetics.

Building on Fraser's 'Another Reading of *The Great Gatsby*' (see pp. 130–34), Kerr first explores what she sees as Nick's ambivalent sexual and gender identity: Nick wants to be like his father but is aware of a tendency to femininity, to unmanly emotions, within himself. 'Nick's fear of being perceived as feminine and the secret knowledge that he *is* feminine create the troubling fissures in his personality that we have traditionally described as either moral lapses or narrative unreliability'.[26] Like Fraser, Kerr focuses on the Nick and McKee scenes, and acknowledges their ambiguity; in a different emphasis from Fraser, however, she suggests that their 'fragmented subtext' is 'aesthetic and personal' 'homosexual panic' on Nick's part – a complex panic that may consist of what she calls 'a heterosexual man's anxiety about the "femininity" of his personal attributes and/or an incipient awareness of his emotional or erotic attractions to other men'.[27] It may also include a fear of becoming – like McKee – a 'feminine' and therefore weak artist.

We join Kerr's essay at the point at which she moves on from the McKee scene to discuss Nick's relationship with Jordan and his attraction to Gatsby. She then examines what she sees as the emasculation of Gatsby by Tom in the Plaza Hotel scene, and goes on to explore the way in which Nick's elevation of Gatsby to mythic stature enables him to reconcile the figures of the manly hero and the feminine, defeated, emotional dreamer, and also to take an artist's revenge against the brutal man of the world embodied by Tom. Finally, Kerr suggests that there might be a relationship between the techniques of women modernist writers and Fitzgerald's own subtle struggle, in *Gatsby*, with the gender divisions and biases of modernist discourse:

■ The McKee exchange . . . is a generative point in the developing plot: it foreshadows Nick's relationship to Gatsby. McKee is the first of two imaginative, defeated, and 'feminine' (p. 26) men who attract Nick. Nick's romantic odyssey takes him from an unemotional obligation to the Midwest girlfriend, to the feminine Mr. McKee, to the masculine sportswoman Jordan Baker, and finally to Gatsby, who, in the novel's most emotionally brutal scene, is publicly feminized by Tom Buchanan. Because of *Gatsby*'s compressed, lyrical descriptions, it is easy to overlook the few details that reveal Nick's psychology as he shifts his attention from the Midwest girlfriend to Jordan Baker and then to Gatsby. Both shifts depend on the same psychological manoeuvre as Nick justifies his pursuit of what he considers illicit desires.

Nick's attraction to Jordan begins while he is still writing dutiful weekly letters to the young woman at home whom all his relatives expect him to marry. In the midst of fulfilling this obligation, Nick succumbs to more exciting desires and a loss of emotional control: '*all* I could think of was how, when that certain girl [Jordan] played tennis, a faint moustache of perspiration appeared on her upper lip' (p. 48, [Kerr's emphasis and interpolation]). What Nick does publicly (writes responsible letters to his girlfriend) does not match what he feels privately (an obsessive attraction to Jordan's mustache of sweat). In this synecdochical reference to his consuming passion for a transitory masculine feature of Jordan – not an attraction to the *person*, we note – he is speaking metaphorically, he is obsessive, and he has masculinized her.[28] All three of these habits of mind reappear when his obsession with Jordan shifts abruptly to preoccupation with Gatsby.

It is Jordan's 'hard jaunty body' (p. 48) that initially attracts Nick, along with her 'masculine' personal qualities – her self-assurance and careful control over her emotions. No other woman in the novel has such control. Daisy openly reveals her bitterness and anger to Nick, making him scornful and uncomfortable, while Myrtle exudes sentimental foolishness. Although Jordan's masculine appearance and emotional reserve initially appeal to Nick, he is never interested in intimacy. Their exchanges are wooden throughout, marked by Nick's reserve and hesitation and what he suggests is Jordan's arrogant indifference. The lifeless quality of their relationship is most pronounced in the scene of their kiss, which he describes in a stiff, rational voice (p. 63), not the voice of his 'haunting loneliness' (p. 47). When Nick finally terminates the relationship, his remarks lead the reader to believe that it is Jordan's indifference, shallowness, and dishonesty that prompt his move. The psychological subtext of *Gatsby*, however, suggests a motivation altogether different. Nick Carraway identifies with and feels most romantically drawn not to 'masculine' women but to 'feminine' men.

Nick's break with Jordan comes near the end of the novel, as Tom, Daisy, Jordan, and Nick gather at the Buchanans' house after the shock of Myrtle's sudden death. Jordan puts her hand on his arm and says, '"Won't you come in, Nick?"' to which he replies, '"No thanks"'. Nick goes on to explain to the reader, not to Jordan, 'I was feeling a little sick and I wanted to be alone . . . I'd had enough of all of them for one day'. He adds, 'She must have seen something of this in my expression for she turned abruptly away and ran up the porch steps into the house' (p. 111). Most readers have assumed that Nick's estimate of Jordan is accurate, that she is indeed cold, arrogant, and careless. Detached from Nick's interpretation, Jordan's overture tentatively expresses a need for emotional contact and offers Nick the chance to confirm his own need. Her sudden flight is significantly different from her earlier pose of self-contained indifference; it is a spontaneous emotional reaction that reveals her sudden vulnerability. The day's shocking events have apparently broken through her protective pose. Nick, however, is not interested in her emotional change – or in a woman's vulnerability. What Nick reveals at this point is his attraction to vulnerable men.

Immediately after Jordan enters the house, Nick confesses, 'I must have felt pretty weird by that time because *I could think of nothing* except the luminosity of [Gatsby's] pink suit under the moon' (pp. 111–12, [Kerr's emphasis]). Immediately after Myrtle's death, the rest of the characters turn to each other: Tom and Daisy reunite, and Jordan reaches out to Nick. Nick, however, is drawn to Gatsby's pink *suit*, just as he was drawn to Jordan's *'moustache of sweat'* [Kerr's emphasis].

Several things become apparent here, all configured succinctly in the image of the suit of the now socially exiled Gatsby. Nick follows the same fetishistic pattern in disentangling himself from Jordan as he did when ridding himself of the midwest sweetheart. Here, Nick claims to reject Jordan because her upper-class 'carelessness' (p. 139) offends his moral principles, although the more immediate and convincing reason seems to be a fascination with Gatsby's pink clothes. If what Nick was drawn to in Jordan was masculinity in a woman, what he is drawn to in Gatsby is femininity in a man. This attraction to Gatsby follows Nick's second flight from Tom Buchanan's brutality, and it is the second alliance he has formed with a sensitive, alienated, and defeated man. Nick's obsessive interest in Gatsby's suit comes just after Tom's second major display of aggression, when he forces Daisy to leave Gatsby by humiliating them both in a room at the Plaza Hotel. In that spectacular scene, Tom turns Gatsby into the social equivalent of a woman.

Tom's material wealth and physical virility together form the apex of a class-gender hierarchy. In the old American aristocracy of the East, fictionalized by Edith Wharton, the defining component of upper-class manhood was gentility – taste, manners, culture – as much as inherited wealth. As Charles Weir, Jr. aptly notes, '[t]here are no old families in Fitzgerald'.[29] Tom Buchanan represents the new American upper class, whose members value money and material possessions, not the development of character and taste. The kind of interior riches cultivated by the old aristocracy had acquired effete, effeminate connotations in the new century. Tom's 'fractiousness' and 'cruel body' (p. 9), along with his money, women, and 'gonnegtion[s]', (pp. 56, 65, 134) are what constitute his powerful masculinity. He is all physical and material force; he appears to have no emotional interior, and he demonstrates, repeatedly, that he has no manners, taste, or intelligence.

Men's competition in the new upper class is governed by a crucial social binary: the secret and the public. A powerful man maintains his social position by denying his own emotional interior while penetrating the emotional secrets of other men. To lose control of one's woman or one's inner emotions in the presence of others is to risk losing one's masculinity.[30] In his confrontation with Tom Buchanan, Gatsby loses control of both.

Tom's inquisition of Daisy and Gatsby at the Plaza in front of Nick and Jordan is verbal violence aimed at humiliation. Its method is to strip away the public identities of those who threaten him and reveal their secret vulnerability. Tom approaches Gatsby and Daisy in the same manner – as objects for his use, valuable for what they can be manipulated to suggest about Tom himself. When he questions Daisy about '"Kapiolani"' (p. 103), he makes public the essence if not the details of a private sexual experience shared during their marriage. Since Daisy's identity has always depended on her sexual appeal to men, which Tom's numerous affairs have called into question, he moves here to assure her of her position as an enchantress of men while confirming his exclusive access to her. When Tom boasts to Gatsby, '"Why, – there're things between Daisy and me that you'll never know, things that neither of us can ever forget"' (p. 103), he confirms his exclusive knowledge of both his own and Daisy's secrets.

Tom also has secret information about Gatsby. Through his network of powerful men Tom has learned that Gatsby is a bootlegger and a gambler, that his fortune was made illegally in the underworld (p. 104). Gatsby, Tom reveals, has never been '"above the hot struggles of the poor"' (p. 117), like Tom and his set, but is driven by desire. To be a feminine man in *The Great Gatsby* is to nurse, intensely, an emotional interior, as does Mr. McKee. When Tom pronounces Gatsby '"Mr. Nobody from Nowhere"', he ridicules Gatsby's longing, his secret emotional life (p. 101). When Tom renames him, Gatsby's male title of address is – Nothing. His manhood is negated.

Gatsby's splendid dreams, like Daisy's tentative attempt to create a new and independent self, are no match for the reality of Tom's aggression. To be a feminine man in *The Great Gatsby* is to have an emotional interior always threatened with exposure and ridicule in the competition among men that brings material success and social position. It is to dream instead of to have; it is to rely on the imagination instead of the material world. If McKee is by nature a 'pale feminine' (p. 26) artist, Gatsby is the man of imagination feminized against his will. To be feminized is, in Prufrock's words, to find oneself 'fix[ed] . . . in a formulated phrase' by those who have social power. In the terms of modernist aesthetics, it is to be pronounced '"Mr. Nobody from Nowhere"' – a 'trashy novelist' whose romantic hero is a 'sclerotic fat woman' (see pp. 6, 20).

Tom's feminization of Gatsby is the climactic point in the narrative that registers Nick's (and Fitzgerald's) perception of the social and aesthetic values that regulate men's emotional expression in 'a man's world'. The power of Tom's sadistic righteousness over Gatsby's impotent sincerity is what gives this scene its terrifying, sickening quality. Tom's display of power confirms for Nick that a man is most powerless among other men when he admits to an inner emotional life. Nick's immediate response to Gatsby's defeat is pity for Gatsby and fear for himself, emotions that cannot be expressed without weakening his own pose of manly invulnerability. Repressed, these emotions crystallize into obsessive, eroticized concern ('I could think of nothing except the luminosity of his pink suit under the moon' (p. 112)). From this point on, Nick is devoted exclusively to Gatsby; no other character receives his sustained attention, respect, or affection. Once George Wilson murders Gatsby, Nick's language swells to lyrical heights as he transforms the devastated con man with romantic dreams into a mythic American hero, a mythopoesis that powerfully expresses Nick's, and perhaps Fitzgerald's, gender anxiety.

Nick's public masculinity is based throughout on conformity to his father's ideas about upper-middle-class manhood. His elevating Gatsby to mythic stature symbolizes the ambivalence he feels toward his father's expectations of emotional reserve among good men. Gatsby, that is, satisfies some of Mr. Carraway's criteria for the successful man – hard work, devotion to one's goal, good manners. Nick, his father, and Gatsby have these traits in common. But Nick is also drawn to Gatsby by hungers that cannot be revealed to his father. 'There was something gorgeous' about Gatsby, confesses Nick (p. 6). The 'something gorgeous' is everything in Nick himself that he cannot speak about: his tendency towards romantic excess, his undisciplined, impractical and secret interior life with its 'haunting loneliness' and fantasies of 'romantic women' and 'pale feminine' men. Nick's creation of a heroic Gatsby openly confirms his father's ideals while allowing Nick to keep intense imaginative company with defeated, emotional male dreamers like himself. Nick's mythopoesis perfectly captures the split in his gender identity: his Gatsby fortifies Nick's public masculinity while allowing him to engage privately in 'feminine' emotions. Gatsby as myth articulates what Nick cannot openly admit – that he identifies with and is emotionally, and sometimes romantically, attracted to 'feminine' men.

The romantic element in Nick's interest in the feminine McKee and the feminized Gatsby is conditioned by the rules of men's competition and emotional distance. As [Richard A.] Isay explains, heterosexual men who feel uncertain of their ability to compete and perform among other men may fantasize about a sexual or romantic attraction to them, since their social interaction as competitors or partners seems questionable. Such fantasies are a defence against the 'dangers inherent in . . . aggressive, "masculine" strivings'.[31] Nick's fantasizing does not take the form of extended narratives, but the reader becomes aware of his imaginative activity through his impulses and impressions, as in his exchange with McKee in the elevator or his sudden attraction to Gatsby's pink suit. Nick's turning Gatsby into myth at the end is an extension of this kind of fantasy.

Nick's mythopoesis is also retribution, a way for Fitzgerald to criticize what Tom Buchanan represents. As the competitive, brutal man of financial and physical sport, Tom Buchanan will always roughshoulder the man of imagination, the artist. McKee, Gatsby, and Nick are all artist figures – men who invest the world with symbolic meaning by arranging people and objects into narratives or visual patterns of order and significance. All three maintain a secret interior space for the imagination and for the socially inappropriate, dangerous, or outrageous desires to which it gives rise. Nick's symbolic Gatsby is the artist's revenge against the man of the world: by turning Gatsby into a symbol of American Idealism, morally above and intellectually beyond Tom Buchanan, Fitzgerald can validate those qualities in Gatsby and Nick that Tom, dismissing them as feminine, overpowers.

In some respects, Fitzgerald's novel is a challenge to the modernist rhetoric that separated manly emotional vitality from womanly sentiment: by the end of *The Great Gatsby*, Tom Buchanan collapses into sentimentality. Mindless emotional excess, it would seem, is not the exclusive province of women and 'feminine' men. Nick encounters Tom for the last time by chance on Fifth Avenue. To Nick's questions about his role in helping the deranged Wilson locate his victim, Tom says defensively, '"And if you think I didn't have my share of suffering – look here, when I went to give up that flat and saw that damn box of dog biscuits sitting there on the sideboard I sat down and cried like a baby"' (p. 139). Tom's outburst, prompted by dog biscuits, is a reprise of the 'feminine' sentimentality that Myrtle exuded when she demanded that Tom buy her the dog because it was '"cute"' and because '"[t]hey're nice to have – a dog"'. Tom paid money for a dog peddled on the streets as a pure-bred Airedale that was actually, Nick clarifies, of 'an indeterminate breed'. Oblivious to facts, Myrtle had 'fondled' the gift 'with rapture' (p. 24). Later her affection for the animal dissolves. The 'little dog . . . sitting on the table looking with blind eyes through the smoke and from time to time groaning faintly' (p. 31), Fitzgerald suggests, is not cute. Tom's tears over the dog biscuits are not a sign of new emotional depth in his character; they are the sentimental substitute for character. He embraces Myrtle's foolish, selfish sentimentality as a way of avoiding facts.

The Great Gatsby's gender ideology, then, is a disjointed dialectic that never resolves its oppositions. Fitzgerald both observes and dismantles strict divisions between masculinity and femininity, between womanly sentiment and manly vitality. What I believe this divided perspective indicates is Fitzgerald's debt to and discomfort with the distinctions members of his 'intellectually élite' drew between self-expression and artistic detachment, a distinction that encompassed the difference between what Eliot called the 'significant emotion' of art and mere personal feeling . . .

. . .

Although Fitzgerald achieved an impersonal style in *The Great Gatsby*, he did not distance himself from his characters to the degree that Eliot and others advocated. My concern here is not to make an aesthetic judgement but to suggest that Fitzgerald's sensibility and talent may have been more congruent with androgynous models and metaphors for writing in which the concept of emotion was not so laden with implicit cautions against femininity. Perhaps this is what Fitzgerald had in mind in calling himself 'half feminine'.

Recent studies of the modernist period have revealed that not only the Bloomsbury group, but women writers on the Left Bank in Paris, Katherine Mansfield, and others were creating new techniques in fiction based on an idea of impersonality that diverged from the Joyce/Eliot/Pound conception of it.[32] Sydney Janet Kaplan's study of Katherine Mansfield's modernism, for example, describes Mansfield's work as committed to the concept of impersonality but also to a kind of Bergsonian intuition: 'the kind of *intellectual sympathy* by which one places oneself within an object in order to coincide with what is unique in it and consequently inexpressible'.[33] Such intuition and impersonality are not, Kaplan stresses, mutually exclusive. Mansfield herself said, 'All that [a writer] sees must be saturated' in 'an initial emotion'. This emotion 'alone can give . . . [the work] a close and intimate unity'.[34] Fitzgerald placed the same emphasis on the writer's intense emotion as a unifying principle.[35] So, of course, did Eliot, Joyce, and Pound. However, Fitzgerald and Mansfield incorporated their personal sympathies more freely and transparently into their art than did the other three modernists. Although Fitzgerald applied the method of impersonality advocated by his 'intellectually élite', he apparently modified the method in his characterization of Gatsby, Nick, and Mr. McKee to maintain a greater personal intimacy with these characters, a practice similar to what Kaplan sees in Mansfield's work. Fitzgerald's sympathy with these three male characters – along with a concern about his own artistic and personal femininity – may have coloured the novel's characterization and shaped the elements of the plot discussed earlier.

To my knowledge, no critic has conducted a thorough comparison of Fitzgerald's technique in *The Great Gatsby* and the fictional technique of a woman modernist. Placing Fitzgerald in such a context (Mansfield and Jean Rhys come to mind immediately) might provide a new structure for viewing questions about impersonality raised by *The Great Gatsby*. I am not suggesting direct influence but similar fictional methods that modified slightly but significantly the theories of impersonality described and practised by Eliot, Joyce, and Pound.[36]

. . .

Nick Carraway, who embodies a public masculinity of emotional reserve and a transgressive secret femininity of emotional freedom, may be emblematic of the subtle ways that Fitzgerald modified the aesthetic laws regulating men's emotional expression among 'the intellectually élite'.

Upon completing *The Great Gatsby*, Fitzgerald wrote Max Perkins, 'I think that at last I've done something really my own'.[37] In light of my discussion, that announcement rings true, but it is complicated and ironic. *The Great Gatsby* is the product of Fitzgerald's self-assertion at the point in his life when he sensed his creative potential most clearly; at the same time, his purposeful 'attempt at form' bears the imprint of a personal struggle with the gender-inflected standards of modernism.[38] □

The readings of *Gatsby* in the 1990s by Kerr, Berman and White are not only of great intrinsic interest but are also important signposts for future critics of Fitzgerald's novel. There is clearly much scope for further interpretations that would relate *Gatsby* to post-modernism, to feminism, and to a modernism that is being rewritten in the light of cultural, gender and gay studies. But these are by no means the only directions that criticism of the novel could take. In 1985, Matthew J. Bruccoli declared: '*The Great Gatsby* is inexhaustible';[39] today, seventy-two years after its first publication, there seems no reason to quarrel with that claim. As the twenty-first century approaches, it is likely that the literary canon will change and that new approaches to critical and cultural analysis will emerge; but it is difficult to imagine a time when there will not be readers and critics who will want to take the road to West Egg, past the valley of ashes, to Gatsby's blue lawn and to the compelling vision of the fresh, green breast of the new world.

SELECT BIBLIOGRAPHY

Fiction by F. Scott Fitzgerald
This lists original American and English editions, and gives details of the Cambridge edition of *The Great Gatsby* to which page references have been given in this Guide. *Gatsby* is available in a range of paperback editions.

Novels
This Side of Paradise. New York: Scribner's, 1920; London: Collins, 1921.
The Beautiful and Damned. New York: Scribner's, 1922; London: Collins, 1922.
The Great Gatsby. New York: Scribner's, 1925; London: Chatto and Windus, 1926; Cambridge: Cambridge University Press, 1991, ed. Matthew J. Bruccoli.
Tender is the Night. New York: Scribner's, 1934; London: Chatto and Windus, 1934.
The Last Tycoon. With *The Great Gatsby* and five stories. New York: Scribner's, 1941; London: Grey Walls Press, 1949.

Short story collections
Flappers and Philosophers. New York: Scribner's, 1920; London: Collins, 1922.
Tales of the Jazz Age. New York: Scribner's, 1922; London: Colllins, 1923.
All the Sad Young Men. New York: Scribner's, 1926.
Taps at Reveille. New York: Scribner's, 1935.
The Stories of F. Scott Fitzgerald, ed. Malcolm Cowley. New York: Scribner's, 1951.
Afternoon of an Author (stories and essays), ed. Arthur Mizener. Princeton, New Jersey: Princeton University Library, 1957; New York: Scribner's, 1958; London: Bodley Head, 1958.
The Pat Hobby Stories, ed. Arnold Gingrich. New York: Scribner's, 1962; Harmondsworth: Penguin, 1967.
The Apprentice Fiction of F. Scott Fitzgerald, ed. John Kuehl. New Brunswick, New Jersey: Rutgers University Press, 1965.
The Basil and Josephine Stories, eds. Jackson R. Bryer and John Kuehl. New York: Scribner's, 1973.
Bits of Paradise, eds. Matthew J. Bruccoli and Scottie Fitzgerald Smith. London: Bodley Head, 1973; New York: Scribner's, 1974.

Essays
The Crack-Up (also includes selections from Fitzgerald's notebooks and letters), ed. Edmund Wilson. New York: New Directions, 1945.

Letters
The Letters of F. Scott Fitzgerald, ed. Andrew Turnbull. New York: Scribner's, 1963; London: Bodley Head, 1964.
Dear Scott/Dear Max: The Fitzgerald/Perkins Correspondence, eds. John Kuehl and

Jackson R. Bryer. New York: Scribner's, 1971; London: Cassell, 1973.
As Ever, Scott Fitz—: Letters Between F. Scott Fitzgerald and His Literary Agent Harold Ober 1919–1940, eds. Matthew J. Bruccoli and Jennifer M. Atkinson. Philadelphia and New York: J. B. Lippincott, 1972; London: Woburn Press, 1973.
Correspondence of F. Scott Fitzgerald, eds. Matthew J. Bruccoli and Margaret M. Duggan, with Susan Walker. New York: Random House, 1980.

Notebooks and Ledger
F. Scott Fitzgerald's Ledger (A Facsimile), ed. Matthew J. Bruccoli. Washington, D. C.: Bruccoli Clark/NCR Microcard Books, 1973.
The Notebooks of F. Scott Fitzgerald, ed. Matthew J. Bruccoli. New York and London: Harcourt Brace Jovanovich/Bruccoli Clark, 1978.

Manuscript facsimile
F. Scott Fitzgerald's 'The Great Gatsby': A Facsimile of the Manuscript, ed. Matthew J. Bruccoli. Washington, D. C.: Microcard Editions Books, 1973.

Concordance
Crosland, Andrew. *A Concordance to The Great Gatsby*. Detroit, Michigan: Bruccoli Clark/Gale Research, 1975.

Bibliographies
Beebe, Maurice and Bryer, Jackson R. 'Criticism of F. Scott Fitzgerald: A Selected Checklist'. *Modern Fiction Studies*, 7:1 (Spring 1961), pp. 82–94.
Bruccoli, Matthew J. *F. Scott Fitzgerald: A Descriptive Bibliography*. Pittsburgh: University of Pittsburgh Press, 1972. Supplement, 1980.
Bryer, Jackson R. *The Critical Reputation of F. Scott Fitzgerald: A Bibliographical Study*. Hamden, Connecticut: Archon Books, 1967. Supplement I through 1981, 1984.

Biographies
Bruccoli, Matthew J. *Fitzgerald and Hemingway: A Dangerous Friendship*. London: Deutsch, 1995.
Bruccoli, Matthew J. *Scott and Ernest: The Authority of Failure and the Authority of Success*. London: Bodley Head, 1978.
Bruccoli, Matthew J. *Some Sort of Epic Grandeur: The Life of F. Scott Fitzgerald*. London: Hodder and Stoughton, 1981.
Meyers, Jeffrey. *Scott Fitzgerald: A Biography*. London: Macmillan, 1994.
Milford, Nancy. *Zelda Fitzgerald: A Biography*. London: The Bodley Head, 1970.
Mizener, Arthur. *Scott Fitzgerald and His World*. London: Thames and Hudson, 1972.
Mizener, Arthur. *The Far Side of Paradise: A Biography of F. Scott Fitzgerald*. Boston: Houghton Mifflin, 1951; London: Eyre and Spottiswoode, 1951. Revised edition: London: Heinemann, 1969.
Turnbull, Andrew. *Scott Fitzgerald*. New York: Scribner's, 1962.

Critical books
General critical works on Fitzgerald

Allen, Joan. *Candles and Carnival Lights: The Catholic Sensibility of F. Scott Fitzgerald*. The Gotham Library series. New York: New York University Press, 1978.

Callahan, John F. *The Illusions of a Nation: Myth and History in the Novels of F. Scott Fitzgerald*. Urbana: University of Illinois Press, 1972.

Chambers, John B. *The Novels of F. Scott Fitzgerald*. London: Macmillan, 1989.

Cross, K. G. W. *Scott Fitzgerald*. Writers and Critics series. Edinburgh and London: Oliver and Boyd, 1964.

Eble, Kenneth E. *F. Scott Fitzgerald*. Twayne's United States Authors series, no. 36. New York: Twayne, 1963. Revised edition: Boston: Twayne, 1977.

Fryer, Sarah Beebe. *Fitzgerald's New Women: Harbingers of Change*. Studies in Modern Literature series, no. 86. Ann Arbor: UMI Research Press, 1988.

Gallo, Rose Adrienne. *F. Scott Fitzgerald*. Modern Literature Monographs. New York: Frederick Ungar Publishing Co. Inc., 1978.

Hindus, Milton. *F. Scott Fitzgerald: An Introduction and Interpretation*. American Authors and Critics series. New York: Holt, Rinehart and Winston, 1968.

Hook, Andrew. *F. Scott Fitzgerald*. Modern Fiction series. London: Edward Arnold, 1992.

Lehan, Richard. *F. Scott Fitzgerald and the Craft of Fiction*. Carbondale: Southern Illinois University Press, 1966.

Miller, James E., Jr. *The Fictional Technique of F. Scott Fitzgerald*. The Hague: Martinus Nijhoff, 1957. Revised edition, under new title: *F. Scott Fitzgerald: His Art and His Technique*. New York: New York University Press, 1964.

Perosa, Sergio. *The Art of F. Scott Fitzgerald*. Translated by Charles Matz and Sergio Perosa. Ann Arbor: University of Michigan Press, 1965.

Piper, Henry Dan. *F. Scott Fitzgerald: A Critical Portrait*. New York: Holt, Rinehart and Winston, 1965.

Sklar, Robert. *F. Scott Fitzgerald: The Last Laocoön*. New York: Oxford University Press, 1967.

Stern, Milton R. *The Golden Moment: The Novels of F. Scott Fitzgerald*. Urbana: University of Illinois Press, 1970.

Way, Brian. *F. Scott Fitzgerald and the Art of Social Fiction*. New York: St. Martin's Press, 1980.

Critical books on *The Great Gatsby*

Berman, Ronald. *'The Great Gatsby' and Modern Times*. Urbana: University of Illinois Press, 1994.

Lehan, Richard. *'The Great Gatsby': The Limits of Wonder*. Twayne's Masterwork Studies, no. 36. Boston: Twayne, 1990.

Long, Robert Emmet. *The Achieving of 'The Great Gatsby': F. Scott Fitzgerald 1920–1925*. Lewisburg, Philadelphia: Bucknell University Press, 1979.

Matterson, Stephen. *The Great Gatsby*. The Critics Debate series. Basingstoke: Macmillan, 1990.

Pendleton, Thomas. *I'm Sorry About The Clock: Chronology, Composition, and*

Narrative Technique in 'The Great Gatsby'. Selinsgrove: Susqhehanna University Press, 1993.

White, Patti. *Gatsby's Party: The System and the List in Contemporary Narrative*. West Lafayette, Indiana: Purdue University Press, 1992. (This book also discusses fiction by Julian Barnes, John Barth, Don DeLillo and Thomas Pynchon.)

Whitley, J. S. *F. Scott Fitzgerald: 'The Great Gatsby'*. Studies in English Literature series, no. 60. London: Edward Arnold, 1976.

Other books that discuss Fitzgerald and *Gatsby*

Allen, Walter. *The Modern Novel in Britain and the United States*. New York: E. P. Dutton and Co., Inc., 1965, pp. 86–92. Published in England under the title *Tradition and Dream*.

Bradbury, Malcolm. *The Modern American Novel*. Revised edition. Oxford: Oxford University Press, 1992, pp. 83–93.

Fiedler, Leslie A. *Love and Death in the American Novel*. London: Paladin, pp. 291–95.

Geismar, Maxwell. *The Last of the Provincials: The American Novel 1915–1925*. New York: Hill and Wang, 1959, Chapter Five, 'F. Scott Fitzgerald: Orestes at the Ritz', pp. 287–352.

Hoffman, Frederick J. *The Modern Novel in America 1900–1950*. Chicago: Henry Regnery Company, 1951, pp. 120–30.

Minter, David. *A Cultural History of the American Novel: Henry James to William Faulkner*. Cambridge: Cambridge University Press, 1994, pp. 110–17.

Tuttleton, James W. *The Novel of Manners in America*. Chapel Hill: University of North Carolina Press, 1972, Chapter Seven, 'F. Scott Fitzgerald: The Romantic Tragedian as Moral Fabulist', pp. 162–83.

Washington, Bryan R. *The Politics of Exile: Ideology in Henry James, F. Scott Fitzgerald, and James Baldwin*. Boston: Northeastern University Press, 1995, pp. 35–54.

Essay collections

Bloom, Harold, ed. *Modern Critical Interpretations of 'The Great Gatsby'*. New York: Chelsea House, 1986.

Bruccoli, Matthew J., ed. *New Essays on 'The Great Gatsby'*. The American Novel series. Cambridge: Cambridge University Press, 1985.

Donaldson, Scott, ed. *Critical Essays on F. Scott Fitzgerald's 'The Great Gatsby'*. Boston: G. K. Hall, 1984.

Eble, Kenneth E., ed. *F. Scott Fitzgerald: A Collection of Criticism*. Contemporary Studies in Literature series. New York: McGraw-Hill, 1973.

Hoffman, Frederick J., ed. *'The Great Gatsby': A Study*. New York: Scribner's, 1962.

Kazin, Alfred, ed. *F. Scott Fitzgerald: The Man and His Work*. New York: World Publishing, 1951.

Lee, Robert A. *Scott Fitzgerald: The Promises of Life*. Critical Studies series. London: Vision Press, 1989.

Lockridge, Ernest H., ed. *Twentieth Century Interpretations of 'The Great Gatsby'*. Englewood Cliffs, New Jersey: Prentice-Hall, Inc., 1963.

Mizener, Arthur, ed. *Scott Fitzgerald: A Collection of Critical Essays*. Twentieth Century Views series. Englewood Cliffs, New Jersey: Prentice-Hall, Inc., 1963.

Piper, Henry Dan, ed. *Fitzgerald's 'The Great Gatsby': The Novel, The Critics, The Background*. Research Anthologies series. New York: Scribner's, 1970.

Review collection
Bryer, Jackson R. *F. Scott Fitzgerald: The Critical Reception*. The American Critical Tradition series, no. 5. New York: Butt Franklin and Co., Inc., 1978.

Journals
Fitzgerald Newsletter (1958–1968). Washington, D. C.: NCR Microcard Editions, 1969.

Fitzgerald/Hemingway Annual. Washington, D. C.: NCR Microcard Editions, 1969–1973; Englewood, Colorado: Information Handling Services, 1974–1976; Detroit: Gale Research, 1977–1979.

Essays in journals and books
Berryman, John. 'F. Scott Fitzgerald'. *Kenyon Review*, 8 (Winter 1946), pp. 103–112.

Bewley, Marius. 'Scott Fitzgerald's Criticism of America'. *Sewanee Review*, 62 (Spring 1954), pp. 223–46. Reprinted in Hoffman (1962), pp. 263–85; Lockridge (1968), pp. 37–53; Bloom (1986), pp. 11–27.

Bicknell, John W. 'The Waste Land of F. Scott Fitzgerald'. *Virginia Quarterly Review*, 30 (Autumn 1954), pp. 556–72. Reprinted in Eble (1973), pp. 67–80.

Bryer, Jackson R. 'Four Decades of Fitzgerald Studies: The Best and the Brightest'. *Twentieth Century Literature*, 26 (Summer 1980), pp. 247–67.

Corrigan, R. A. 'Somewhere West of Laramie on the Road to West Egg: Automobiles, Fillies, and the West in *The Great Gatsby*'. *Journal of Popular Culture*, 7 (1973), pp. 152–58.

Doyno, Victor A. 'Patterns in *The Great Gatsby*'. *Modern Fiction Studies*, 12 (1969), pp. 415–26. Reprinted in Piper (1970), pp. 160–67; Donaldson (1984), pp. 94–105.

Dyson. A. E. '*The Great Gatsby* Thirty-Six Years After'. *Modern Fiction Studies*, 7:1 (Spring 1961), pp. 37–48. Reprinted in Mizener (1963), pp. 112–24.

Eble, Kenneth E. 'The Craft of Revision: *The Great Gatsby*'. *American Literature*, 36 (November 1964), pp. 315–26. Reprinted in Piper (1970), pp. 110–17; Eble (1973), pp. 81–92; Donaldson(1984), pp. 85–94.

Fiedler, Leslie A. 'Notes on F. Scott Fitzgerald'. *New Leader*, 34 (9 April 1951), pp. 20–1. Reprinted in Fiedler, *An End to Innocence*. Boston: Beacon Press, 1955, pp. 174–82; Mizener (1963), pp. 70–6.

Forrey, Robert. 'Negroes in the Fiction of F. Scott Fitzgerald'. *Phylon: The Atalanta University Review of Race and Culture*, 48 (1967), pp. 293–98.

Foster, Richard. 'The Way to Read *Gatsby*' in Brom Weber, ed. *Sense and Sensibility in Twentieth-Century Writing: A Gathering in Memory of William Van O'Connor*. Carbondale and Edwardsville: Southern Illinois University Press, 1970, pp. 94–108.

Fraser, Keath. 'Another Reading of *The Great Gatsby*'. *English Studies in Canada*, 5 (Autumn 1979), pp. 330–43. Reprinted in Donaldson (1984), pp. 140–53; Bloom (1986), pp. 57–70.

Fussell, Edwin S. 'Fitzgerald's Brave New World'. *ELH: A Journal of English Literary History*, 19:4 (December 1952), pp. 291–306. Reprinted in revised form in Hoffman (1962), pp. 244–62; Mizener (1963), pp. 43–56.

Godden, Richard. 'Glamour on the Turn'. *Journal of American Studies*, 16:3 (1982), pp. 343–44.

Holquist, Michael. 'Stereotyping in Autobiography and Historiography: Colonialism in *The Great Gatsby*'. *Poetics Today*, 9:2 (1988), pp. 460–61.

Jacobson, Dan. 'F. Scott Fitzgerald'. *Encounter*, 14:6 (June 1960), pp. 71–7.

Kerr, Frances. 'Feeling "Half Feminine": Modernism and the Politics of Emotion in *The Great Gatsby*'. *American Literature*, 68:2 (June 1996), pp. 405–31.

Korenman, Joan S. '"Only Her Hairdresser . . . ". Another Look at Daisy Buchanan'. *American Literature*, 46 (January 1974), pp. 574–78.

Long, Robert E. '*The Great Gatsby* and the Tradition of Joseph Conrad'. *Texas Studies in Language and Literature*, 8:2, 3 (Summer and Fall 1966), pp. 257–76, 407–22.

McDonnell, Robert F. 'Eggs and Eyes in *The Great Gatsby*'. *Modern Fiction Studies*, 7:1 (Spring 1961), pp. 32–6.

McKendrick, Paul L. '*The Great Gatsby* and Trimalchio'. *The Classical Journal*, 45:7 (April 1950), pp. 307–14.

MacPhee, Laurence E. '*The Great Gatsby*'s Romance of Motoring'. *Modern Fiction Studies*, 18 (Summer 1972), pp. 207–12.

Mizener, Arthur. 'The Poet of Borrowed Time' in Willard Thorp, ed. *Lives of Eighteen from Princeton*. Princeton: Princeton University Press, 1946. Reprinted in Kazin (1962), pp. 23–45.

Neuhaus, Ron. '*Gatsby* and the Failure of the Omniscient "I"'. *The Denver Quarterly*, 12:1 (Spring 1977), pp. 303–12. Reprinted in Bloom (1986), pp. 45–55.

Ornstein, Robert. 'Scott Fitzgerald's Fable of East and West'. *College English*, 18 (1956–57), pp. 139–43. Reprinted in Lockridge (1968), pp. 54–60; Eble (1973), pp. 60–6.

Paulson, A. B. '*The Great Gatsby*: Oral Aggression and Splitting'. *American Imago: A Psychoanalytic Journal for Culture, Science and the Arts*, 35 (Fall 1978), pp. 311–30. Reprinted in Bloom (1986), pp. 71–85.

Person, Leland R., Jr. '"Herstory" and Daisy Buchanan'. *American Literature*, 50 (May 1978), pp. 250–57.

Ross, Alan. 'Rumble Among the Drums – F. Scott Fitzgerald (1896–1940) and the Jazz Age'. *Horizon*, 18 (December 1948), pp. 420–35.

Scrimgeour, Gary J. 'Against *The Great Gatsby*'. *Criticism*, 8 (Winter 1966), pp. 75–86. Reprinted in Lockridge (1968), pp. 70–81.

Slater, Peter Gregg. 'Ethnicity in *The Great Gatsby*'. *Twentieth Century Literature*, 19 (1973), pp. 53–62.

Stallman, R. W. 'Conrad and *The Great Gatsby*'. *Twentieth Century Literature*, 1 (April 1955), pp. 5–12. Reprinted in Stallman, R. W. *The Houses that James Built and Other Literary Studies*. Michigan: Michigan State University Press (1961), pp. 150–57.

Stallman, R. W. '*Gatsby* and the Hole in Time'. *Modern Fiction Studies*, 1:4 (November 1955), pp. 2–16. Reprinted in Stallman (1961), pp. 131–50.

Thornton, Laurence. 'Ford Madox Ford and *The Great Gatsby*'. *Fitzgerald/Hemingway Annual* (1975), pp. 57–74.

Trilling, Lionel. 'F. Scott Fitzgerald', in *The Liberal Imagination: Essays on Literature and Society*. London: Secker and Warburg, 1951, pp. 243–54. Reprinted in Hoffman (1962), pp. 232–43; Kazin (1962), pp. 195–205; Mizener (1963), pp. 11–19; Donaldson (1984), pp. 13–20.

Troy, William. 'Scott Fitzgerald – The Authority of Failure'. *Accent*, 6 (Autumn 1945), pp. 56–60. Reprinted in Hoffman (1962), pp. 224–31; Kazin (1962), pp. 188–94; Mizener (1963), pp. 20–4.

Wasiolek, Edward. 'The Sexual Drama of Nick and Gatsby'. *The International Fiction Review*, 19 (1992), pp. 14–22.

Westbrook, J. S. 'Nature and Optics in *The Great Gatsby*'. *American Literature*, 32 (March 1960), pp. 79–84.

Films of *The Great Gatsby*

There have been three films of *The Great Gatsby* to date, two partly based on the Owen Davis stage adaptation. For discussions of the films and/or the stage adaptation, the following are useful.

Margolies, Alan. 'Novel to Play to Film. Four versions of *The Great Gatsby*' in Donaldson (1984), pp. 187–200.

Morsberger, Robert E. 'Trimalchio in West Egg: *The Great Gatsby* Onstage'. *Prospects: An Annual Journal of American Cultural Studies*, 5 (1980), pp. 489–506.

Phillips, Gene D., S. J. *Fiction, Film and Scott Fitzgerald*. Chicago: Loyola University Press, 1986, pp. 101–24.

The details of the films below are from Phillips (1986), pp. 205, 206, 208.

1. *The Great Gatsby*. Famous Players-Lasky-Paramount, 1926
Director: Herbert Brenon.
Screenwriters: Becky Gardiner and Elizabeth Meehan (based on the novel and the Owen Davis play).
Cast: Warner Baxter (Jay Gatsby); Lois Wilson (Daisy Buchanan); Hale Hamilton (Tom Buchanan); Neil Hamilton (Nick Carraway); Carmelita Geraghty (Jordan Baker); Georgia Hale (Myrtle Wilson); William Powell (George Wilson); George Nash (Charles Wolf [this film's version of Wolfsheim]).

Running time: Eight reels.
The print of this film is now apparently lost.

2. *The Great Gatsby*. Paramount, 1949
Director: Elliott Nugent.
Screenwriters: Cyril Hume and Richard Maibaum (based on the novel and
the Owen Davis play).
Cast: Alan Ladd (Jay Gatsby); Betty Field (Daisy Buchanan); Barry Sullivan
(Tom Buchanan); MacDonald Carey (Nick Carraway); Ruth Hussey (Jordan
Baker); Shelley Winters (Myrtle Wilson); Howard da Silva (George Wilson);
Elisha Cook, Jr (Klipspringer); Ed Begley (Myron Lupus [this film's version of
Wolfsheim]); Henry Hull (Dan Cody); Carole Mathews (Ella Cody); Nicholas
Joy (Owl Man); Tito Vuolo (Mavromichaelis).
Running time: 92 minutes.

3. *The Great Gatsby*. Paramount, 1974.
Director: Jack Clayton.
Screenwriter: Francis Ford Coppola (based on the novel).
Cast: Robert Redford (Jay Gatsby); Mia Farrow (Daisy Buchanan); Bruce
Dern (Tom Buchanan); Sam Waterston (Nick Carraway); Lois Chiles (Jordan
Baker); Karen Black (Myrtle Wilson); Scott Wilson (George Wilson); Edward
Hermann (Klipspringer); Howard da Silva (Meyer Wolfsheim); Roberts
Blossom (Mr Gatz).
Running time: 145 minutes.

NOTES

INTRODUCTION

1 F. Scott Fitzgerald, 'Early Success', in *The Crack-Up* (Harmondsworth: Penguin, 1965), p. 58.

2 Matthew J. Bruccoli, *Some Sort of Epic Grandeur: The Life of F. Scott Fitzgerald* (London: Hodder and Stoughton, 1981), p. 119.

3 Andrew Turnbull ed., *The Letters of F Scott Fitzgerald* (New York: Scribner's, 1963), p. 144.

4 Fitzgerald (1965), p. 39.

5 Fitzgerald (1965), p. 39.

6 Edmund Wilson, 'Thoughts on Being Bibliographed', in Wilson, *Classics and Commercials: A Literary Chronicle of the Forties* (New York: Farrar, Straus and Co., 1950), p. 110.

7 See Jackson R. Bryer, *F. Scott Fitzgerald: The Critical Reception*. The American Critical Tradition series, no. 5 (New York: Butt Franklin and Co., Inc., 1978), pp 1-32. This quotation, p. 27.

8 Edmund Wilson, *Letters on Literature and Politics, 1912-1972* (New York: Farrar, Straus and Giroux, 1977), p. 46.

9 Bryer (1978), p. 107.

10 Bryer (1978), p. 109.

11 Matthew J. Bruccoli and Margaret M. Duggan, eds., *Correspondence of F. Scott Fitzgerald* (New York: Random House, 1980), p. 112.

12 Matthew J. Bruccoli, 'Introduction' to F. Scott Fitzgerald, *The Great Gatsby* (Cambridge: Cambridge University Press, 1991), p. ix.

13 John Kuehl and Jackson R. Bryer, eds., *Dear Scott/Dear Max: The Fitzgerald–Perkins Correspondence* (London: Cassell, 1971), p. 70.

14 Kuehl and Bryer (1971), p. 80.

15 Kuehl and Bryer (1971), pp. 82-4.

16 For a discussion of the exchange with Perkins, see Bruccoli (1991), pp. xv-xx.

17 Ron Neuhaus, 'Gatsby and the Failure of the Omniscient "I"', *The Denver Quarterly*, 12:1, (Spring 1977), pp. 303-12. Reprinted in Harold Bloom, ed., *Modern Critical Interpretations of The Great Gatsby* (New York: Chelsea House, 1986), pp. 45-55.

CHAPTER ONE

1 Bryer (1978), p. 195.

2 Bryer (1978), p. 196.

3 Bryer (1978), p. 197.

4 Bryer (1978), p. 223.

5 Bryer (1978), p. 223.

6 Bryer (1978), p. 224.

7 Bryer (1978), p. 195.

8 Bryer (1978), p. 217.

9 Bryer (1978), p. 205.

10 Bryer (1978), pp. 198, 199.

11 Bryer (1978), p. 246.

12 Bryer (1978), p. 248.

13 Bryer (1978), p. 228.

14 Bryer (1978), p. 236.

15 Bryer (1978), p. 195.

16 Bryer (1978), p. 207.

17 Bryer (1978), p. 203.

18 Bryer (1978), p. 218.

19 Bryer (1978), p. 245.

20 Bryer (1978), p. 246.

21 Bryer (1978), p. 249.

22 Bryer (1978), p. 249.

23 Bryer (1978), p. 224.

24 Bryer (1978), p. 237.

25 Bryer (1978), pp. 195-249.

26 Bryer (1978), p. 200.

27 Bryer (1978), p. 203.

28 Bryer (1978), p. 205.

29 Bryer (1978), p. 227.

30 Bryer (1978), p. 233.

31 Richard Foster, 'The Way to Read Gatsby', in Brom Weber, ed., *Sense and Sensibility in Twentieth-Century Writing: A Gathering in Memory of William Van O'Connor* (Carbondale and Edwardsville: Southern Illinois University Press, 1970), pp. 94-108. See also Lawrence Thornton, 'Ford Madox Ford and *The Great Gatsby*', Fitzgerald/Hemingway Annual (Englewood, Colorado: Information Handling Services, 1975), pp. 57-74.

32 For Isabel Paterson's review of *Gatsby* in *McNaught's Monthly*, see Bryer (1978), pp. 233-34.

33 Bryer (1978), p. 202.

34 Kazin (1962), p. 11.

35 T. S. Eliot, 'Ulysses, Order, and Myth', *The Dial*, 75 (1923), pp. 480–83. Reprinted in Richard Ellmann and Charles Feidelson, Jr, eds., *The Modern Tradition: Backgrounds of Modern Literature* (New York: Oxford University Press, 1965). This quotation, Ellmann and Feidelson (1965), p. 681.

36 See, for example, Paul L. MacKendrick, 'The Great Gatsby and Trimalchio', *The Classical Journal*, 45:7 (April 1950), pp. 307–14; James W. Tuttleton, *The Novel of Manners in America* (Chapel Hill: University of North Carolina Press, 1972), pp. 172–3; Brian Way, *F. Scott Fitzgerald and the Art of Social Fiction* (London: Edward Arnold, 1980), pp. 115–16; reprinted Bloom (1986), pp. 105–06. Fitzgerald disliked *The Great Gatsby* as a title. Returning the proof of the title page to Maxwell Perkins, he said 'my heart tells me I should have named it Trimalchio'. He felt that *Trimalchio in West Egg* was a possible, though less preferable, compromise title. See Turnbull (1963), pp. 169, 170, 177.

37 Isabel Paterson, 'Up to the Minute', *New York Herald Tribune Books* (19 April 1925), p. 6. Reprinted in Bryer (1978), pp. 200–02.

38 Kenneth E. Eble, 'The Great Gatsby and the Great American Novel' in Matthew J. Bruccoli, ed., *New Essays on 'The Great Gatsby'*, The American Novel series. (Cambridge: Cambridge University Press, 1985), p. 95.

39 'E. K.', Untitled, *Literary Digest International Book Review*, 3 (May 1925), pp. 426–27. Reprinted in Bryer (1978), pp. 208–09.

40 Bruccoli (1981), p. 106.

41 Turnbull (1963), p. 509. Bruccoli (1991, p. 205) says that 'Absolution' 'was written as part of a lost early version of a novel which became *The Great Gatsby*' but he warns against any facile identification of its protagonist, Miller, with Gatsby.

42 H. L. Mencken, 'As H. L. M. Sees it', *Baltimore Evening Sun* (2 May 1925), p. 9.

Reprinted in Kazin (1962), pp. 89–92; Henry Dan Piper, ed., *Fitzgerald's The Great Gatsby: The Novel, The Critics, The Background*, Scribner's Research Anthology series (New York: Scribner's, 1970), pp. 121–23; Bryer (1978), pp. 211–14.

43 William Rose Benét, 'An Admirable Novel', *Saturday Review of Literature*, 1 (9 May 1925), pp. 739–40. Reprinted in Bryer (1978), pp. 219–21.

44 See Henry Dan Piper, *F. Scott Fitzgerald: A Critical Portrait* (London: The Bodley Head, 1965), pp. 103–07.

45 For a discussion of links between the work of Fitzgerald and Norris, see, for example, Richard Astro's essay '*Vandover and the Brute* and *The Beautiful and Damned*: A Search for Thematic and Stylistic Reinterpretations', *Modern Fiction Studies*, 14 (Winter 1968–69), pp. 397–413.

46 Carl Van Vechten, 'Fitzgerald on the March', *The Nation*, 120 (20 May 1925), pp. 575–76. Reprinted in Bryer (1978), pp. 229–30.

47 The *Vanity Fair* page – in which Fitzgerald's photo is the largest – is reproduced in Arthur Mizener, *Scott Fitzgerald and His World* (London: Thames and Hudson, 1972), p. 59.

48 See Piper (1970), p. 125.

49 Gilbert Seldes, 'Spring Flight', *The Dial*, 79 (August 1925), pp. 162–64. Reprinted Bryer (1978), pp. 239–41; Scott Donaldson, ed., *Critical Essays on F. Scott Fitzgerald's The Great Gatsby* (Boston: G. K. Hall, 1984), pp. 271–73.

50 Turnbull (1963), p. 342.

51 Turnbull (1963), p. 480. Mencken apparently wrote: 'My one complaint is that the basic story is somewhat trivial – that it reduces itself to an incident'. Quoted in Donaldson (1984), p. 265.

52 T. S. Eliot, 'A Letter on *The Great Gatsby*' in Alfred Kazin, ed., *F. Scott Fitzgerald: The Man and His Work* (New York: Collier Books, 1962), pp. 93–4. Partly reprinted in Donaldson (1984), p. 268.

53 Bruccoli (1981), pp. 220–21.

54 Bruccoli (1985), p. 4. As Bruccoli pointed out back in 1981, Fitzgerald's work was not out of print when he died (1981, p. 489). The claim that it was continues to be made, however, perhaps showing the continued force of the myth of Fitzgerald: in 1990, Stephen Matterson said of *Gatsby*: '[w]hen Fitzgerald died in 1940, the novel was out of print'. Stephen Matterson, *The Great Gatsby*, The Critics Debate series (Basingstoke: Macmillan, 1990), p. 61.

55 Bruccoli (1981), p. 489.

56 Piper (1965), p. 159.

57 Bruccoli (1985), p. 4.

58 Bruccoli (1981), p. 248.

59 Arthur Mizener, *The Far Side of Paradise: A Biography of F. Scott Fitzgerald* (London: Eyre and Spottiswoode, 1951), p. 191. For more detailed accounts of the play of *Gatsby*, see Robert E. Morsberger. 'Trimalchio in West Egg: *The Great Gatsby* Onstage', *Prospects: An Annual Journal of American Cultural Studies*, 5 (1980), pp. 489–506; Alan Margolies, 'Novel to Play to Film: Four Versions of *The Great Gatsby*' in Donaldson (1984), pp. 187–200.

60 Mizener (1951), p. 191.

61 Bruccoli (1985), p. 4.

62 Mizener (1951), p. 192. For more detailed accounts of this film, and of the two other films (1949 and 1974) of *Gatsby*, see Margolies (1984) and Gene D. Phillips, S. J., *Fiction, Film, and F. Scott Fitzgerald* (Chicago: University of Loyola Press, 1986), pp. 101–24.

63 Bryer (1978), p. 267.

64 Bryer (1978), p. 255.

65 Bryer (1978), p. 262.

66 Bryer (1978), p. 261.

67 Bryer (1978), p. 257.

68 Bryer (1978), p. 259.

69 Bryer (1978), p. 260.

70 Bryer (1978), p. 275.

71 Bryer (1978), p. 276.

72 Bryer (1978), pp. 267–68. This quotation, p. 268.

73 Quoted Piper (1965), p. 159.

74 Edward Shanks, 'Fiction', *London Mercury* (13 April 1926), pp. 656–8. This quotation, p. 657.

75 Bryer (1978), pp. 243–44.

76 *Times Literary Supplement* (18 February 1926), p. 116.

77 L. P. Hartley, 'New Fiction', *The Saturday Review* (20 February 1926), pp. 234–35. This quotation, p. 235. Despite Hartley's criticisms of *Gatsby*, he produced, twenty-eight years later, a novel that features a large and impressive house; a summer of intense heat; two lovers between whom there is a social barrier and who have difficulty in meeting; a participant observer who acts (though unwittingly) as a pander and, after he has retreated from life, tells the story in retrospect; and the fatal blast of a shotgun near the end. This novel is, of course, Hartley's best-known work, *The Go-Between* (1953).

78 Matthew J. Bruccoli. 'Introduction' to *F. Scott Fitzgerald, The Great Gatsby* (London: Scribner's, 1991), pp. xvi, xvii. Hereafter referenced as Bruccoli (1991b).

79 Bruccoli (1985), p. 4.

80 Bruccoli (1991b), p. xvii.

81 Turnbull (1963), p. 79.

82 Bryer (1978), p. 312.

83 Bryer (1978), p. 287.

84 Bryer (1978), p. 290.

85 Bryer (1978), p. 294.

86 Bryer (1978), p. 317.

87 Bryer (1978), p. 292.

88 Fitzgerald may have in mind the remark by the anonymous writer (not specifically identified as a woman) of the New York World review headed 'F. Scott Fitzgerald's Latest a Dud', who said: '*The Great Gatsby* is another one of the thousands of modern novels which must be approached with the point of view of the average tired person towards the movie-around-the-corner'. Bryer (1978), p. 195.

89 F. Scott Fitzgerald. 'Introduction', *The Great Gatsby*, Modern Library Edition (New York: Random House, Inc., 1934), pp. vii–xi. Reprinted in Frederick J. Hoffman, ed., *The Great Gatsby: A Study* (New York: Scribner's, 1962), pp. 165–68;

Ernest H. Lockridge, ed., *Twentieth Century Interpretations of 'The Great Gatsby'* (Englewood Cliffs, New Jersey: Prentice-Hall, Inc., 1968), pp. 108–10; Piper (1970), pp. 108–09.

90 Bruccoli (1981), p. 392.

91 Bryer (1978), p. 349.

92 Bryer (1978), pp. 337, 338.

93 Bryer (1978), pp. 338, 339.

94 Fitzgerald (1965), p. 46.

95 Vernon Louis Parrrington, *Main Currents in American Thought*, Volume 3, *The Beginnings of Critical Realism in America 1860–1920: Completed to 1900 Only* (New York: Harcourt, Brace, and Co., 1930), p. 386. Quoted in Piper (1965), p. 288. Piper does not mention that Parrington's sudden death prevented his completion of this volume and that Parrington's judgements on Fitzgerald are brief notes, not developed arguments.

96 Harlan Hatcher, *Creating the Modern American Novel* (New York: Farrar and Rinehart, 1935), p. 72. Quoted in Piper (1965), p. 288.

97 'Not Wholly Lost', *New York Times* (24 December 1940), p. 14. Quoted in Bruccoli (1985), p. 4.

98 James Gray, 'A Last Salute to the Gayest of Sad Young Men', *St. Paul Dispatch* (24 December 1940), p. 4. Quoted in Bruccoli (1985), pp. 4–5.

99 *The New Yorker* (4 January 1941), p. 9. Quoted in Bruccoli (1985), p. 5.

100 John Dos Passos, 'Fitzgerald and the Press', *The New Republic*, 104 (17 February 1941), p. 213. Quoted in Bruccoli (1985), p. 5.

101 Bryer (1978), pp. 360–61. The other review which used the term 'masterpiece' in a non-committal way was by Robert J. Conklin who called *Gatsby* 'the long short-story which is generally regarded as Fitzgerald's masterpiece'. Bryer (1978), pp. 361–62.

102 Bryer (1978), pp. 369–70.

103 Bryer (1978), p. 369.

104 Bryer (1978), pp. 356–57.

105 Bryer (1978), pp. 358, 359.

106 Bryer (1978), p. 364.

107 Bryer (1978), p. 374.

108 Bruccoli (1985), pp. 5–6.

109 Bruccoli (1991b), p. xvii.

110 Bruccoli (1985), p. 6.

111 Carl Van Doren, *The American Novel, 1789–1930* (New York: Macmillan, 1940), p. 326. Quoted in Piper (1965), p. 288.

112 Joseph Warren Beach, *American Fiction 1920–1940* (New York: Macmillan, 1941). Discussed in Piper (1965), p. 288.

113 George Snell, *The Shapers of American Fiction, 1798–1947* (New York: Dutton, 1947), p. 158. Quoted in Piper (1965), p. 288.

114 Alexander Cowie, *The Rise of the American Novel* (New York: American Book Co., 1948), p. 747. Cited in Piper (1965), p. 288.

115 Maxwell Geismar, *The Last of the Provincials: The American Novel, 1915–1925* (New York: Hill and Wang, 1959), p. 351.

116 William Troy, 'Scott Fitzgerald – The Authority of Failure', *Accent*, 6 (Autumn 1945), pp. 56–60. Reprinted in Hoffman (1962), pp. 224–31; Kazin (1962), pp. 188–94. Further Troy page references to Kazin (1962). This quotation, pp. 188–89.

117 T. S. Eliot, 'Hamlet' (1919) in *Selected Essays*, 2nd edition (London: Faber and Faber, 1934), p. 145.

118 Kazin (1962), pp. 189–91.

119 Kazin (1962), pp. 23–4.

120 Robert E. Long, '*The Great Gatsby* and the Tradition of Joseph Conrad'. *Texas Studies in Language and Literature: A Journal of the Humanities*, 8:2, 3 (Summer and Fall 1966), pp. 257–76, 407–22.

121 Arthur Mizener, 'F. Scott Fitzgerald 1896–1940: The Poet of Borrowed Time', in Willard Thorp, ed., *The Lives of Eighteen from Princeton* (Princeton: Princeton University Press, 1946), pp. 333–53. Jackson R. Bryer observes that this is an only slightly revised version of Mizener's essay 'Scott Fitzgerald and the Imaginative Possession of American Life', *Sewanee Review* 54 (Winter 1946), pp. 66–86. See Jackson R. Bryer, *The Critical Reputation of F. Scott Fitzgerald: A Bibliographical Study* (Hamden, Connecticut:

Archon Books, 1967), pp. 213, 306. 'The
Poet of Borrowed Time' was reprinted in
Kazin (1962), pp. 23–45 and in John W.
Aldridge ed., *Critiques and Essays on
Modern Fiction, 1920–1951* (New York:
Ronald Press, 1952), pp. 286–302.
Mizener page references below are to
Kazin (1962). This quotation, Kazin, p. 31.
122 Kazin (1962), pp. 34–8.
123 Bryer (1967) lists, in his selective
'Articles about Fitzgerald', 114 items in all
between 1940 and 1950 (this excludes
pieces, such as Mizener's 'The Poet of
Borrowed Time', published in books).
There are thirty-nine items for 1940, the
year of Fitzgerald's death; fifteen items for
1941; two items for 1942; no items for
1943; three items for 1944; fifteen items
for 1945, including William Troy's essay;
five items for 1946; four items for 1947;
five items for 1948 (two of the 1948 items
are responsive to Zelda Fitzgerald's death
in that year in a fire at Highland Hospital
Asheville, where she was an inmate);
eight items for 1949; and eighteen items
for 1950. A number of these articles – by
Malcolm Cowley, Alfred Kazin, Mark
Schorer, Andrews Wanning, Charles
Weir, Jr, and the anonymous *Times Literary
Supplement* writer – were given wider currency when they were collected in Kazin
(1962), first published in 1951. Among
other significant articles not included in
Kazin's collection were John Berryman's
'F. Scott Fitzgerald', *Kenyon Review*, 8
(Winter 1946), pp. 103–12, and, in
England, Alan Ross's 'Rumble Among the
Drums – F. Scott Fitzgerald (1896–1940)
and the Jazz Age', *Horizon* (18 December
1948), pp. 420–35.

CHAPTER TWO

1 See Maurice Beebe and Jackson R.
Bryer, 'Criticism of F. Scott Fitzgerald: A
Selected Checklist'. *Modern Fiction Studies*,
7 (Spring 1961), p. 88. According to Bryer
(1967, p. 212), Trilling's *Crack-Up* review
article, called 'F. Scott Fitzgerald', was
published in *The Nation*, 161 (25 August
1945), pp. 182–84.

2 Lionel Trilling, *The Liberal Imagination:
Essays on Literature and Society* (London:
Secker and Warburg, 1951), p. xii.
3 Trilling (1951), p. ix.
4 Trilling (1951), p. xiv.
5 Trilling (1951), p. xv.
6 Trilling (1951), p. 246.
7 Ezra Pound, 'A Few Don'ts by An
Imagiste', in Peter Jones ed., *Imagist Poetry*
(Harmondsworth: Penguin, 1972), p.
130. 'A Few Don'ts By An Imagiste', pre-
ceded by F. S. Flint's 'Imagisme', was
originally published in the magazine
Poetry, 1 (March 1913), pp. 198–206.
8 See Daniel T. O'Hara, *Lionel Trilling: The
Work of Liberation* (Madison, Wisconsin:
University of Wisconsin Press, 1988), for
discussion of what O'Hara calls 'Trilling's
radical ambivalence about being a Jew in
America' (p. xi). The issue of Fitzgerald's
representation of Jews had already been
raised by Milton Hindus, 'F. Scott
Fitzgerald and Literary Anti-Semitism: A
Footnote on the Mind of the 20's',
Commentary, 3 (June 1947), pp. 508–16.
For later discussion of this issue, see also:
William Goldhurst, 'Literary Anti-
Semitism in the 20's', *American Jewish
Congress Bi-Weekly*, 29 (24 December
1962), pp. 10–12; William Goldhurst, *F.
Scott Fitzgerald and his Contemporaries*
(Cleveland: Cleveland World Publishing,
1963); Barry Edward Gross, 'F.'s "Anti-
Semitism" – A Reply to William
Goldhurst', *Fitzgerald Newsletter*, no. 21
(Spring 1963), pp. 3–5, collected in
Matthew J Bruccoli, ed., *Fitzgerald News-
letter* (Washington, D. C.: NCR Microcard
Editions, 1969), pp. 118–19; William
Goldhurst, 'An Answer to Barry Edward
Gross', *Fitzgerald Newsletter* no. 22
(Summer 1963), pp. 1–2, in Bruccoli
(1969), pp. 125–26, Josephine Z. Kopf,
'Meyer Wolfsheim and Robert Cohn: A
Study of Jewish Type and Stereotype',
Tradition, 10 (Spring 1969), pp. 93–104,
and Forrey (1967) and Slater (1973) in
this Guide.
9 Trilling (1951), pp. 251–54. Trilling's
whole essay is reprinted in Hoffman

(1962), pp. 232–43; Kazin (1962), pp. 195–205; Arthur Mizener, ed., *F. Scott Fitzgerald: A Collection of Critical Essays*, Twentieth Century Views series (Englewood Cliffs, New Jersey: Prentice-Hall, Inc., 1963), pp. 11–19; Donaldson (1984), pp. 13–20.

10 Edwin S. Fussell. 'Fitzgerald's Brave New World'. *ELH: A Journal of English Literary History*, 19:4 (December 1952), pp. 291–306. This quotation, p. 291. Reprinted in revised form in Hoffman (1962), pp. 244–62; Mizener (1963), pp. 43–56.

11 Marius Bewley, 'Scott Fitzgerald's Criticism of America', *Sewanee Review*, 62 (Spring 1954), pp. 223–46. Bewley, *The Eccentric Design: Form in the Classic American Novel* (New York: Columbia University Press, 1959), pp. 259–87.

12 These anthologies are, in order of date of publication: Hoffman (1962), pp. 263–85; Mizener (1963), pp. 125–41; Lockridge (1968), pp. 37–53; and Bloom (1986), pp. 11–27. Bewley page references below are to Lockridge (1968).

13 F. R. Leavis, 'Introduction' to Marius Bewley, *The Complex Fate: Hawthorne, Henry James and Some Other American Writers* (London: Chatto and Windus, 1968), pp. x–xi.

14 Lockridge (1968), p. 40.

15 Lockridge (1968), p. 41.

16 Lockridge (1968), p. 41.

17 Lockridge (1968), p. 45.

18 Lockridge (1968), p. 46.

19 Lockridge (1968), p. 46.

20 Fussell (1952), p. 298.

21 Lockridge (1968), pp. 42–4.

22 John W. Bicknell, 'The Waste Land of F. Scott Fitzgerald', *Virginia Quarterly Review*, 30 (Autumn 1954), pp. 556–72. Reprinted in Kenneth E. Eble, ed., *F. Scott Fitzgerald: A Collection of Criticism*, Contemporary Studies in Literature series (New York: McGraw-Hill, 1973), pp. 67–80.

23 R. W. Stallman, '*Gatsby* and the Hole in Time'. *Modern Fiction Studies*, 1:4 (November 1955), pp. 2–16. Reprinted in Stallman, *The Houses that James Built and Other Literary Studies* (Michigan: Michigan State University Press, 1961), pp. 131–50. Page references below to Stallman (1961). This quotation, p. 131.

24 Stallman (1961), p. 133.

25 Stallman (1961), p. 137.

26 Stallman (1961), p. 131.

27 Stallman (1961), pp. 140–42.

28 Bicknell (1954), p. 557.

29 Richard P. Blackmur, 'Introduction' to Henry James, *The Art of the Novel: Critical Prefaces* (New York: Scribner's, 1947), p. xxix.

30 Henry James, 'The New Novel', in *Notes on Novelists* (New York: Scribner's, 1916), p. 347.

31 James (1947), p. 324. 'To project imaginatively, for my hero, a relation [with a *ficelle*] that has nothing to do with the matter (the matter of my subject) but has everything to do with the manner (the manner of my presentation of the same) and yet to treat it, at close quarters and for fully economic expression's possible sake, as if it were important and essential – to do that sort of thing and yet muddle nothing may easily become, as one goes, a signally attaching proposition . . .'. Fitzgerald, it seems, has met and overcome this 'signally attaching proposition' admirably: Jordan Baker, who belongs more to the treatment than to the subject, is yet given a well-defined character and a significant role in the action. [*Editor's Note:* The French word *ficelle* can mean a string used to control a puppet or a crafty trick. James applies the term to a fictional character who plays the role of confidant(e) and can thus be used by the author to supply the reader with information without authorial intervention. See Chris Baldick, *The Concise Oxford Dictionary of Literary Terms* (Oxford: Oxford University Press, 1991), p. 83.]

32 Fitzgerald, (1934), p. x.

33 Fitzgerald, *The Last Tycoon* (New York: Scribner's, 1941), pp. 139–140.

34 Conrad, 'Preface' to *The Nigger of the 'Narcissus': A Tale of the Sea* (New York: Doubleday, Doran and Company, Inc.,

1935), p. xiv.
35 Ford Madox Ford, *Joseph Conrad: A Personal Remembrance* (Boston: Little, Brown and Company, 1924), pp. 136–37.
36 Joseph Warren Beach, *The Twentieth-Century Novel: Studies in Technique* (New York: Appleton-Century-Crofts, Inc., 1932), p. 363.
37 F. Scott Fitzgerald, 'The Note-Books', in *The Crack-Up*, ed. Edmund Wilson (New York: New Directions, 1945), p. 179.
38 James E. Miller, Jr, *The Fictional Technique of F. Scott Fitzgerald* (The Hague: Martinus Nijhoff, 1957). Reprinted in an enlarged edition with the title *F. Scott Fitzgerald: His Art and His Technique* (London: Peter Owen, 1965). This passage, 1965 edition, pp. 106–14. The section in which Miller discusses *Gatsby*, and which includes this passage, is in Lockridge (1968), pp. 19–36.
39 Bruccoli (1969), 'A Personal Foreword', no page number.

CHAPTER THREE

1 Beebe and Bryer (1961), pp. 82–94.
2 Robert F. McDonnell, 'Eggs and Eyes in *The Great Gatsby*', *Modern Fiction Studies*, 7:1 (Spring 1961), pp. 32–6.
3 A. E. Dyson, '*The Great Gatsby*: Thirty-Six Years After', *Modern Fiction Studies*, 7:1 (Spring 1961), pp. 37–48. Reprinted in Mizener (1963), pp. 112–24.
4 J. B. Priestley, 'Introduction', *The Bodley Head Scott Fitzgerald*, Volume 1 (London: The Bodley Head, 1958), p. 15.
5 Walter Allen, *The Modern Novel in Britain and the United States* (New York: E. P. Dutton & Co., Inc., 1965), p. 90.
6 Fitzgerald's debt to *The Waste Land* has been generally recognised by critics, but the spirit of the poem is adapted to materials so unique that the originality of the novel is in no way impaired.
7 J. S. Westbrook, 'Nature and Optics in *The Great Gatsby*'. *American Literature* (March 1960), vol. 32, pp. 79–84. [*Editor's Note:* It is interesting, and perhaps more than incidental, to see that, in the original

version of an essay that focuses on what it calls 'ocular confusions', the initials of 'Doctor T. J. Eckleburg', and the 'le' of his surname, are transposed. This particular 'ocular confusion', the repeated misspelling of 'Carraway' as 'Carroway', and a number of misquotations, have been corrected in the essay as printed in this Guide.]
8 Kenneth E. Eble, 'The Craft of Revision: *The Great Gatsby*', *American Literature*, 36 (November 1964), pp. 315–26. Reprinted in Piper (1970), pp.110–17; Donaldson (1984), pp. 85–94. This quotation from Piper (1970), p. 116.
9 Sergio Perosa, *The Art of F. Scott Fitzgerald*, translated by Charles Matz and Sergio Perosa (Ann Arbor: University of Michigan Press, 1965), p. 60.
10 Robert Sklar, *F. Scott Fitzgerald: The Last Laocoön* (New York: Oxford University Press, 1967), p. 195.
11 Sklar (1967), p. 196
12 Milton Hindus, *F. Scott Fitzgerald: An Introduction and Interpretation*, American Authors and Critics series (New York: Holt, Rinehart and Winston, Inc., 1968), p. 35.
13 Hindus (1968), p. 39.
14 R. W. Stallman, 'Conrad and *The Great Gatsby*', *Twentieth Century Literature*, 1 (April 1955), pp. 5–12. Reprinted Stallman (1961), pp. 150–57.
15 Baldick (1991), p. 121.
16 Baldick (1991), pp. 110–11.
17 Turnbull (1963), p. 163.
18 Piper (1970), p. 160.
19 Mizener (1951), p. 174.
20 The cancelled *c* is followed by what appears to be the first vertical curve of a *u*.
21 [*Editor's Note:* An unidentified review in Fitzgerald's scrapbook did not explicitly criticise the 'plot manipulation' for making Daisy run down her husband's mistress, but it did observe, in its generally very favourable account of *Gatsby*, one imperfection: '[t]he disposition of the characters in the automobiles before the tragic accident was difficult to contrive

and the ingenuity of the author is apparent' (Bryer, 1978, p. 248).]

22 The complete passage, which begins with the setting and is too long to quote, has several complicating aspects; it also includes allusion to such religious matters as Jacob's ladder and the incarnation (see pp. 86–7 of *Gatsby*).

23 For another example of the use of folklore in the novel see Tristram P. Coffin, 'Gatsby's Fairy Lover'. *Midwest Folklore*, 10 (Summer 1960), pp. 79–85.

24 Victor A. Doyno, 'Patterns in *The Great Gatsby*', *Modern Fiction Studies*, 12 (1969), pp. 415–26. This extract from pp. 416–26. The essay is reprinted in Piper (1970), pp. 160–67; Donaldson (1984), pp. 94–105. The Fitzgerald quotation at the end of the extract (which is also the end of the essay) is from Bruccoli and Duggan (1980), p. 112.

25 Robert Forrey, 'Negroes in the Fiction of F. Scott Fitzgerald', *Phylon: The Atalanta University Review of Race and Culture*, 48 (1967), pp. 293–98. This quotation from p. 293.

26 Forrey (1967), p. 295.

27 [*Editor's Note:* In his essay, 'The Sexual Drama of Nick and Gatsby', *The International Fiction Review*, 19 (1992), pp. 14–22, Edward Wasiolek observes: 'I know of no defense of Tom, whatever the reservations about *Gatsby*' (p. 14).

28 Gary J. Scrimgeour, 'Against *The Great Gatsby*', *Criticism*, 8 (Winter 1966), pp. 75–86. Reprinted Lockridge (1968), pp. 70–81. Scrimgeour page references below are to Lockridge (1968). This quotation, Lockridge (1968), p. 70.

29 Joseph Conrad, 'Heart of Darkness' (London: Penguin, 1983), p. 57.

30 Lockridge (1968), pp. 76–81.

31 Mizener (1963), p. 70.

32 Mizener (1963), p. 73.

33 Mizener (1963), p. 70.

34 Leslie A. Fiedler, *Love and Death in the American Novel* (London: Paladin, 1970), p.276.

35 Fiedler (1970), pp. 291–95.

CHAPTER FOUR

1 Milton R. Stern, *The Golden Moment: The Novels of F. Scott Fitzgerald* (Urbana: University of Illinois Press, 1970), p. xii.

2 Stern (1970), pp. 253–58.

3 John F. Callahan, *The Illusions of a Nation: Myth and History in the Novels of F. Scott Fitzgerald* (Urbana: University of Illinois Press, 1972), p. 3.

4 Kenneth E. Eble, *F. Scott Fitzgerald*. Twayne's United States Authors series, no. 36 (New York: Twayne, 1963). Revised edition (Boston: Twayne, 1977), p. 173.

5 Richard Lehan, *The Great Gatsby: The Limits of Wonder*, Masterwork Study no. 36 (Boston: Twayne, 1990), p. 19.

6 Thomas Jefferson as quoted by Bewley (1959), p. 265.

7 Callahan (1972), pp. 45–9.

8 Peter Gregg Slater, 'Ethnicity in *The Great Gatsby*', *Twentieth Century Literature*, 19 (1973), pp. 53, 55.

9 Slater (1973), pp. 58–9. For a more recent discussion relating to ethnicity in *Gatsby*, see Bryan R. Washington, *The Politics of Exile: Ideology in Henry James, F. Scott Fitzgerald, and James Baldwin* (Boston: Northeastern University Press, 1995), pp. 35–54.

10 [*Editor's Note:* One explanation of this – it could have interesting implications – would be that Daisy sometimes dyes her hair.]

11 Sheilah Graham, 'Casting *The Great Gatsby*'. *Washington Evening Star* (10 January 1972), p. B-7.

12 For example, in 1973 I posed the question of Daisy's hair colour to two of my American literature classes; of the seventy-five students responding, sixty-one thought Daisy was blonde. So, too, ultimately, did those responsible for casting the 1974 Paramount film [with Mia Farrow as Daisy].

13 For one extensive discussion of Fitzgerald's use of white and gold, see Stern (1970), pp. 267–88.

14 For further discussion of dark and fair women in romantic fiction, see Frederic I. Carpenter, 'Puritans Preferred Blondes:

The Heroines of Melville and Hawthorne', *New England Quarterly*, 9 (June 1936), pp. 253–72; Philip Rahv, 'The Dark Lady of Salem', *Partisan Review*, 8 (September–October 1941), pp. 362–81; Perry Miller, 'The Romance and the Novel' in *Nature's Nation* (Cambridge, Massachusetts: The Belknap Press of Harvard University Press, 1967), pp. 241–78.

15 *Gatsby MS facsimile*, p. 221.

16 Joan S. Korenman, '"Only Her Hairdresser . . .": Another Look at Daisy Buchanan', *American Literature*, 46 (January 1974), pp. 574–78.

17 Lockridge (1968), pp. 44, 45.

18 Robert Ornstein, 'Scott Fitzgerald's Fable of East and West', *College English*, 18 (1956–57), pp. 139–43. Reprinted in Lockridge (1968), pp. 54–60; Eble (1973), pp. 60–6. Ornstein in fact refers to 'the criminal amorality of Daisy Buchanan', and does not actually use the phrase 'criminally amoral' that Person attributes to him. See Lockridge (1968), p. 55.

19 Kazin (1962), p. 179.

20 Two excellent arguments against Nick's reliability are R. W. Stallman's famous essay (Stallman, 1961) and Gary J. Scrimgeour, 'Against *The Great Gatsby*' in Lockridge (1968).

21 See Jan Hunt and John M. Suarez, 'The Evasion of Adult Love in Fitzgerald's Fiction', *Centennial Review*, 18 (Spring 1973), pp. 156–62.

22 Leland S. Person, Jr, '"Herstory" and Daisy Buchanan', *American Literature* (May 1978), vol. 46, pp. 250–57.

23 J. Laplanche and J. B. Pontalis, *The Language of Psychoanalysis*, translated by Donald Nicholson-Smith (London: The Hogarth Press and the Institute of Psycho-Analysis, 1973), p. 430.

24 Kuehl and Bryer (1971), pp. 92–3.

25 Ernest H. Lockridge, 'Introduction' in Lockridge (1968), pp. 1–18, especially pp. 9–10.

26 Sigmund Freud, 'On The Universal Tendency to Debasement in the Sphere of Love' in *On Sexuality*, translated James Strachey, Pelican Freud Library, Volume 7 (Harmondsworth: Penguin, 1977), p. 254.

27 Turnbull (1963), p. 341.

28 Fitzgerald (1965), p. 39.

29 A. B. Paulson, '*The Great Gatsby*: Oral Aggression and Splitting', *American Imago: A Psychoanalytic Journal for Culture, Science, and the Arts*, 35 (Fall 1978), pp. 311–30. Reprinted Bloom (1986), pp. 71–85. These extracts from Bloom (1986), pp. 74–5, 78–83.

30 Freud (1977), p. 209.

31 Bloom (1986), p. 88.

32 Ken Kolb, *Getting Straight* (London: Barrie and Rockliff, 1968), p. 175. The novel was later adapted into a film with the same title, starring Elliott Gould and directed by Richard Rush, which came out in 1970. The film retained the oral examination scene, and the exchange about homosexuality in *Gatsby*.

33 Kolb (1968), pp. 179, 180.

34 Keath Fraser, 'Another Reading of *The Great Gatsby*', *English Studies in Canada*, (Autumn 1979), 5. pp. 330–43. Reprinted in Bloom (1986), pp. 57–70. Page references below to Fraser (1979). This quotation, p. 331.

35 Fraser (1979), p. 334.

36 Fraser (1979), p. 341.

37 Fraser (1979), p. 342.

38 Quoted in Jackson R. Bryer and John Kuehl, eds., *The Basil and Josephine Stories by F. Scott Fitzgerald* (New York: Scribner's, 1973), p. xxi.

39 Turnbull (1963), p. 173.

40 Fraser (1979), pp. 334–38.

CHAPTER FIVE

1 Bruccoli (1985), p. 77.

2 Bruccoli (1985), p. 67.

3 Richard Godden, '*The Great Gatsby*: Glamour on the Turn', *Journal of American Studies*, 16:3 (1982), pp. 343–44.

4 See Bruccoli's note, Fitzgerald (1991), p. 197.

5 Bertolt Brecht, 'Alienation Effects in Chinese Acting', in John Willett, ed. and translated, *Brecht on Theatre: The Development of an Aesthetic* (London: Methuen, 1974), pp. 96–7.

6 Thorstein Veblen, *The Theory of the Leisure Class* (London: Unwin, 1970), p. 164.

7 Mikhail Bakhtin, *Problems of Dostoevsky's Poetics*, translated by R. W. Rotsel (New York: Ardis, 1973), pp. 162–63.

8 Fredric Jameson, *Marxism and Form* (Princeton: Princeton University Press, 1971), p. 96.

9 Godden (1982), pp. 346–49.

10 Michael Holquist, 'Stereotyping in Autobiography and Historiography: Colonialism in *The Great Gatsby*', *Poetics Today*, 9:2 (1988), pp. 460, 461.

11 Holquist (1988), pp. 469–71.

12 Lehan (1990), p. 132.

13 Fraser (1989), p. 341.

14 Wasiolek (1992), p. 19.

15 Patti White, *Gatsby's Party: The System and the List in Contemporary Narrative* (West Lafayette, Indiana: Purdue University Press, 1992), p. 3.

16 Jean Baudrillard, *Simulations*, translated by Paul Foss, Paul Patton, Philip Beitchman (New York: Semiotext(e), 1983), p. 16.

17 White (1992), pp. 132–39.

18 Bruccoli (1985), p. 11.

19 Long (1979), p. 143.

20 Hugh Kenner, *A Homemade World: The American Modernist Writers* (New York: William Morrow, 1975), p. 42.

21 According to Bruccoli (1991), p. 184, Jordan Baker's name 'combines two automobile makes: the sporty Jordan and the conservative Baker electric'. See also Laurence E. MacPhee, 'The Great Gatsby's Romance of Motoring: Nick Carraway and Jordan Baker', *Modern Fiction Studies*, 18 (Summer 1972), pp. 207–12 and R. A. Corrigan, 'Somewhere West of Laramie on the Road to West Egg', *Journal of Popular Culture*, 7 (1973), pp. 152–58.

22 JoAnne Olian, *Authentic French Fashions of the Twenties* (New York: Dover, 1990), p. v.

23 Ronald Paulson, *Hogarth: His Life, Art, and Times* (New Haven: Yale University Press, 1974), p. 138.

24 Ronald Berman, *The Great Gatsby and Modern Times* (Urbana: University of Illinois Press, 1994), pp. 2–11.

25 Andrew Turnbull, *Scott Fitzgerald* (Harmondsworth: Penguin, 1970), pp. 263–64.

26 Frances Kerr, 'Feeling "Half Feminine"; Modernism and the Politics of Emotion in *The Great Gatsby*', *American Literature*, 68:2 (June 1996), pp. 403–31.

27 Kerr (1996), p. 416.

28 [*Editor's Note:* It is, in fact, ambiguous as to whether the phrase 'that certain girl' refers to Jordan Baker or to the Midwest girlfriend. Critics have tended to interpret it as referring to the latter. Roger Lewis, for example, seems to assume that it refers to the latter when he writes that '[e]ven Nick seems unsure about his feelings for the tennis girl back in the Midwest' (Bruccoli, 1985, p. 48). Jordan Baker is not otherwise associated with playing tennis in *The Great Gatsby*, but with the less physically active game of golf, nor is she otherwise linked at all with perspiration; indeed, she is described in such a way as to distance her from any such manifestation of warmth and moistness – she has a 'cool' smile and a 'hard' body (p. 48). If 'that certain girl' is the Midwest girlfriend, it is possible to interpret the 'moustache of perspiration' as a feature that Nick finds repulsive rather than attractive. This is Callahan's reading: '[Nick's] admiration for the poster girl in Jordan comes out in his revulsion from the "faint moustache of perspiration" ungracing the old flame's upper lip after tennis' (Callahan, 1972, p. 37). It would, of course, be possible to interpret this revulsion as repressed attraction! It is perhaps significant that, according to Andrew Crosland's *A Concordance to F. Scott Fitzgerald's 'The Great Gatsby'* (Detroit: Gale Research Company, 1975), the only other references to perspiration in the novel are associated with heat and with female abandonment and prostration, and that both occur in the climactic Chapter VII. Near the start of that chapter, as Nick takes the train out of New

York to have lunch with Gatsby, 'the woman next to me perspired delicately for a while into her white shirtwaist and then, as her newspaper dampened under her fingers, lapsed despairingly into deep heat with a desolate cry' (p. 89). Here, perspiration is associated with a public abandon, to some extent mimicking erotic abandon, which would be very uncharacteristic of Jordan. Later in the chapter, we have this account of the discovery of Myrtle Wilson's body: 'Michaelis and this man reached her first but when they had torn open her shirtwaist still damp with perspiration they saw that her left breast was swinging loose like a flap and there was no need to listen for the heart beneath' (p. 107). In this highly charged description, perspiration, eroticism, violence and death mix together in a complex way. If the 'moustache of perspiration' is a source of revulsion rather than direct attraction, it could signify Nick's uneasiness about both heterosexual and homosexual abandonment – his aversion to the girl from the Midwest is focused in an image in which she is both feminine (insofar as femininity is associated with perspiration in *Gatsby*) and, because of the 'moustache', masculine.]

29 Charles Weir, Jr, '"An Invite with Gilded Edges": A Study of F. Scott Fitzgerald', *Virginia Quarterly Review*, 20 (Winter 1944), pp. 100–13. Reprinted in Kazin (1962), pp. 133–46. This quotation, Kazin (1962), p. 141.

30 For the generative paradigm of these social dynamics in British literature, see Eve Sedgwick, *Between Men: English Literature and Male Homosocial Desire* (New York: Columbia University Press, 1985).

31 Richard A. Isay, *Being Homosexual: Gay Men and Their Development* (New York: Farrar, Straus and Giroux, 1989), p. 99.

32 See Shari Benstock, *Women of the Left Bank: Paris, 1900–1940* (Austin: University of Texas Press, 1987).

33 Henri Bergson, *An Introduction to Metaphysics*, translated by T. E. Hulme (New York: G. P. Putnam's, 1912), p. 7; quoted in Sydney Janet Kaplan, *Katherine Mansfield and the Origins of Modernist Fiction* (Ithaca: Cornell University Press, 1991), p. 182.

34 Katherine Mansfield, *Novels and Novelists* (New York: Knopf, 1930), p. 236; quoted in Kaplan (1991), p. 183.

35 'I must start out with an emotion – one that's close to me and that I can understand.' F. Scott Fitzgerald, 'One Hundred False Starts', in *Afternoon of an Author: A Selection of Uncollected Stories and Essays by F. Scott Fitzgerald*, ed. Arthur Mizener (New York: Scribner's, 1957), p. 152.

36 We now understand some of the ways that Eliot and Pound actually violated their own theories of impersonality in their major works, but in the Twenties this understanding was decades away. See James E. Miller, Jr, *T. S. Eliot's Personal Waste Land* (University Park: Pennsylvania State University Press, 1977); and Robert Casillo, *The Genealogy of Demons: Anti-Semitism, Fascism, and the Myths of Ezra Pound* (Evanston, Illinois: Northwestern University Press, 1988).

37 Turnbull (1963), p. 168.

38 Kerr (1996), pp. 417–23, 425–26, 427.

39 Bruccoli (1985), p. 12.

ACKNOWLEDGEMENTS

The editor and publishers wish to thank the following for their permission to reprint copyright material: University of Illinois Press (for material from *The Great Gatsby and Modern Times* and *The Illusions of a Nation: Myth and History in the Novels of F. Scott Fitzgerald*); Johns Hopkins University Press (for material from *Modern Fiction Studies* and *American Imago: A Psychoanalytic Journal for Culture, Science and the Arts*); Penguin Books (for material from *Love and Death in the American Novel*); Random House Inc. (for material from *The Great Gatsby*); Association of Canadian Teachers of English (for material from *English Studies in Canada*); Duke University Press (for material from *Poetics Today* and *American Literature*); New York University Press (for material from *The Fictional Technique of F. Scott Fitzgerald*); Princeton University Press (for material from *The Lives of Eighteen from Princeton*); Wayne State University Press (for material from *Criticism*); University of Illinois Press (for material from *The Golden Moment: The Novels of F. Scott Fitzgerald*); Secker & Warburg (for material from *The Liberal Imagination*); Purdue University Press (for material from *Gatsby's Party: The System and the List in Contemporary Narrative*).

Every effort has been made to contact the holders of any copyrights applying to the material quoted in this book. The publishers would be grateful if any such copyright holders whom they have not been able to contact, would write to them.

Nicolas Tredell teaches American and English literature, art history, and cultural and film studies for Sussex University. He has contributed widely to journals in the UK and the USA, and his recent books include *Uncancelled Challenge: The Work of Raymond Williams, The Critical Decade: Culture in Crisis, Conversations with Critics* and *Caute's Confrontations: The Novels of David Caute*.

INDEX